"So m[...] and [...] megalli[...] [...] [...] forget the rich histories of preservation that led to their creation in the first place. Danny Childs breaks down those walls, and with a methodical attention to detail, presents traditional recipes for botanical fermentation along with inventive applications for them. Raise a glass to this gem of a book that feels as much like a reference guide as it does an inspiration."

—**DAVID ZILBER**, author of *The Noma Guide to Fermentation*

"It turns out that years of ethnobotanical research in the Peruvian Amazon and the mountains and deserts of Chile can serve as the perfect foundation for building a bar program in southern New Jersey. *Slow Drinks* isn't just a collection of extraordinary cocktail recipes, but a guide to understanding and appreciating the flora we have all around us—wherever we live."

—**NICHOLAS GILL**, food writer and co-author of *Central* and *The Latin American Cookbook*

"Danny Childs takes beverage making to a whole new level by drawing upon his ethnobotanical, foraging, and bartending experience. His innovative approach to cocktails and drinks of all kinds provides a superb complement to the Slow Food movement."

—**PATRICK E. MCGOVERN**, author of *Ancient Brews: Rediscovered and Re-created* and *Uncorking the Past: The Quest for Wine, Beer, and Other Alcoholic Beverages*

"Fans of bitters and amari are going to love using the tips in this book to create fresh and foraged seasonal versions of their favorite beverages. Danny Childs provides readers with information on specific botanicals and a toolkit of techniques with which to preserve them in the form of fermented sodas, shrubs, liqueurs, and more. *Slow Drinks* serves up both specific recipes and endless possibilities."

—**CAMPER ENGLISH**, author of *Doctors and Distillers: The Remarkable Medicinal History of Beer, Wine, Spirits, and Cocktails*

SLOW DRINKS

SLOW DRINKS

A Field Guide to Foraging and Fermenting Seasonal Sodas,
Botanical Cocktails, Homemade Wines, and More

BY DANNY CHILDS

Photos by Katie Childs
Illustrations by Molly Reeder

Hardie Grant
NORTH AMERICA

CONTENTS

INTRODUCTION

It was a snowy night in mid-January and the wind was beating against the canvas walls of the converted military tent. I looked through the opening into the white void and across the fields that stretched to the edge of the Jersey Pine Barrens. This is where we lived, my wife and I, in a tent on a two-hundred-acre farm, not far from the house where I grew up.

It had been a particularly brutal winter, and I couldn't help but feel isolated and lost. Not only were the living conditions incredibly difficult, but I was in the middle of upending both my personal and professional life, and I hadn't the faintest clue what my next step would be. After spending the previous four years conducting anthropological and ethnobotanical research in South America, I was now afraid that we were going to freeze in a town to which I'd vowed to never return. And even though we *chose* to live in the tent, it felt, at times, like we were, well, homeless.

Our initial decision to live there was based on equal parts opportunity and necessity. We saw the chance to live and work on a farm and learn something new in the process. However, we also really needed a cheap place to live after moving home from South America. After sinking the last of our savings into buying the tent, equipping it with a wood-burning stove, and building the necessary infrastructure to survive these conditions, I realized that I desperately needed another way to make money. So I went out to do what I had done before in this situation: work at a restaurant. The Farm and Fisherman Tavern was only seven miles away, and one day on a whim I walked in and filled out an application. I had no idea that it would change my life forever.

The Farm and Fisherman Tavern is co-owned by chefs Josh Lawler and Todd Fuller in Cherry Hill, New Jersey, just twenty minutes east of Philadelphia. When it first opened, it was hailed as "Blue Hill South" due to Chef Lawler's six years as chef de cuisine at Dan Barber's farm-to-table mecca Blue Hill at Stone Barns in Westchester County, New York. The Farm and Fisherman translated the philosophy of Stone Barns to a more approachable suburban tavern setting, showcasing the agricultural bounty that southern New Jersey has to offer. It didn't take long before I realized that this restaurant was quite different from places I had worked before. The staff was professional, the chefs were talented in a way I had only seen in films and on TV, and the focal point of the entire endeavor was the ingredients and farmers.

I became enthralled with the operation and immersed myself, learning as much as I could about the restaurant, how to operate at the highest level of hospitality, and how to educate our guests about our values in the process. When I wasn't waiting tables at the restaurant, I was farming the food we were serving and exploring the surrounding forests in an effort to discover and understand the wild foods and flavors that were hidden in plain sight. I also began to delve into fermentation and other types of food preservation as a way to capture the season's bounty. Noticing my newfound passion, Chef Todd proposed that I move behind the bar to create a beverage program that felt cohesive with our restaurant's principles and my interests. I happily obliged and quickly took to my new position.

As I began to think about what type of cocktail program I wanted to build, a theory began to take shape. I wanted to build a bar program that highlighted the bounty to be discovered in and around New Jersey, and to do so in a way that was rooted in my previous fields of study, anthropology and ethnobotany. I began with a mission, which I scrawled on the back of a bar napkin one night after a shift: "cocktails through an anthropological lens." This idea has evolved over the years to express a method of crafting beverages with botanical, historical, and cultural significance using only what our foodshed has to offer.

THE EARLY DAYS

When I tell people about my job, they often assume that I grew up foraging; however, this couldn't be further from the truth. I was born in a densely populated suburb of Philadelphia known as Delaware County ("Delco" for short). My mom had me at a very young age, and we lived in a house along with my grandparents for the first few years of my life until we could afford to move elsewhere. Although my grandfather worked as a printer for most of his career, he was a self-taught naturalist who instilled in me an appreciation for the natural world. As the years passed, I turned to *National Geographic* and *Smithsonian* magazines, TV programs on PBS and the History Channel, and movies like *Motorcycle Diaries* to serve as my portals to these subjects I desperately wanted to know more about.

When I was in the sixth grade, my mom married my stepdad, and despite my best efforts to stop it, we moved to his home state of New Jersey. We settled in a town in South Jersey called Marlton, located about fifteen minutes east of where the Farm and Fisherman stands today. While Marlton is relatively unimpressive upon first glance, I soon came to appreciate how it sits on a divide between two very distinct ecospheres: northeastern coastal forests and the Atlantic coastal pine barrens. I could walk on a trail just outside of my new neighborhood and watch as the landscape changed from deciduous forest to the coniferous pine barrens in a matter of a mile or two. And, as I soon discovered, Marlton was surrounded by cultural hubs, too: Philadelphia, Pennsylvania Dutch country, Jersey shore coastal communities, the Appalachian Mountains, New York City, Baltimore, Washington D.C.

While I see my home as exotic today, I didn't always feel that way. Growing up in Marlton, I dreamed of living in a faraway place filled with different sights, tastes, sounds, and people, and when I went to the University of Delaware in 2007, I designed my college education around the goal of doing just that. Although I wasn't sure how I would accomplish it, my objective was to live and work with South American Indigenous populations. I wanted to learn about their traditional medical practices and ultimately merge them with Western medicine in a holistic practice of my own. Early in my sophomore year, I was sharing late-night drinks with my roommate and telling him about this vision, and he recommended I take an anthropology course. The next morning, I signed up for Anthropology 101 with Dr. Peter G. Roe.

Dr. Roe (who I later learned was lovingly referred to as the University of Delaware's Indiana Jones) was a towering figure with a bellowing voice. His larger-than-life presence was further accentuated with Amazonian bead bracelets, textiles stitched into the back of denim or khaki shirts, and caiman-tooth necklaces hanging from his neck. After my second day of Dr. Roe's class, I was so captivated by his stories of shamans curing patients with plants and flying through the universe with the aid of hallucinogenic brews that I immediately enrolled in another class with him. One day after class, I worked up the courage to ask him if I could accompany him to South America and study under one of these shamans. After some initial skepticism and questioning, he recommended I visit him during his office hours to discuss further.

Later that week, I visited his office and stared in wonder at the anaconda skin, masks, headdresses, spears, and ceramic vessels that adorned his office. After telling him more about the project I had in mind, he told me about a subset of anthropology, known as ethnobotany, focused on how humans use plants for a variety of purposes including medicine. Over the next few months, Dr. Roe helped me apply for a scholarship to fund the trip and helped me refine my curriculum to include classes in biology, anthropology, Spanish, and botany to meld a pre-med education with an anthropological focus on South American ethnobotany. After being awarded the scholarship, I was off to Lima, Peru, that summer where I met Dr. Roe in the airport for a connecting flight to the Amazonian city of Pucallpa, located on the banks of the Ucayali River.

After a long canoe trip to a remote village upriver, Dr. Roe left me to find my way as a twenty-year-old aspiring ethnobotanist. Over the next two months, I worked with Shipibo medicine men and women, shamans, and elders to document all aspects of medicinal plant usage. In exchange, I later provided this Shipibo community with a Spanish-language compendium of ethnobotanical information I collected, including plant names, usages, and preparation methods, to protect this information for future generations.

After I completed my fieldwork in Peru, I continued southward for shorter stays with the Likan-antai people in the Atacama Desert in northern Chile, as well as the Mapuche tribe located in the temperate climates of northern Chilean Patagonia. I began to see how people adapted to their environments in three extremely different biomes: the wettest rainforest in the world, the driest desert in the world, and a temperate environment. Over the course of the next few years, I returned various times to work with the Mapuche and Shipibo to continue learning about medicinal plants and to volunteer in medical clinics to better understand which factors shaped their view of health, sickness, and medicine, and how interaction with the surrounding world affected each of these factors.

During my time in Peru and Chile, I collected specimens shown to me by each group and transported them back to the United States with a USDA permit to study them in the lab at the Delaware Biotechnology Institute. I was looking for their effectiveness against a lethal, drug-resistant human pathogen known as *Enterococcus faecalis*. While working in the lab and attending classes, I got a restaurant job at an Irish pub in town where I waited tables and was occasionally paid to dress up as a leprechaun, drink Guinness, and socialize with guests. This is where I met my wife, Katie. Although Katie wasn't fond of me at first due to my (alleged) negligence at work, I managed to win her over on Saint Patrick's Day after climbing on the bar in full leprechaun regalia and delivering an Irish toast to our patrons.

A few months later, after Katie graduated and I finished my undergraduate research and thesis, we packed our bags and moved to South America together. I wanted to share with her some of the experiences that I'd had before we met, and to make new unforgettable memories of our own. We ended up traveling from the southern tip of Patagonia all the way up into Central

America and finally Cuba and Mexico, via every available mode of transportation—bus, boat, train, hitchhiking, flying, and hiking. We visited twelve countries in total and had a great mix of urban and rural immersion, which allowed us to experience foreign cultures, see vastly different environments, enjoy new cuisines, and realize we made a damn good team.

When we returned home, I didn't feel fully ready to commit to the next phase of my academic career, and we were riding a wave of confidence and adventurousness from our South American trek. So when an opportunity presented itself to live and work on a two-hundred-acre farm in my hometown, we decided to try homesteading in a fifteen-foot-square canvas military tent on the property for the next nine months. I had worked on that same farm during high school, and I knew the family well. Since the 1960s, they had been operating as an agritourism operation, mainly focused on pumpkin patches, haunted hayrides, and cut-your-own Christmas trees. Talking with one of the sons around a campfire one night, we mused about the amount of food that could be grown on a farm that size. I told him how we had worked on some farms in exchange for room and board while we were backpacking and floated the idea of doing the same there.

We moved in on my birthday, September 1, during the height of the summer's bounty, and watched as everything died off in the fall to give way to the coldest winter in thirty-seven years. While we thought that we would be "glamping," there was very little glam about it, and the adventure turned out to be our toughest yet. However, we learned much about ourselves and gained an intimate familiarity with the cycles of our environment in the process. I began to see the region of my childhood in an entirely new light. Though we ended up leaving that particular farm, I went on to work on other farms over the next few years. Katie and I have now moved into a house with a sprawling garden and central heat. We welcomed our first child, Leo, into the world in March of 2020, our second, Sonny, in September of 2021.

THE ORIGIN OF SLOW DRINKS

While living with the Shipibo in Peru, I inadvertently drank contaminated drinking water and found myself battling a nasty case of dysentery. So, I decided to seek the help of a particularly well-regarded village medicine woman. After some questioning, she examined me, then disappeared inside her straw thatch hut. Moments later, she returned with a collection of different plastic bottles filled with herbs infusing in *aguardiente de caña* (a high-proof distillate made from sugarcane). She took a little of each tincture, mixed them together, and gave me a bottle full of the resulting mixture to consume three times a day until the dysentery was gone. To my surprise, my GI symptoms disappeared in a day or two. Although I didn't know it then, this woman essentially gave me an amaro that she made by using high-proof alcohol to extract the therapeutic compounds from different rainforest plants. As I continued my travels, I saw the same process being used again by the Likan-antai and Mapuche in Chile and elsewhere throughout Central and South America.

Another first was trying different wild fermented brews prepared using ancient practices. With the Shipibo, I drank *masato de yuca*, which has been prepared for hundreds, if not thousands, of years by village women who boil the fibrous tubers of the yuca plant, then mash it, and chew the mashed yuca for up to thirty minutes before spitting it into a vat of water. As they chew, enzymes in the saliva break down the yuca's starch molecules into fermentable sugars, which in turn feed the yeast and allow fermentation to occur. Later, while in the Andes Mountains with Quechua-speaking Incan descendants, I tried the corn-based *chicha de jora*, which is made by the same process of chewing and spitting the corn into a fermentation vat filled with water. In Chile, a Mapuche shaman gave me a different type of chicha that was made by wild-fermenting local crabapples into a hard cider. Each of these were unique and unlike anything I had ever tasted before. They were very much alive and reflective of the people and places that produced them.

I also saw many urban drinking customs in South America that were so different from what I was familiar with. In Peru and Chile, I visited one-hundred-year-old pisco distilleries and drank minimal-intervention wines made with Pais grapes planted by missionaries centuries prior. In Argentina, home to many Italian immigrants, I was introduced to Fernet-Branca and Campari for the first time. I drank aguardiente in Colombia, delicious terroir-driven rums in Cuba, and mezcal in Mexico made from wild agave plants. I came to realize how botanical ingredients, Indigenous knowledge, and colonialism were all interwoven in the backstory of spirits. And that these were inextricably linked to the culinary customs in each of these countries.

Later, when living in Santiago de Chile, I landed my first ever bartending gig at my friend Felipe's restaurant, La Casa de la Luna Azul, located in the Lastarria neighborhood. Chile's bartending culture is full of techniques and recipes that arrived with emigrating bartenders after prohibition was enacted in the United States. These practices were enhanced by Chile's own rich agricultural and culinary history. Up to that point, I had experienced only cloying cocktails made with artificially flavored and colored ingredients; however, Felipe and I went to the market nearly every day and purchased fresh fruit, herbs, and produce that we'd use in the drinks that evening. We juiced all our citrus fresh each day, made syrups for that night's service, measured ingredients to ensure precision, and made classic cocktails that were worlds apart from the neon-colored libations I was used to consuming in college bars.

Felipe and I began to include traditional Chilean botanical ingredients, such as the infused leaves of the boldo tree that we foraged around the city to use in place of mint in our Mojito Chileno, and the native pepper species known as *ají cacho de cabra* that was featured on the rim of our house Michelada. Not only did it make us happy to incorporate these ingredients, but it made the guests happy to see familiar parts of the national cuisine incorporated in cocktails.

A few years later, when I took over the bar program at the Farm and Fisherman, I was able to pick up where I left off while bartending in Chile. I realized, however, that while I had a pretty firm grasp of many different South American plant species, my knowledge of the local flora in my own native region was lacking. Unlike my time in South America, I was not able to study with and learn from the local indigenous populations about our regional flora and its ethnobotanical significance to their culture.

Instead, I began immersing myself in ethnobotanical literature to learn what was available to forage, while simultaneously delving into farming and gardening to learn about what could be cultivated here. I could feel a shift occurring as I began to look at the botanical makeup of my hometown through the same lens that I had brought to my fieldwork in South America.

It became clear early on that between farming and plumbing the wilds of South Jersey, I was going to have more ingredients than I could reasonably use all at once. Out of necessity, I began exploring different preservation techniques, including infusions, pickling, and fermentation. We brewed our first batches of ginger beer and kombucha, infused our first amari, amassed a large inventory of tinctures and bitters, and lined the shelves of the restaurant with

pickles. Soon we had assembled a sizable larder and the only thing left to do was to figure out how to use them in our bar program, which meant learning how to make a proper drink.

However, I lived and worked in southern New Jersey, where the cocktail scene at the time seemed stuck in the 1980s. This meant I had to learn from books and online publications on cocktails, as well as conversations with other bartenders, chefs, foragers, and farmers, and a seemingly endless amount of trial and error.

Over time, my ethos of creating "cocktails through an anthropological lens" started to come to fruition, and my thoughts of going back to school faded. I had developed an approach to drink-making that encompassed ethnobotany, foraging, and farming, and when I poured a drink into a glass, it could act as a small story that wove together all those threads.

SLOW DRINKS

The title *Slow Drinks* contains several meanings. A slow drink is a carefully crafted cocktail with a unique backstory, whether it's about an ingredient, region, person, or technique. In the literal sense, these drinks are "slow" in that they take time and patience. This includes the preservation processes, as well as the growing time for the ingredients. Many of these ingredients have specific seasonal windows of availability, and when they run out, the long wait for them to reappear the following year begins. Finally, *Slow Drinks* can be interpreted as an extension of the principles put forth by Slow Food International, an organization in which I am extensively involved.

The cocktail revival did not happen in a vacuum, it occurred in concert with an international food renaissance. Chef-driven restaurants emerged, the Slow Food movement was started in Italy by Carlo Petrini in 1986, and the modern locavore ethos began to take shape. It was a monumental moment in history where people in the Western world reconsidered how they ate, where their food came from, and ultimately how they imbibed. As a result, new trends began to enter the drinking landscape that had much more in common with the food movement of the time.

Slow Drinks teaches readers how to take ingredients that grow in or near their backyard and transform them into a delicious beverage. Often, these are ingredients that have been historically important in the production of food, drinks, and medicine for centuries, but have been forgotten in the industrialized age due to many factors including colonialism and cultural erasure.

I hope you can implement the information here wherever you live. My ultimate goal is for this book to be a springboard; to adapt this information to any number of different environments all over the planet. Remember to take it slow, have fun, and embrace the unknown. Not every experiment or cocktail will work out the way you hoped, but at least you'll get to spend time outside and in the kitchen and sip some delicious drinks along the way. Enjoy.

A Note on Cultural Context

I always do my best to mention the role ingredients have played in different cultures' foodways throughout history. These ingredients don't exist in a vacuum and cannot be divorced from their historical contexts. Approaching from the perspective of curiosity and admiration rather than exploitation allows us to draw inspiration from an ingredient or tradition while simultaneously honoring the people who helped popularize it. Educating ourselves on the cultural origins of ingredients and techniques, and, when possible, connecting with these communities to help ensure accurate representation of their cuisine is key.

This is especially important when talking about foraging, where so much of our knowledge comes to us from marginalized Indigenous, Black, and rural, often poor, populations whose traditions taught us which ingredients are safe, nutritious, and/or medicinally beneficial to consume, as well as the processes needed to transform them from their raw state.

Here in the United States, Indigenous Americans were the original stewards of the land and possessed an intricate understanding of the delicate balance between humans and their environments. After a devastatingly large percentage of Indigenous communities were wiped out by disease, warfare, and genocide, many were then forcibly removed from their land. As Western "civilization" encroached on Native homelands and destroyed ancient, thriving forests, Congress began establishing National Parks, in which foraging and hunting were prohibited. These events nearly put an end to the traditional foodways that were inextricably linked to Native American identity, with most historical anecdotes we see today collected from anthropologists and

ethnobotanists in the nineteenth and twentieth centuries. However, it has been wonderful to see the rise in recent years of Indigenous voices such as Oglala Lakota Sioux chef Sean Sherman, who have helped lead the way in reclaiming and revitalizing Native American cuisine.

For Black communities, foraging has long been a part of their foodways in both the North and South, with much of this knowledge originally taught to them by local Indigenous populations. In the North, it was a free, abundant means of finding food, and in the antebellum South, enslaved Black communities foraged, hunted, fished, and trapped to bulk up the rations they were given by plantation owners.

After the Civil War, many Black people in the North and South consumed and sold foraged food as a means of sustenance and a way to make a living. However, trespass laws were soon put in place that permitted foraging only on land that the forager owned. By making foraging illegal in public parks and private land, it became largely seen as taboo by the general public. Overtime, many Black people became disconnected from foraging as they migrated out of the rural countryside and into cities. Plus there was the harsh reality that being alone in the woods wasn't always safe. There are many people working to change the disconnect, including Alexis Nikole Nelson, the wild food educator known on TikTok as the Black Forager, who has been an inspiration for millions of people with her contagious enthusiasm and mastery of wild cuisine.

In the last few decades, we've seen foraging return to the spotlight but it's far too often that BIPOC are excluded from the conversation, despite the fact that much of this information is their intellectual property. I realize full well the privilege I occupy as a white person who forages on Lenni Lenape land, and it is my duty to give credit for the traditions that have paved the way for me to do so.

CHAPTER 1

THE BASICS

For me, when making drinks, everything begins with the ingredients. Often, these are foraged, so I need to know where to find them; or they are grown in the garden, which means the seeds were started months before I'll ever be able to harvest and taste it. Or they were grown by a farmer, in which case I'll need to know that they have grown it in previous years, or I'll have to convince one to try growing it for that upcoming season. In any case, this is an exercise in patience and one of the truly slow elements of this practice.

Sourcing ingredients when they are in season at peak ripeness and freshness, then transporting them the short distance to your kitchen, and finally, to the plate or the glass, ultimately results in a final product that tastes better.

I realize that many people (my former self included) shop for all of their food at the supermarket where the concept of seasonality doesn't really exist. I still get food from the supermarket; however, I also supplement a large portion of my diet with food I've grown, harvested from the wild, or purchased from my farmers in my region.

Many of the ingredients called for in this book require you to venture outside of the supermarket. Speaking from experience, this is a process that takes time and patience. However, if you tend a garden of any size, visit a farmer's market, or forage in any capacity, then you are already eating and drinking better, fresher, and more flavorfully. If you don't, my hope is that once you immerse yourself in this pursuit, it won't take long to see that it's worth the extra bit of effort. There is no moment more sublime than tasting the year's first ripe strawberry, peach, tomato, or almost any other ingredient that was allowed to ripen in its own proper way. It also allows us to revel in the ebbs and flows of the seasons and know that where one ingredient's window of availability ends, another's begins.

Foraging is no longer necessary for our survival, but for many, it offers a rare opportunity to connect to nature and take pause from modern society. In that way, foraging is a revolutionary act, one that allows us to reclaim autonomy from the industrialized food system that has profoundly influenced the modern diet. And yet for others, foraging is alluring for the thrill of discovering new, delicious ingredients and flavors that exist right under our noses.

While foraging can make us more conscious and respectful of our natural environment, it can harm an ecosystem. To ensure that the ingredients we are foraging are there for future generations to enjoy, it is of vital importance to not overharvest, making sure that we are encouraging new growth, and always keeping the overall health and vitality of the environment in mind. To accomplish this, we need to learn which plants are endangered, rare, or require a long time to establish themselves, and harvest them in a responsible way, if at all.

Equally important is learning which plants are safe for us to consume. Use foraging guidebooks and plant identification apps (I recommend iNaturalist), take a foraging class, join a local foraging club, and try to connect with an online community of foragers in your area. I subscribe to an email-based group of local foragers known as the Wild Foodies of Philly. I also subscribe to several plant- and mushroom-identification groups on Facebook and follow many foragers on Instagram and TikTok. I've learned as much, if not more, from social media as I have from books over the years.

Another safe foraging practice is to avoid harvesting food next to heavily traveled roadways or where chemicals are sprayed. Staying slightly off the beaten path is generally a good idea.

Although this book reads as a snapshot of the foraging calendar here in the mid-Atlantic, I have made the conscious effort to choose plants that are widespread and likely to be found throughout much of North America and, in many cases, the world. For the most part, I've also tried to include wild foods that are easy to identify and hopefully easy to find. If you are unsure if what you're harvesting is the desired ingredient, play it safe and do not consume it. To assist you as you begin your foraging journey, I have included each ingredient's native range, tips for identifying them, as well as regional substitutes when possible.

A Note on Pregnancy and Safety

The recipes in this book are a mix of alcoholic and nonalcoholic recipes. It goes without saying that the alcoholic recipes should be avoided during pregnancy, but it's also important to check with your doctor to make sure the nonalcoholic recipes are safe to consume while pregnant. The general consensus is that fermented foods and nonalcoholic drinks are safe and potentially good for the mom and baby during pregnancy, but it's a good idea to check with your healthcare provider to be safe. Also, certain herbs and botanical ingredients should be avoided during pregnancy. These include hibiscus, rhubarb, juniper, sassafras, wormwood, mugwort, horehound, and yarrow, as well as many others not included in this book.

Gardening is the other main way that I have access to unique ingredients that I wouldn't be able to source otherwise. I have two gardens I manage, one behind my home and the other behind the restaurant, and it is not something I take for granted. In the years before I had my own garden, I was a proud member of a community garden and absolutely loved the experience of sharing knowledge and ingredients with other people from my community.

Start by choosing a site that gets ample sunlight. Growing ingredients in raised beds or even pots gives you better control over the conditions in the soil and, most important for me, there are far less weeds. Five years ago, I started with wooden raised beds that are now starting to rot. Next year I will switch to galvanized steel beds, which should last me a minimum of thirty years.

I like to use a 50/50 mix of topsoil and compost to fill my beds and top them off with a few inches of fresh compost each spring (bonus points if you composted it yourself). Compost is truly a miracle amendment that doubles as a fertilizer and weed-reducing mulch. Of course, there will still be weeds. For manual weed removal, I highly recommend buying yourself a stirrup hoe, which will save your body a lot of wear and tear over time.

Buy seeds and starts specific to your area. In addition to being best suited to your local growing conditions, you are also helping ensure the survival of an at-risk, endangered, or possibly even functionally extinct ingredient. The greatest resource that I have found for learning about these varieties is the Slow Food Ark of Taste, which has an extensive, international list of heritage ingredients broken down by country.

If you're starting your own seeds, it's worth investing in a simple grow light setup and a heated seedling mat, which will aid germination. You can use seedling starter cells to start seeds and "pot them up" into larger cells as they grow, or you can do what I do and use plastic cups with soldered holes in the bottom and keep them in there until they're ready to be set out. For seed starting, I layer about 1 inch/2.5 cm of extremely nitrogen-rich potting soil on the bottom, then top with a more broad-spectrum potting soil for the upper 3 inches/7 cm. After planting your seeds, my advice is water once a day, add organic fertilizer once a week, and keep the grow lights only about 4 inches/10 cm above your seedlings.

Farmers' markets are another wonderful resource for sourcing fruits, vegetables, and anything else that you can't grow yourself. As you go more frequently, you will get to learn more about your farmer, which varieties they grow, which ones are your favorites, and when they come into season. It's a wonderful thing to be able to build a relationship with the person who is growing your food and know that you are helping them sustain their family and livelihood as they help sustain yours.

Supermarkets certainly have their time and place. Use your best judgment to make sure you are getting the freshest ingredients and, when possible, opt for organic over conventional produce.

STOCKING YOUR BAR

Many people find making cocktails intimidating. Part of the blame can be placed on leather apron–clad, mustachioed "mixologists" who make drinks feel unapproachable and complicated. Cocktail books can make it seem as though you need to spend a small fortune in order to stock your home bar with dozens of bottles that you may very likely never use again.

Unlike many other cocktail books that rely heavily on hard-to-find brands, I talk instead about classes of spirits. If I do include a brand, and you have another producer that you prefer, use the one you like the best. Once this book is in your hands, you're making drinks for *you*, not me.

The following list includes brands that I find to be both well-made and well-priced.

Base Spirits

GIN
Made by distilling neutral grain alcohol with juniper and other botanicals, including citrus, herbs, and spices.

Shopping List: Although there are quite a few styles of gin, you'll need only a bottle of London dry gin to complete the recipes in this book. I prefer either Tanqueray or Beefeater.

WHISK(E)Y
A distilled beverage made from fermented, malted grains, most commonly barley (Irish, Scotch, and Japanese whiskys), corn (bourbon), and rye (rye whiskey). It's almost always aged in charred oak casks to make it palatable, as unaged whiskey is quite harsh.

Shopping List: There are so many incredible whiskeys from around the world, but those I stock in my home bar are Buffalo Trace Bourbon, Old Overholt Rye, Redbreast Irish Whiskey, Famous Grouse Blended Scotch, peaty Laphroaig ten-year Islay single-malt Scotch, and Japanese Akashi White Oak single-malt whisky.

VODKA
A neutral spirit made from grains, potatoes, beets, and/or grapes.

Shopping List: Any vodka of suitable quality will do, such as Tito's, or one of the countless locally made options available today. You'll also need a 151-proof vodka, such as Everclear, for crafting liqueurs throughout the rest of the book.

TEQUILA AND MEZCAL

Mezcal, meaning "cooked agave," is the name given to all agave spirits produced throughout Mexico, including tequila. However, most people think of mezcal as the smoky agave spirit produced in Oaxaca, and tequila as the distillate produced in Jalisco.

Tequila can be made only from a large, spiky succulent known as blue agave that is either steamed in stainless-steel pressure cookers or baked in neutral clay ovens to convert its starches to fermentable sugars. Mezcal, on the other hand, is made from any one of roughly thirty different agaves, wild or cultivated, that are roasted in underground pits with hot stones for days or weeks, which imparts a smoky flavor.

Both tequila and mezcal can be broken down into blanco (unaged), reposado ("rested" in barrels for two to twelve months), and añejo (aged in oak from one to three years). With blanco mezcal and tequila, you can really taste the agave, whereas aged agave spirits are more similar to whiskey.

Shopping List: One bottle each of blanco, reposado, and añejo from a solid brand, such as Cazadores, will do, although you'll definitely taste the difference with top-shelf brands like Siembra Azul. For mezcal, you'll need one good blanco, such as Del Maguey's Vida.

RUM

Rum is a distillate produced from sugarcane juice, cane sugar, or molasses, bottled aged or unaged. Rum is mainly produced in the Caribbean, and the styles often can be traced back to the colonizing European country. There are lighter, molasses-distilled Spanish rums, grassy French rums (known as rhum agricole), and richer English rums, including funky, ester-rich Jamaican rums. Each is so different that it's not recommended to swap styles, however, using them in concert with each other can often produce magical results, hence the old adage "what one rum can't do, three rums can."

Shopping List: Rum is the most varied spirit in the world. That's why it's good to have one brand you know you can trust. For me, that brand is Plantation. By stocking your bar with a bottle of their 3 Stars white rum, Original Dark, and Xaymaca, a funky, ester-rich Jamaican rum, you can cover most of your rum bases. Having a molasses-heavy black rum on hand, such as Goslings Black Seal or Hamilton Jamaican Pot Still Black, for Dark 'n' Stormys is also nice.

BRANDY

Brandy is an umbrella term used to describe any spirit distilled from fermented fruit juice. This can include French cognac, Italian grappa, and Peruvian and Chilean pisco (all wine-based brandies), American applejack (made from distilled cider), or one of the many aromatic *eau de vie* distillates made from any number of other fermented fruit products.

Shopping List: Laird's Applejack, pisco (for Peruvian, I like BarSol Acholado, for Chilean, Espíritu del Elqui), H by Hine VSOP Cognac.

Modifiers

Modifiers, including amaro, bitters, liqueurs, and vermouths, refer to alcoholic ingredients used in harmony with base spirits to add depth and complexity to cocktails. For a more in-depth discussion of these categories, see chapter 2 on preservation. Here is a list of modifiers I use in the recipes that follow:

Amaro: Amaro Averna, Aperol, Campari, Fernet-Branca, Zucca Rabarbaro.

Bitters: Angostura, Peychaud's, orange.

Liqueurs: Green and Yellow Chartreuse, Pierre Ferrand Dry Curaçao, Luxardo Maraschino.

Vermouth: The three main styles of vermouth you want in your home bar are sweet red vermouth, dry white vermouth, and blanc/bianco, which is a white sweet vermouth. French-produced Dolin makes expressions of each that are both affordable and delicious, making them an excellent choice. Additionally, it's worth picking up a bottle of Carpano Antica Formula, a rich, full-bodied vermouth that makes an exceptional Manhattan.

Other Ingredients

ICE

For the recipes in this book, you really only need two types of ice: large cubes (2 inches/5 cm) and small cubes (1 inch/2.5 cm). In addition to serving drinks over small cubes, I also use these for shaking and stirring cocktails.

Occasionally, I splurge and use pebble ice for tiki drinks, Juleps, and Smashes. Some fast-food chains will sell you bags of pebble ice for next to nothing.

CITRUS

All citrus juice should be freshly squeezed. When garnishing with citrus peels, make sure to use the freshest fruit that is firm to the touch and unblemished.

Sweeteners

Sweeteners are an integral part of creating a balanced cocktail. In addition to sweetening, they also add body and mouthfeel to a drink. Sweeteners can be neutral, like simple syrup, or they can affect the overall flavor of a drink, like maple syrup, honey, or a less-refined sugar syrup, that uses demerara or brown sugar.

Water is a critical component of syrups, functioning to dissolve sugar, as well as to thin out thicker sweeteners, such as honey and agave. Simple syrups are composed of one part sugar to one part water; however, sometimes the goal is to sweeten with as little dilution as possible, in which case you will use a "rich syrup" of two parts sugar to one part water. Thicker syrups with a higher sugar content, such as honey and agave, are often thinned with three parts by volume of the sweetener to one part boiling water to make them easier to work with. Maple syrup is thin enough that it doesn't need to be thinned further. Here is a list of the most commonly used syrups:

SIMPLE SYRUP

Combine equal parts white, brown, or demerara sugar and hot water by volume (or weight for a more precise ratio) in a saucepan over medium-low heat and stir frequently until the sugar dissolves. Will keep for one month when stored in the refrigerator. If a recipe says "simple syrup" it always refers to a 1:1 syrup made with white sugar unless otherwise specified.

RICH SYRUP

Combine two parts white, brown, or demerara sugar and one part hot water by volume (or weight for a more precise ratio) in a saucepan over medium-low heat and stir frequently until the sugar dissolves. Will keep for six months stored in the refrigerator.

HONEY SYRUP

Combine three parts wildflower honey and one part boiling water by volume in a container and stir until well incorporated. Will keep for six months stored in the refrigerator.

AGAVE SYRUP

Combine three parts raw blue agave nectar and one part boiling water by volume in a container and stir until well incorporated. Will keep for six months stored in the refrigerator.

Botanical Flavor Components

The list of possible botanical ingredients for use in cocktails is endless and impossible to fully list here. However, I've included this list of some of those I use most, broken down by category and flavor profile.

BOTANICAL FLAVORING AGENTS

Bitter Ingredients

Dandelion (*Taraxacum* spp.)
Chicories (*Cichorium* spp.)
Artichoke and cardoon (*Cynara* spp.)
Wormwood and mugwort (*Artemisia* spp.)
Hops (*Humulus* lupulus)
Sorrel (*Rumex acetosa*)
Horehound (*Marrubium* vulgare)

Acidic Ingredients

Sumac (*Rhus* spp.)
Citruses (*Citrus* spp.)
Lemongrass (*Cymbopogon* spp.)
Rhubarb (*Rheum* spp.)
Hibiscus (*Hibiscus* spp.)
Lemon balm (*Melissa officinalis*)

Ingredients for Spice

Coriander seed (*Coriandrum sativum*)
Fig leaves (*Ficus carica*)
Fennel seed (*Foeniculum vulgare*)
Birch (*Betula* spp.)
Sassafras (*Sassafras albidum*)
Spruce (*Picea* spp.)
Pine (*Pinus* spp.)
Juniper (*Juniperus* spp.)

Floral Ingredients

Yarrow (*Achillea millefolium*)
Elderflower (*Sambucus* spp.)
Honeysuckle (*Lonicera* spp.)
Valerian (*Valeriana officinalis*)
Chamomile (*Chamaemelum nobile*)

Hardy (Woody) Herbs

Rosemary (*Salvia rosmarinus*)
Sage (*Salvia officinalis*)
Thyme (*Thymus* spp.)
Oregano (*Origanum vulgare*)
Lavender (*Lavandula* spp.)

Tender Herbs

Mint (*Mentha* spp.)
Fennel (*Foeniculum vulgare*)
Hyssop (*Hyssopus officinalis*)
Dill (*Anethum graveolens*)
Celery leaf (*Apium graveolens*)
Basil (*Ocimum basilicum*)

CUCURBITS

ROSE FAMILY

CONI

*spp. indicates several species in the same genus

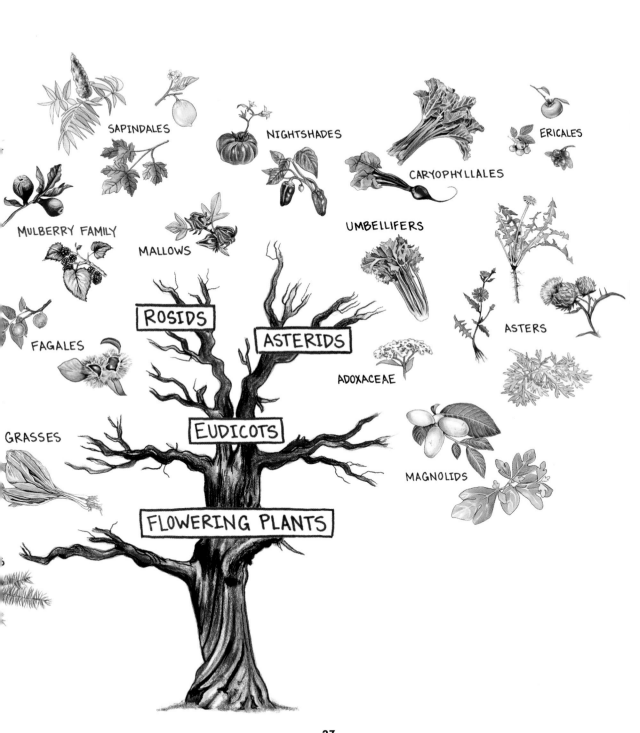

SAPINDALES

NIGHTSHADES

ERICALES

CARYOPHYLLALES

MULBERRY FAMILY

UMBELLIFERS

MALLOWS

ROSIDS

ASTERIDS

ASTERS

FAGALES

ADOXACEAE

EUDICOTS

GRASSES

MAGNOLIDS

FLOWERING PLANTS

MAKING A COCKTAIL

Making a proper cocktail is easy to do at home, keeping in mind a few key points.

SHAKING AND STRAINING

In general, cocktails with citrus juice, cream, eggs, and/or muddled ingredients are shaken in order to chill, dilute, and aerate them. If a drink is served "up" (with no ice), I recommend shaking for 15 seconds, 10 seconds for one that's going to be served over a large ice cube, and for about 5 seconds if it's going to be served over small cubes.

Drinks that are served up or over large cubes should also be *double strained* through both a Hawthorne strainer as well as a mesh strainer to remove ice shards. Double straining is not necessary when straining shaken drinks over small cubes, but make sure that you are always using fresh ice and not recycling the cubes you used to shake the drink.

Cocktails with egg white should be shaken with ice to dilute and chill, then double strained and shaken again without ice for an additional 5 seconds to emulsify the egg white. This is called *dry shaking*.

Last but certainly not least, when shaking a cocktail, put your back into it and shake as hard as you can. The famous bartender Harry Craddock once said, "Don't just rock it, you are trying to wake it up, not put it to sleep!" and I couldn't agree more.

STIRRING

Drinks that contain only spirits or spirits and a sweetener are stirred in a mixing glass with the addition of ice. Stirring is meant to chill and dilute a drink without aerating it, resulting in a cocktail that is ice cold and silky smooth. Drinks that are served up should be stirred for around 30 seconds, and those that are served over a large cube need be stirred for only around 15 seconds. After stirring, the drink can be strained into your glass of choice using a Hawthorne strainer. Some ice shards are bound to sneak through the strainer, and if these bother you, you can either scoop them out or use a mesh strainer to strain the drink again.

GARNISHING

A citrus peel garnish is as much an ingredient as it is an aesthetic component. The oils in the citrus add brightness, aroma, and flavor to a drink. To make a citrus garnish, remove a swath of the peel using a Y-peeler, trying not to dig too deep down into the bitter pith layer. Next, with the skin side facing the drink, squeeze the peel to release the oils. You should be able to see and smell these immediately. Next, rub the peel around the rim of the glass and either drop it inside the drink, arrange it on the rim, or discard the peel.

Aside from citrus, there are an infinite number of possible garnishes. As a rule of thumb, they should be used to enhance the drink's flavor, aroma, or aesthetic presentation. They can be arranged on the rim of a drink, skewered with a pick, or laid across the top of a large cube. If garnishing with fresh herbs, whether a single leaf or a small bouquet, be sure to give it a light smack to release the herb's aroma. When garnishing with wedges of fruits, including citrus or apple, attach them to the glass via a notch cut in the center, or skewer with a pick. Maraschino cherries, olives, or cocktail onions can be skewered or placed in the bottom of the glass depending on your preference.

Types of Cocktails

Having a solid foundation of some of history's most popular recipes will better set you up to create your own beverages. Here are what I believe to be the five most important types of cocktails and some popular riffs that can be made by modifying one or more of their ingredients.

SOURS
Formula: 2 oz/60 ml spirit, ¾ oz/22 ml citrus juice, ¾ oz/22 ml simple syrup (or other syrup)

Examples: Daiquiri, Gimlet, Whiskey Sour, Bee's Knees, Gold Rush, Pisco Sour, Jack Rose, Lemon Drop Martini, Margarita, Sidecar, Cosmopolitan

MARTINIS AND MANHATTANS
Formula: 2 oz/60 spirit, 1 oz/30 ml aromatized wine, bitters

Examples: Classic Martini and Manhattan, Martinez, Bronx, Bobby Burns, Black Manhattan, Gibson, Vesper

OLD FASHIONED–STYLE COCKTAILS
Formula: 2 oz/60 ml spirit, ½ oz/15 ml simple syrup (or other syrup), bitters

Examples: Old Fashioned, Julep, Smash, Sazerac, Oaxaca Old Fashioned

HIGHBALLS
Formula: 2 oz/60 ml spirit, sparkling mixer for topping

Examples: Cuba Libre, Pimm's Cup, Americano, Moscow Mule, Dark & Stormy, Collins, Fizz, Buck, Cooler

NEGRONIS
Formula: 1 oz/30 ml spirit, 1 oz/30 ml amaro, 1 oz/30 ml aromatized wine

Examples: Negroni, Boulevardier, Old Pal, Kingston Negroni, Mezcal Negroni, Bijou

Tools and Equipment

Cocktail Shakers

Spice Grinder, Mortar and Pestle, and/or Molcajete

Silicone Ice Cube Trays

Barspoons

Glass Jars

Cone Strainers

Hawthorne Strainers

Mixing Glasses

Measuring Cups

1 Cup / 235 ml
1/2 Cup / 118 ml
1/3 Cup / 79 ml
1/4 Cup / 59 ml

Measuring Spoons

Citrus Press

Spice Grater

Jiggers

Muddler

Y-Peeler

Digital Scale

Glassware

Glassware is an essential element of a well-composed beverage. Here is a list of drinking vessels I recommend having on hand. Also, keep in mind the temperature of your drink. An easy bartending trick to incorporate at home is to chill glassware before pouring your drink into it. This can be done by placing your glass in the freezer or filling it with ice and water for a few minutes beforehand before emptying it out. For hot drinks, you can preheat your mug or glassware with hot water before pouring the drink in the glass.

COLLINS GLASS: Also known as a highball glass, this is the go-to for most tall drinks served over ice.

COUPE GLASS: A stemmed glass with a broad, shallow bowl, it is a wonderful choice for both shaken and stirred "up" drinks.

HEATPROOF MUG: For hot drinks.

NICK AND NORA: A stemmed glass with a deeper, more rounded bowl than a coupe, that's great for shaken and stirred "up" drinks.

PILSNER GLASS: Good for beer cocktails such as Micheladas and Shandies, as well as tall drinks served over pebble ice.

PUNCH BOWL WITH LADLE AND CUPS: Although this isn't technically necessary, treating yourself to a punch bowl will amplify the presentation of serving a large format cocktail for communal consumption. I promise that it is something that you (and your guests) won't regret.

ROCKS GLASS: Also known as an Old Fashioned glass, this is the preferred vessel for serving drinks on, you guessed it, the rocks, whether over one large cube or smaller cubes.

WINEGLASS: For spritzes, certain beers, wines, and meads.

Fermentation Tools

SWING-CAP BOTTLES: I use 750 ml (25 oz) swing-cap bottles for all of my soda, beer, wine, mead, and kombucha ferments. They are perfect for checking the pressure inside by opening the cap and "burping" the bottle ever so slightly (see page 45). You can purchase them new, or recycle brands that use them, such as Stateside Vodka or Grolsch beer, although the Grolsch bottles are only 500 ml (17 oz).

GLASS CARBOY OR PLASTIC FERMENTATION BUCKET: A carboy is a large glass jug used for brewing beer, wine, cider, and mead. It's worth it to have a few sizes depending on what volume you are brewing. I recommend starting with 1-gallon/1 L, 3-gallon/3 L, and 5-gallon/5 L carboys. Plastic fermentation buckets are a cheaper, more lightweight alternative that will accomplish the same task. Both need to be equipped with airlocks.

AIRLOCK: An airlock consists of a two-chambered vent plugged into a rubber stopper known as a bung. It allows excess carbon dioxide that builds up inside the carboy as a result of fermentation to escape without allowing air to enter.

WOODEN BARREL: Aging amari, other liqueurs, beer, wine, mead, and vinegars in a barrel helps them absorb flavors from the barrel's wood while simultaneously mellowing harsh, undesirable flavors.

CERAMIC FERMENTATION CROCK OR PLASTIC FOOD-SAFE CONTAINER: Ceramic crocks are the most traditional containers for fermenting foods and drinks. Food is usually fermented in cylindrical crocks with a moat that acts as an airlock, whereas liquid brews, such as kombucha, soda, and beer, are often fermented in crocks with a spigot on the bottom that are great for tasting your brew as it progresses. Any food-safe plastic or glass container could be used instead.

FERMENTATION WEIGHTS: Fermentation weights, typically made from ceramic or glass, are used in lacto-fermentation to keep ingredients submerged in the brine to avoid contact with air (and mold formation).

FUNNELS: A set of stainless-steel funnels for decanting liquid into various size bottles and/or carboys to avoid spillage.

CHAPTER 2

PRESERVATION TECHNIQUES AND BASE RECIPES

Preserving food halts the process of decay by inhibiting the growth of harmful microorganisms, including bacteria and fungi. This can either be achieved by creating an environment that is inhospitable to their growth, or by creating the right conditions for beneficial microbes to thrive. There are dozens of ways to achieve this goal, but I focus on just a few here: fermentation, vinegar preserves, alcoholic infusion, and sugar preserves. Though many of these processes may sound intimidating, with a little patience you will see that they are safe and easy.

Each preservation technique that follows will include a broad foundation recipe that can be adapted to nearly any ingredient. In the flowchart on page 71, you can see how many directions you can go with a single ingredient. The main takeaway from this chart is that there is no one right way to treat any ingredient, but rather an infinite world of possibilities to experiment with.

FERMENTATION

Fermentation is one of humankind's oldest modes of preservation, dating back millennia. The word *fermentation* is derived from the Latin word *fervere*, meaning "to boil." This was the name given to the process by the Romans upon seeing vats of grapes naturally bubbling as the juices were converted to wine by alcoholic fermentation.

Alcohol is just one of dozens of fermented products. They can be explained as the transformation of ingredients by bacteria, yeasts, or mold. I focus on soda, beer, wine, mead, vinegar, lacto-fermented pickles, and kombucha.

Sometimes, we rely solely on wild fermentation, which uses only the microbes already present on the surface of whatever we're fermenting. More commonly, we introduce the desired microorganisms by adding a starter culture known as a SCOBY "symbiotic culture of bacteria and yeast." I use three types: kombucha mother, vinegar mother, and most important of all, the ginger bug.

Ginger Bug

A ginger bug is a wild yeast starter consisting of grated, skin-on ginger, sugar, and water. This slurry is rich in "bugs" from the ginger skin, mainly ambient yeasts (including *Saccharomyces cerevisiae*, used in brewing beer) and lactic acid bacteria (LAB). Making the bug is pretty simple. Mix grated organic ginger, simple syrup, and water in a clean food-safe container, stir well to incorporate, and cover with cheesecloth or tea towel secured with a rubber band or other non-airtight lid, so that the gasses can escape but no insects can enter. Each day for the next four days (or until the bug is vigorously bubbling), you'll need to feed it with simple syrup and fresh grated ginger. Soon you will see the ginger rise to the top and the slurry will begin to bubble.

I have been using my current ginger bug now for about six years, and my wife and I often joke that it is like our pet. We regularly feed it, monitor it to make sure it looks healthy and active, and have even helped it reproduce by packaging it for other aspiring fermenters to use at home. Not all ginger bugs are created equal, however. Depending on its environment, your starter culture will take on various ambient microbes over time. In this way, each bug will develop its own *microbial terroir*, to use a term coined by David Chang, and develop flavor profiles specific to their surroundings. You may even notice slight changes in the flavor of your ferments depending on the time of year.

Once your bug is well-established, it is time to put it to work doing your microbial bidding. I like to think of fermenting with the ginger bug as a sort of "choose your own adventure" story where you can change the nature of your final product by altering the variables. Take a base *wort* (the name given to an unfermented liquid) and couple it with a short fermentation, and you have nonalcoholic soda (1% alcohol or less). Increase the time of fermentation, and you'll have made alcoholic beer. Increase the time and sugar, and you have wine. Swap sugar for honey, and you have mead. Let the soda, beer, wine, or mead ferment for three to six months longer, and you'll end up with vinegar. All these incredible variations in flavor from the unassuming, yet mighty, ginger bug.

HOW TO GROW A GINGER BUG

DAY 1

½ cup/48 g grated organic unpeeled fresh ginger (use a Microplane or the smallest hole on a box grater)

1¼ cups/300 ml simple syrup (see page 25)

1½ cups/360 ml filtered water

Add all the ingredients to a food-safe container, stir to incorporate, and cover with cheesecloth or a tea towel secured with a rubber band or other non-airtight lid, so that the gasses can escape but no insects can enter. Store at room temperature (between 65 and 70° F/18 and 21° C).

DAYS 2, 3, 4

An additional ¼ cup/24 g grated ginger, each day

An additional ½ cup/120 ml simple syrup (see page 25), each day

Stir to incorporate the ingredients.

By day 4, you should start to see signs of microbial activity—it should bubble when you stir it and smell mildly alcoholic.

DAY 5 AND BEYOND

¼ cup/24 g grated ginger

½ cup/120 ml simple syrup (see page 25)

Add this on day 5. Your bug should be active by now and ready to be stored. Continue to add this same amount of ginger and simple syrup once or twice per week moving forward to keep the bug alive.

If your ginger bug is not showing signs of life after a week, the problem likely lies in either the ginger or the water. It is very important to use organic ginger in your recipe, as much of the ginger available in grocery stores has been irradiated, a process that kills the bacteria and yeasts necessary to produce a healthy bug.

CONTINUED

HOW TO GROW A GINGER BUG, CONTINUED

The preferred way to do this would be to source ginger in bulk from a local grower and freeze it for the months when it is no longer available (even in the colder climates, farmers can successfully produce a ginger crop in a hot house). If you live somewhere where this isn't accessible, any health food store will be sure to have organic ginger.

If you are using organic ginger and your ginger bug has still not become active after a week, it could be because the water you are using has a high amount of chlorine, which will inhibit microbial growth. Typically, chlorine is removed using any standard water filter, but if you are still experiencing problems, using distilled or bottled water should remedy the issue.

Variation: You can swap out other yeast-rich ingredients for the ginger, like conifer needles, wildflowers, and wild berries. Just add the same amount of fresh ingredients and sugar as you would with the ginger bug, and within a few days you should have an active-enough culture to inoculate your soda wort. I have experimented with other starters, but I've found the ginger bug to make the best ginger beer, which is kind of the most important criteria for me. Plus, I find it to be the easiest to keep healthy and alive year-round, and I have had tremendous success in brewing all kinds of sodas, beers, wines, and meads from it.

A Note on Hygiene:

Hygiene is an important element of fermentation, but it isn't any more complicated than washing your dishes. Though some books recommend using bleach, sterilization tablets, or other chemicals, I have always found the combination of dish soap, hot water, and a sponge or bottle brush does the trick. It is important to remember that people have been brewing for thousands of years in conditions that were much less hygienic than what can be achieved using these three things. To this day, I have never had a single issue with any one of my ferments.

Nonalcoholic Sodas and Tonics: Ginger Beer

When I started tending bar at the Farm and Fisherman, the first thing our chef tasked me with was figuring out a recipe for fermented homemade ginger beer. We tried using brewer's yeast and baker's yeast, but both yielded a soda that was too explosive. Next, we tried using a kombucha mother, but we just ended up making ginger kombucha in our naivete. Once we tried the ginger bug method, we knew that we had something special. The bubbles were tight, it was perfectly balanced, and it had just the right amount of spice from the ginger. Now this ginger beer recipe is the base recipe for almost every soda I make.

The formula is roughly ten parts water, three parts simple syrup, two parts freshly squeezed lemon juice, one part grated fresh ginger, and one-half part ginger bug. We generally make this in 5 qt/5 L batches with 100 oz/296 ml water, 32 oz/.95 L simple syrup (see page 25), 20 oz/591 ml freshly squeezed lemon juice, 10 oz/284 g grated skin-on fresh ginger, and 4 oz/118 ml Ginger Bug (see page 39). This recipe is scalable and can be adjusted to make a larger or smaller batch.

All these ingredients are mixed into a wort and put into a non-airtight vessel and allowed to sit for 2 days while the primary fermentation occurs. As this first phase implies, there are multiple stages of fermentation needed to reach the desired final product (two in this case). You can get very technical with this step and ferment the wort in an airlocked container, but in all my years of brewing sodas I have never had a problem brewing in 6-quart/6 L plastic food-safe containers as long as I'm following proper sanitation practices and starting with a healthy ginger bug.

Note: Nonalcoholic sodas were traditionally known as "small beers" because they were fermented in the same style of alcoholic beers but stopped short before high amounts of alcohol accumulated. As a result, many common sodas today still have the word "beer" in them, including ginger beer, root beer, and birch beer, which may be confusing, especially for readers trying to avoid alcohol.

GINGER BEER MASTER RECIPE

Makes approximately six 750 ml bottles

---

3 qt/2.8 L water

1 qt/950 ml simple syrup (see page 25)

2½ c/590 ml freshly squeezed lemon juice

1¼ c/120 g grated organic unpeeled fresh ginger (use a Microplane or the smallest holes on a box grater)

½ c/160 ml Ginger Bug, liquid only (see page 39)

PRIMARY FERMENTATION

In a thoroughly cleaned 6 qt/6 L food-safe container, mix all the ingredients together to create the base. Cover with cheesecloth or a tea towel secured with a rubber band or other non-airtight lid, and allow to sit at room temperature for 2 days to ferment. After the first 24 hours, you should begin to see signs of fermentation: The liquid will turn cloudy, the grated ginger will begin to rise and fall in the suspension, and if you put your ear close enough, you may even be able to hear bubbles faintly popping.

SECONDARY FERMENTATION

After 2 days have passed, it is time for the secondary fermentation. Pass your soda through a fine-mesh strainer to remove the solids and decant the strained ginger beer into six swing-top bottles. Add 1 Tbsp simple syrup (see page 25) to each 750 ml bottle (or 1 tsp per cup/240 ml if using another size bottle). This additional simple syrup is known as a *primer*, which both sweetens the brew to the desired level and functions as an additional food source for the yeast as it undergoes further fermentation. The naturally occurring carbon dioxide produced in this step will build pressure and cause the gas to be absorbed by the liquid in the bottle, resulting in a naturally carbonated beverage. This process is known as *bottle conditioning*.

Shake the bottle to incorporate and allow it to ferment at room temperature for an additional 1 to 2 days (or longer as needed). The soda should be sufficiently bubbly after this time but may take an additional day or two. Burp the bottle (see page 45) to see if it is carbonated, and once carbonated, store it in the refrigerator and drink within a few weeks.

CONTINUED

GINGER BEER MASTER RECIPE, CONTINUED

FUTURE SODA EXPERIMENTS

This ginger beer recipe can be used as the base recipe for any other soda that you want to make.

Taste your wort before primary fermentation to make sure it has a good balance of acidity, sweetness, and dilution. Some sodas (like Root Beer, page 119) benefit from less citrus in the wort, so as not to overpower the delicate flavors of the main ingredient.

Taste your wort again before secondary fermentation. It will likely be drier (less sweet) at this stage. If this is the case, it will require additional simple syrup prior to bottling. If it is still very sweet, or if you notice it's really active (i.e., very carbonated), you will not need to add any sugar primer for secondary fermentation.

Another variable to keep in mind when brewing sodas is that each ingredient will add different strains of wild yeasts, which can greatly affect the flavor of the final product, potentially making it sour, dry, and/or funky. This potential for variation in flavor is one of my favorite elements of fermentation. It is a reminder that these ingredients are very much alive and will result in beverages as varied as life itself. Approach brewing experimentally and be open to the fact that each fermented beverage is part of your learning experience.

Bottling and Carbonation

The process outlined earlier is what I have found to be the most effective in producing sodas that have consistently balanced flavors and the right amount of carbonation, but this is not a one-size-fits-all approach. Just as different strains of yeast can result in a wide variation in flavors, they may also result in differences in fermentation and carbonation. The sugar present in sodas will interact differently with the yeast strains, causing some to carbonate more quickly (like the Celery Tonic on page 225 and the Fermented Watermelon Soda on page 175), whereas others (like the Juniper Tonic on page 293) may require more time to bottle condition and carbonate.

In my early days of experimentation, I bottled many sodas and beers only to open them and have the liquid explode out of the bottle. Unfortunately, this has even happened to me in the middle of a busy dinner service, spraying me or another bartender in the face in front of a bar full of guests. While mistakes like this are bound to happen, there are some simple principles to follow to try to prevent it.

The first is choosing the right bottle type. For the recipes in this book, I usually recommend using a 750 ml glass swing-cap bottle. I find the swing cap makes it easier to check the carbonation levels inside than a traditional crown-capped bottle. To check the carbonation, hold the cap firmly with one hand, release the metal latch, and slowly crack the seal from the bottle opening. What you hope for is a slight hiss or pop, followed by the bubbles rising to the top of the bottle in a controlled manner. If you are greeted with a forceful expulsion of gas, or the liquid lunges towards the mouth of the bottle, it is likely overcarbonated and needs to be *burped*, which refers to opening and quickly closing the bottle a few times to release some of the excess carbonation.

If too much pressure builds up inside of a bottle, it is possible for the glass to explode. This can be dangerous, so it is important to regularly check on the bottles to prevent this. I recommend checking on bottles every 12 to 24 hours. In the case of highly active ferments, like Celery Tonic (see page 225) or Fermented Watermelon Soda (see page 175), bottles should be checked more frequently, every 3 to 6 hours. If your soda is not quite as carbonated as you want it to be, give it more time. Once you are happy with the level of carbonation, placing your bottles in the refrigerator will essentially freeze the fermentation in time by reducing it to a very, very slow crawl. Refrigeration can also diminish the opening "pop," so if you refrigerate when the bottle is slightly more carbonated than desired, it should settle down once it's thoroughly chilled.

If you are a beginner and are intimidated by gauging carbonation using glass bottles, it may be helpful to start with plastic bottles, which allow you to judge the carbonation level by squeezing on the sides of the bottle. When the sides feel rigid and resist when you push on them, the liquid inside is sufficiently carbonated.

Temperature is another factor to keep in mind to either speed or slow fermentation. Whereas placing your bottles in the refrigerator will stop fermentation, warmer temperatures speed up the process. For example, fermentations that take place in the winter or in a cool cellar will take longer than the same process in the summer or at room temperature.

Fermentation is an inexact science. When dealing with microscopic living organisms, there is only so much you can do to control what they are biologically programmed to do. Like anything else, it will get easier with more experience. Just take careful notes when you are beginning, especially when dealing with new ingredients, trying your best to learn from your mistakes and enjoy the process.

ALCOHOLIC FERMENTATION

There is an obsession with alcoholic nomenclature these days, but it is a relatively recent development. Until only a few centuries ago, alcohol was produced on a small scale by home brewers or village experts (oftentimes women) using a wide variety of sweeteners, such as honey, tree saps, malted grains or other starchy crops, and sugar. These primitive brews were fermented along with all types of botanical ingredients, including berries, grains, flowers, bittering herbs, barks, roots, and seeds, as well as medicinal and narcotic plants. Names didn't matter quite as much because fermented beverages were just what many people drank, since they were safer than water, which was frequently contaminated. Alcohol also offered a coveted source of calories, nutrients, and even medicine.

This all changed in sixteenth-century Europe, as alcohol production became industrialized and laws were put in place to govern and standardize its production. Examples include the German beer purity law of *Reinheitsgebot*, as well as the later-formed governing bodies of wine production including the French *appellation d'origine côntrolée* (AOC) and Italian *Denominazione di origine controllata* (DOC), which both outline very strict parameters for permitted grape varieties, labeling practices, designations of origin, and many other variables.

In this book, I depart from traditional definitions and follow a more free-form approach to brewing and fermentation, similar to the practices people used to follow for thousands of years. For simplicity's sake, I will refer to brews with lower alcohol levels as beer, those with higher alcohol levels as wine, and those brewed with honey as mead.

The good news is that if you have successfully brewed a soda, all you need to do to make your brew alcoholic is just give it more time. Unlike sodas, which have relatively no alcohol (less than 1%) and still contain plenty of sugar from their quick fermentation, the goal with beers, wines, and meads is to allow the fermentation to reach completion over a longer period, so that almost all the sugars have been converted to alcohol by the bacteria and yeast. That means that any soda recipe in this book can be used to make alcohol, and, conversely, that any beer, wine, or mead recipe can be stopped short to make a soda.

One caveat when brewing alcoholic beverages as compared to sodas is that the amount of citrus should be greatly reduced. Another variable to keep in mind is that the bottle-conditioning stage for carbonation will take longer due to the lower amount of activity that remains after fermentation (anywhere from 1 to 4 weeks, or even longer).

Wild Beer

The beer purity law *Reinheitsgebot*, which originated in sixteenth-century Germany, stated that beer could be brewed with only barley malt, yeast, hops, and water. Although *Reinheitsgebot* is not considered law outside of Germany, it has set the worldwide precedent for what is considered beer. These narrow parameters obscure the fact that for centuries beer was brewed with many different sweeteners and bittering agents. Some of these bitter herbs and barks included the "trinity" of yarrow, bog myrtle/sweet gale, and mugwort, as well as dandelion, juniper, horehound, wormwood, and many more. Sweeteners included malted grains, honey, and tree saps such as maple.

Although I'm not overly concerned with alcohol percentage, a rough guide is that using 1 quart/950 ml of 1:1 sugar syrup (as with the master recipe, page 49) will yield a beer that is roughly 5% alcohol by volume. Increasing that sugar syrup quantity to 1½ quarts/1.2 L will yield approximately 7.5%, 2 quarts/1.9 L will yield 10%. After that, we're beginning to get into wine territory by our loose definitions. Which sugar you use will also impact the flavor of your final brew, with white sugar creating lighter beers and unrefined sugars such as brown or demerara creating more dark, bitter beers.

When it comes to how to best extract flavor when brewing, you must decide whether to employ a hot- or cold-brewing method. As a rule of thumb, ingredients with stronger, more bitter flavors are best extracted by either boiling them in water (see Root Beer, page 119), or by covering them with boiling or close-to-boiling water as if you're brewing tea (see Dandelion Mead, page 95). Other, more delicate flavors are best prepared by cold-brewing them (see Spruce Beer, page 113, or sumac wine, page 299), or extracting their juice (see Blueberry Country Wine, page 165, and Wild Fermented Cider on page 220) via what I call the "blender method," in which you place your ingredient (chopping into chunks, if necessary) into a blender along with water from the wort recipe. Just make sure to measure the amount of water you add to the blender in order to subtract that volume from the total called for in the wort recipe. Blend on high until smooth, then pass through a cheesecloth-lined fine-mesh strainer, squeezing as much liquid from the solids as possible. Discard the solids.

BEER MASTER RECIPE

Makes approximately six 750 ml bottles

---

1 gal/3.8 L water

4 to 6 c/950 ml to 1.4 L bittering or flavoring ingredient (see chart, page 26)

1 qt/950 ml simple syrup (made from white, brown, or demerara sugar, see page 25), plus 1 Tbsp syrup per bottle for priming (see page 43)

½ c/120 ml Ginger Bug, liquid only (see page 39)

3 oz/89 ml freshly squeezed lemon or lime juice

HOT-BREWING DIRECTIONS

Bring the water to a boil. Add the bittering ingredient of choice to a large heatproof bowl. Turn off the heat, let the water stand for 3 minutes, then pour it over the bittering ingredient. Allow to infuse at room temperature until cool, or until the desired flavor extraction is complete. Once cool, add 1 qt/950 ml sugar syrup, the ginger bug, and citrus and stir well to incorporate. Let sit for a few days until signs of active fermentation appear.

Once active, you can strain out the solids, or leave them in if you think the brew will benefit from a prolonged infusion. Pour everything into your fermentation vessel. This can be a rudimentary setup like a food-grade container covered with cheesecloth or a tea towel secured with a rubber band or other non-airtight lid, or you can use a carboy or fermentation bucket outfitted with an airlock. If using an airlock, fill it with water and a splash of vodka (vodka helps avoid any microbial contamination in the water) to the designated lines and place it into the container opening.

Once bubbling subsides, after 4 to 6 weeks, rack the liquid into a new container, being careful not to disturb the yeast on the bottom. Pour the racked beer into bottles primed with the remaining 1 Tbsp of sugar syrup. Close the lid, shake to incorporate, and store in a cool, dark place. Wait 1 to 4 weeks for the beer to carbonate, checking every so often by "burping" the bottles to make sure they haven't overcarbonated. Once sufficiently carbonated, move to the refrigerator. This will keep for 1 year or more and will continue to change and evolve with time.

CONTINUED

COLD-BREWING DIRECTIONS

Combine the water, bittering ingredient, 1 qt/950 ml syrup, the ginger bug, and citrus in your fermentation vessel and mix well to incorporate. This can be a rudimentary setup like a food-grade container covered with cheesecloth or a tea towel bound with a rubber band or other non-airtight lid, or a carboy or fermentation bucket outfitted with an airlock. If using an airlock, fill it with water and a splash of vodka (vodka helps avoid any microbial contamination in the water) to the designated lines and place it into the container opening. The fermentation should be active and bubbling within a few days.

After 1 week, strain out the solids, or leave them in if you think the brew will benefit from a prolonged infusion. Pour the liquid back into the fermentation container. After the bubbling subsides, an additional 3 to 5 weeks, rack the liquid into a new container, being careful not to disturb the yeast on the bottom.

Pour the racked liquid into 750 ml bottles primed with the remaining 1 Tbsp of sugar syrup. Close the lid, shake to incorporate, and store in a cool, dark place. Wait 1 to 4 weeks for the beer to carbonate, checking every few days by "burping" the bottles to make sure they haven't overcarbonated. Once sufficiently carbonated, move to the refrigerator. This will keep for 1 year or more and will continue to change and evolve with time.

Racking

One thing you will notice with making beer and wine is the amount of sediment that forms as a byproduct of the primary fermentation. This sediment, referred to as *trub* with beer and *lees* with wine, is made up of deposits of dead yeast that precipitate to the bottom of the fermentation vessel. If left to sit on the sediment for too long, your wine or beer may develop off-flavors. For this reason, it is usually recommended to separate the liquid from the sediment before bottling through a process known as "racking," wherein the wine or beer is moved to a new container. Racking aids in the clarification and stabilization of the final product.

Racking can be accomplished by using a racking cane and tube or by siphoning through a hose. To start, place the lower end of the racking cane or hose midway between the surface and the sediment. Begin siphoning and gradually lower the cane or hose as the volume decreases. There will come a point when the clarified liquid approaches the yeast on the bottom and the sediment will start to be siphoned. This is when you stop racking and discard any remaining sediment so that it doesn't make it into the bottle.

Country Wine

Like beer, wine can be extremely complicated and governed by strict rules and guidelines, or it can be made the way people have made it for thousands of years: with various ingredients, wild yeast, and minimal intervention. I prefer the latter approach, because it results in a product that is unique, expressive of terroir, and very much alive. To avoid confusion with the wine that most people are used to drinking, we will refer to those in this book as country wines. Country wines, or *vin de pays* in French, can either mean a wine that doesn't meet the standards designated for a particular *appellation d'origine contrôlée* (AOC), or it can refer to wine made with something other than grapes, such as the juice from a different fruit (such as apple cider), flowers, herbs, or vegetables. None of the wines featureed in this book will be made with grapes.

Fermenting country wines differs from beer fermentation in two ways: The wines require more sugar and more time. This increased fermentation time also results in an increase in the probability that your wine may spoil, which is why I typically recommend fermenting in a carboy or fermentation bucket equipped with an airlock. Airlocks allow carbon dioxide to escape from inside the vessel, while simultaneously preventing oxidation and contamination during the long fermentation period.

While we will be making wine using raw ingredients that are inherently covered in ambient yeast, I still like to add just a bit of ginger bug. The ginger skin is rich in lactic acid bacteria (LAB), which helps acidify the environment, protecting the wine from spoilage. It also aids in the process of malolactic fermentation, which occurs when the LAB converts harsh-tasting malic acid into the softer, subtler lactic acid. This process is used in most conventional red wine production, and though it's less frequently employed with white wines, there are cases where it is desirable (malolactic fermentation is what gives some Chardonnays their characteristic buttery flavor). In addition, I also like the idea of all of my ferments having some trace of my ginger bug in them, like a biochemical DNA strand that ties them all together.

An all-purpose base recipe for country wine is difficult to provide given the great variety of ingredients one can start with, but the process described here can be followed as a rule of thumb. Typically, I use white sugar when making wine, although the amount of sugar should be adjusted depending on the sweetness of your fruit. If you are making strawberry wine, for example, only 2 quarts/1.9 L simple syrup is needed, whereas if you are making rhubarb or herb wine where your starting ingredients have virtually no sugar, 3 quarts/2.8 L simple syrup should be used to achieve the same final alcohol content. Feel free to taste your wines as they are fermenting and adjust as you see fit. If you think they could benefit from more sweetness, add sugar at any point. If they need more acid, try adding a bit of citrus juice to the carboy. If you think the wine you've made would be better as a pét-nat (from the French *pétillant naturel*, meaning "naturally sparkling") wine, try adding 1 Tbsp simple syrup to your bottles at bottling as a primer for a secondary fermentation.

COUNTRY WINE MASTER RECIPE

Makes approximately nine 750 ml bottles

The following recipe outlines how to make wine using fruit juice; however, wine can be made using many other ingredients including flowers, herbs, and/or vegetables. If using another ingredient, you can either juice it or cold or hot brew it, following the guidelines outlined with beer above.

6 to 8 c/1.4 to 3.8 L chopped fresh fruit

1 gal/3.8 L water

2 to 3 qt/ 1.9 to 2.8 L simple syrup
(see page 25), plus 1 Tbsp per bottle,
if making sparkling wine

3 oz/89 ml freshly squeezed lemon
or lime juice

½ cup/120 ml Ginger Bug, liquid only
(see page 29)

DIRECTIONS

Juice the fruit in a large bowl using your hands, a juicer, or using the "blender method" on page 48.

Strain the juice from the solids into a large container, passing it through a tea towel or cheesecloth-lined fine-mesh strainer to ensure that no particulate matter passes through. Add all the remaining ingredients and stir to combine. Pour the liquid into a carboy or fermentation bucket equipped with an airlock and let it ferment in a cool, dark place until signs of fermentation have all but stopped (2 to 3 months).

Once fermentation is complete, carefully rack the liquid into a new container, being careful not to disturb the yeast on the bottom. Pour the racked liquid into sterilized bottles and let sit for another 3 to 6 months before enjoying. If you can't wait that long, open a bottle after a few weeks to drink as a nouveau-style wine, leaving the rest to age. If you decide to carbonate the wine into a pét-net, add 1 Tbsp of sugar to each bottle as a sugar primer prior to sealing the bottles, and make sure to check periodically to ensure the bottles haven't overcarbonated. Wine will keep for 1 year or more and will continue to change and evolve over time.

Mead

Mead is one of humankind's oldest fermented beverages. It is made, in the simplest terms, by mixing honey with water and letting the ambient yeasts present in the honey consume the sugar to produce alcohol. Since honeybees are present in many regions around the world, honey was the most widespread sugar source available to ancient humans worldwide. As a result, there are countless ancient examples of mead fermentation, many of which are still intact today. A few examples can be seen with the pre-Columbian Mexican tradition of fermenting balché, the Filipino mead known as bais, and iQhilika made by the Xhosa of South Africa. There are numerous other examples of fermented honey beverages that can be found throughout European cultures, though its popularity was supplanted by beers, wines, and ciders after the advent of permanent settlements and agriculture.

However, this replacement did not mean that the categories would never again intersect. Meads often overlap with beer, wine, and cider. Braggot is the name given to the beer-mead hybrid made by fermenting honey, hops, and malt, whereas melomel refers to mead made with fruit. This latter category is the one to which pyments (mead fermented with grapes) and cysers (mead fermented with apple juice) are classified. There were also meads brewed for therapeutic purposes, as with metheglin (Welsh for "healing liquor"), made by fermenting mead with medicinal ingredients, including herbs, flowers, and spices.

In addition to the wide range of ingredients that can be added to mead, there is an equally wide-ranging definition for its ABV and flavor. Alcohol can range from 3 to 18%; it can be sweet, dry, semisweet, sparkling, still, and just about everything in between. In my Mead Master Recipe 4 cups/950 ml of honey are added to produce a mead with around 12% alcohol that tastes more similar to wine. If you reduce the honey to 3 cups/720 ml, it will be closer to 9% ABV, 2 cups/475 ml will yield 6%, and so on.

MEAD MASTER RECIPE

Makes approximately seven 750 ml bottles

1 gal/3.8 L water

4 to 6 c/950 ml to 1.4 L chopped bittering or flavoring ingredient (see chart, page 26)

2 to 4 c/475 ml to 950 ml honey

½ c/120 ml Ginger Bug, liquid only (see page 39)

3 oz/89 ml freshly squeezed lemon or lime juice

1 Tbsp honey syrup, (see page 25) for priming (see page 43, optional for sparkling mead)

DIRECTIONS

Decide if you want to cold- or hot-brew the bittering ingredient following the guidelines outlined with beer, pages 49–50. Strain out the solids or leave them in if you think your brew will benefit from a prolonged infusion.

Pour into a large food-safe container along with the remaining ingredients and stir well to incorporate. For a more rudimentary setup, leave the wort to ferment in the container covered with cheesecloth or a tea towel bound with a rubber band, or another non-airtight lid. For a more sterile setup, transfer the liquid into a carboy or fermentation bucket equipped with an airlock and let it ferment in a cool, dark place until signs of fermentation have all but stopped (2 to 3 months, less for lower-ABV meads). If using an airlock, fill it with water and a splash of vodka to the designated lines and place it into the container opening.

Once fermentation is complete, carefully rack the liquid into a new container, being careful not to disturb the yeast on the bottom. Pour the racked liquid into sterilized bottles and let sit for another 3 to 6 months before enjoying. If you can't wait that long, open a bottle after a few weeks to drink young, leaving the rest to age. If you decide to carbonate the mead, add 1 Tbsp honey syrup as a primer prior to sealing the bottles, and make sure to check periodically to ensure the bottles haven't overcarbonated. Mead will keep for 1 year or more and will continue to change and evolve over time.

Vinegar

The word *vinegar* comes from the Latin *vinum acer*, literally "sour wine," which is a good hint of how it is made. Vinegar is the product of the acetification of alcohol by acetic acid bacteria (also known as *acetobacter* or AAB). Much like lactic acid bacteria (LAB), AAB are present almost everywhere in nature and very little is needed to encourage them to work their magic, just a liquid environment with an alcohol percentage between 3 and 9%, oxygen, and time, usually between 3 and 6 months.

Although only one recipe is included for vinegar in this book (Cider Vinegar, page 221), the reality is that you could make incredibly unique vinegars from any of the soda, beer, wine, or mead recipes.

Although the AAB are almost certainly present on the ginger bug as well as the raw ingredients used in making the alcoholic ferment, I always add a starter culture to ensure a healthy fermentation. This can come from a previous batch of homemade vinegar, or an unpasteurized "raw" vinegar, such as Bragg apple cider vinegar. A good rule of thumb is to add 20 to 25% unpasteurized vinegar to the total volume of the alcohol you want to acetify.

Another key to a successful vinegar fermentation is having a gelatinous SCOBY, known as a "vinegar mother," on top as fermentation occurs. Unlike the ginger bug SCOBY, which is more of a slurry, the vinegar mother is a type of biofilm composed of cellulose and AAB. Although they are rather unsightly, they are truly amazing products of nature. If you don't have a vinegar mother as you embark on your vinegar-making journey, fret not; the SCOBY should form spontaneously at the liquid-air interface as your first batch of vinegar ferments, which is also a good indicator of a healthy vinegar fermentation. Over time, this SCOBY will give birth to new baby SCOBYs as the chemical composition of the vinegar begins to change. Once you have several vinegar mothers, you can separate them to use in additional ferments. An inventory of my current vinegar projects includes juniper, peach, mulberry, celery, and apple cider. Here is a basic recipe to make any vinegar. It can be scaled up or down to make a larger or smaller batch.

VINEGAR MASTER RECIPE

Makes approximately 1 qt/950 ml

---

3 c/720 ml alcoholic beverage (beer, wine, mead, cider, or other) with an ABV of 3 to 9%

1 c/240 ml vinegar starter culture (from a previous batch of homemade vinegar or a store-bought unpasteurized "raw" brand)

Vinegar mother SCOBY (optional, but preferable. If you don't have a vinegar mother, one should form on its own)

DIRECTIONS

Add your alcohol and vinegar starter culture to a food-safe glass or plastic container. If you have a vinegar mother, place it on top of the liquid; if you don't, one should form within a few weeks. Cover with cheesecloth or a tea towel secured with a rubber band or other non-airtight lid. Allow to ferment for 3 months, or until it tastes like vinegar. Once you're happy with the flavor, decant into lidded bottles. The vinegar can be stored at room temperature indefinitely.

Once your vinegar is complete, you can use it to brighten any number of dishes, or use it as a medium for preservation. The easiest way to do this is by simply infusing your vinegar with fruits, vegetables, or herbs, or you can use them to create more involved preserves, such as pickles and shrubs.

Note: It's not uncommon during the vinegar fermentation for the odor to smell a bit like nail polish remover. This is totally normal and occurs when acetaldehyde forms as an intermediate step during the conversion of alcohol to acetic acid. Replacing the lid with cheesecloth and occasionally mixing the vinegar with a whisk to help aerate it should solve the problem within a few weeks.

Shrubs

Shrubs refer to a type of sweet and sour syrup most commonly made from a mix of vinegar, sugar, and fruit or even vegetables. Herbs and spices can also be included as flavoring agents. Shrubs are the most enduring example in a long line of drinking vinegars consumed throughout history as medicinal tonics, cooling refreshments, and a safer alternative to water. Examples include a diluted mixture of honey and vinegar known as *oxymel* in ancient Greece, or *sekanjabin* in Iran. *Posca* was the name given to a mix of vinegar and water consumed during the time of the Roman Empire, and *switchel* was a popular drink in colonial New England made from a mix of apple cider vinegar, ginger, and either honey, maple syrup, or molasses. Today, drinking vinegars are also very popular in various Asian cuisines.

The word *shrub* comes from the Middle Eastern custom of drinking *sharbats* (from the Arabic word *shariba*, meaning "to drink"). Sharbats were a large class of sweetened nonalcoholic drinks that gave rise to many different offshoots whose names we know today, including syrups, sherbets, sorbets, and vinegar-laced shrubs.

I love shrubs; they are easy to make, are excellent nonalcoholic refreshments when diluted with water or club soda, and make incredible additions to cocktails.

Again, master recipes are difficult considering the variability inherent in the ingredients; however, I typically start with a 1:1:1 mix of fruit, sugar, and vinegar by weight and adjust as needed.

SHRUB MASTER RECIPE

Makes approximately 1 qt/950 ml

---

1 lb/450 g sugar (approximately 2 c)

1 lb/450 g vinegar (approximately 2 c)

1 lb/450 g fresh fruit or other ingredient

DIRECTIONS

To a medium saucepan over medium heat, add the sugar and vinegar and stir frequently, until the sugar dissolves. Once the sugar dissolves, remove from the heat and let cool until it reaches room temperature. Add the vinegar syrup to a blender along with the fruit and blend on high until all the fruit is liquefied, working in batches if necessary. If you are using berries, you can add them whole, but if using a larger ingredient (like apples), cut it into 1 in/2.5 cm cubes to make it easier to work with.

Strain using a fine-mesh strainer, making sure to squeeze as much liquid from the fruit as possible before discarding the solids. Pour the shrub into an airtight bottle or jar and move to the refrigerator where it will keep indefinitely, although flavors may dull with time.

Pickles

Pickles are one of humankind's oldest preserved foods. They got their start more than 4,000 years ago when ancient Mesopotamians began soaking cucumbers in brine to preserve them for longer-term storage. They are mentioned in the Bible, were prized among ancient Egyptians, and played an integral part in feeding crews and preventing scurvy on countless transoceanic voyages, including Columbus's journey to America.

In the most generic terms, pickling refers to the process of preserving an ingredient in an acidified solution—either a vinegar brine or a lactic acid–rich environment produced by the fermentation of sugars by LAB in salt brine. From there, the addition of herbs, spices, sugar, and other fresh ingredients creates a world of pickles that you could spend a lifetime exploring.

There are lots of ways to incorporate pickles into your cocktails. The most obvious is preserving an ingredient to be used later as a cocktail garnish, but you can also use the brine as a cocktail ingredient to lend bright acidity, salinity, and a savory element that many drinks lack. Examples can be seen with the Dirty Ramp Martini (see page 105), the Fermented Tomato Water (see page 180), and, of course, Dirty Martinis.

Although there are many examples of pickling from around the world, the two main types of pickles we'll use are lacto-fermented pickles and vinegar pickles.

LACTO-FERMENTED PICKLES

Making lacto-fermented pickles is a true exercise in submitting to what I like to refer to as our "microbial overlords." Lacto-fermentation is a wild fermentation, relying solely on the ingredient and their ambient bacteria to produce the preservation agent, lactic acid. Each of these ambient microbes produces unique and complex flavors that vinegar pickles can't achieve. Lacto-fermentation helps add nutritional value to foods by preserving the beneficial nutrients and vitamins in the pickled ingredients and adding additional B vitamins and probiotics produced as a byproduct of fermentation. This is the process responsible for fermented favorites including kimchi, sauerkraut, and sour cucumber pickles.

All that is needed is to place your ingredient in a 2% saline environment and give them anywhere from a few days to a few months (or longer!) to ferment at room temperature. From there, the LAB present will begin to convert sugars into lactic acid, thus acidifying the environment and preventing the growth of harmful microorganisms in the process.

Lactic-acid fermentation is an anaerobic process, meaning that you want to starve the ingredients of oxygen. To accomplish this, your ingredients should be fully submerged in the brine in order to avoid contact with the air. You can use glass or ceramic weights, or a plastic zip-top bag filled with water and placed on top works as well.

My preferred vessel is a ceramic fermentation crock, which usually comes equipped with weights to keep the ingredient submerged, or a large glass jar, but any food-safe container will do. Just like with bottles for soda and alcoholic ferments, cleanliness is key to a healthy ferment, but don't obsess too much over this facet. A good scrub with hot soapy water prior to adding ingredients will suffice.

DRY SALTED VS. BRINED LACTO-FERMENTS

If the ingredient that you're fermenting contains sufficient moisture, it can be chopped or grated to expose as much surface area as possible. It can then be dry salted with 2% of its weight in kosher salt in order to coax the water out of its cells through the process of osmosis. In order to calculate this 2% weight in salt, start by weighing your ingredient in grams (using the metric system will make for an easier conversion here). Next, multiply the weight of the ingredient by .02 to calculate how many grams of salt to add.

In as little as an hour or two (sometimes longer) you should notice your ingredient starting to sweat. Once you see this, you can begin to pound the ingredients with a muddler or squeeze the vegetables by hand until liquid is released and the cell walls break down. Next, pack the ingredient plus its liquid into a clean, food-safe container or fermentation vessel and press down until the ingredients are submerged under the brine. Add weights or a plastic bag filled with water to weigh down the ingredients, and loosely cover with cheesecloth or a tea towel secured with a rubber band or other non-airtight lid. This is the process for making cabbage ferments, like sauerkraut and kimchi, as well as lacto-fermented tomatoes (see page 180) and the Fermented Long Hot Sauce (see page 187).

However, it's also possible that your ingredient doesn't contain enough moisture (like a carrot, for instance), or perhaps you want to preserve the ingredient whole, rather than chopping and muddling it beyond recognition. In this case, the ingredient should be brined to create the saline environment. To accomplish this, ingredients are placed in a fermentation vessel and covered with water before weighing the contents. Next, use the steps outlined above to calculate 2% of the total weight of the ingredient and the water, then add that amount of kosher salt into a large bowl. Pour the water out of the fermentation vessel into to the bowl with the salt and stir to create the brine. Pour this back over the ingredient, making sure to scrape any residual salt into the fermentation vessel, before weighting the solids down and loosely covering with cheesecloth or a tea towel secured with a rubber band or other non-airtight lid.

As for how long to ferment, that's totally up to you, but I find the sweet spot to be between a week or two, keeping in mind variables such as activeness of certain ingredients and ambient temperature (warmer temperatures will cause the ferment to move at a quicker pace, just like with sodas). I'm looking for a nice balance between acidity and sweetness that still maintains the flavor of the original ingredient. The best way to know when to pull your ferment is by tasting it. Once you're pleased with the flavor, you can move it to the refrigerator. Fermentation will continue in the refrigerator, but at a very slow pace. Ferments in the refrigerator are still good to be consumed for months or even years, though they may gradually change over time.

As your ferment progresses, it's not uncommon for some white yeast bloom to form at the air-liquid interface. This is called Kahm yeast, and while it is totally harmless, it will change the flavor of your ferment if it mixes into the brine. When you see it form, just scrape away as much of it as possible with a stainless-steel spoon, trying not to mix it into the liquid too much (some mixing is inevitable). Kahm yeast can be avoided by sufficiently salting, fermenting in cooler temperatures (like a basement), submerging ingredients, and if you really want to get technical, using an airlock, which is not something I do often.

It is important to be able to distinguish between Kahm yeast and mold. Mold can come in a variety of colors, most commonly green, black, blue, or white, and it will be fuzzy or hairy, whereas Kahm yeast is white and smooth. If mold forms, nine times out of ten it's safe to scrape it away and enjoy what lies below the surface. However, if the mold smells bad, or has black, pink, or orange spores, it's best to throw your lacto-ferment away, thoroughly clean your container, and start again.

DRY-SALTED LACTO-FERMENTATION MASTER RECIPE

When I'm weighing ingredients for fermentation, I prefer to use the metric system, since calculating the 2% weight of salt needed is far easier than with the imperial system. If you scale up or down, just make sure to calculate 2% of the weight of the ingredient in salt.

---

1 kg/2.2 lb chopped or grated ingredient   20 g/2 tbsp plus 1 tsp kosher salt

DIRECTIONS

Chop or grate your ingredient to expose as much surface area as possible. Add the salt and let sit for 1 hour (or longer if necessary). Pound the ingredients with a muddler or squeeze the vegetables until liquid is released, then pack into a clean, food-safe container or fermentation vessel. Press down until the ingredients are submerged under the brine. Add weights or a plastic bag filled with water to weight down the ingredients, and loosely cover with cheesecloth or a tea towel secured with a rubber band or another non-airtight lid.

Let ferment for 1 or 2 weeks (or longer!), tasting frequently until the desired flavor is achieved. Move to the refrigerator where it will keep for a few months or longer, gradually changing with time.

BRINED LACTO-FERMENTATION MASTER RECIPE

---

1 kg/2.2 lb ingredient

Water, for topping

2% kosher salt by weight of ingredient plus water

DIRECTIONS

Place your fermentation vessel on a scale, and zero the scale. Add your ingredient to the fermentation vessel, cover with water, and weigh. Calculate 2% of the weight of the water plus ingredients and add that amount of salt into a bowl. Pour the water out of the fermentation vessel and into the bowl with the salt and stir until the salt dissolves to create your brine. Pour this back over the ingredient, add weights, and loosely cover with cheesecloth or a tea towel secured with a rubber band or other non-airtight lid.

Let ferment for 1 or 2 weeks (or longer!), tasting frequently until the desired flavor is achieved. Move to the refrigerator where it will keep for a few months or longer, gradually changing with time.

VINEGAR PICKLES

Whereas lacto-fermentation relies on encouraging growth of beneficial microorganisms, vinegar pickling relies on destroying microbes by heating the ingredient with highly acidic vinegar. When most people think of vinegar pickles, the first thing to jump to mind would be cucumbers, but just about anything can be pickled—vegetables, fruits, nuts, seeds, meat, fish, eggs.

There are essentially two main types of vinegar pickles: quick pickles, also known as refrigerator pickles or simply "quickles," and boiling water bath-processed pickles. Quick pickles are made by preparing a hot vinegar brine (although sometimes the brine isn't heated at all), pouring it over your ingredients, and moving it to the refrigerator once cooled. Processed pickles are also made by pouring a hot brine over the ingredients; however, the ingredients are packed in sterilized mason jars and then transferred to a bath of boiling water to both kill off any microbes present and vacuum-seal the jars.

For pickling recipes in this book, I'll mostly follow quick-pickling procedures since (as the name implies) it's quicker and easier. For longer storage, transfer to canning jars and process in a boiling water bath.

To make quick pickles, follow the basic brine recipe that follows, feeling free to adjust the variables as you see fit, including experimenting with different types of vinegar, as each will impart a unique flavor to the final pickle. From there, bring your brine to a boil, pack the ingredient you want to pickle in a clean jar along with any herbs or spices, cover with brine, and refrigerate once cool. That's it! You'll want to leave the ingredients in the jar for a bit to let them absorb the brine's flavor, but the timing will vary depending on what you're pickling and how you've cut it and packed it in the jar. For example, sliced cucumbers can be ready in a matter of hours, whereas whole cucumbers will need longer to become infused with the flavor of the brine (a few days to a week).

BASIC PICKLE BRINE

This recipe should be scaled up or down to ensure that the ingredient you are pickling is fully submerged under the brine. You can also optionally add different herbs and spices to alter the flavor of your final pickle.

Makes approximately 2 c/475 ml brine

---

1 c/240 ml water   ¼ c/50 g sugar
1 c/240 ml distilled white vinegar   2 Tbsp/17 g salt

DIRECTIONS

Add all the ingredients to a small saucepan and bring to a boil. Meanwhile, pack whatever ingredient you're pickling into clean glass jars or another food-safe container, adding any spices or herbs you are using along with them. Pour the boiling brine on top, put the lid on the jar, and let sit at room temperature until cool. Move to the refrigerator where they will keep for 1 month or more.

Kombucha

Many people have come to know kombucha through its recent rise to health food superstardom. However, many who grew up outside of Asian culture may be surprised to know that the drink's origins stretch back more than two thousand years to northeastern China before spreading to Korea and Japan a few hundred years later. Sometime during the early-twentieth century, kombucha arrived in Europe along with the expansion of Asian trade routes and became especially important in Russia. In the 1960s, kombucha consumption became more widespread throughout Europe, especially among the hippie communities and New Age crowd. Since then, kombucha has made its way around the world and is now valued at over $2 billion per year.

Many kombucha proponents attribute any number of health claims to the brew, many of which are unfortunately unsubstantiated. However, one that can't be disputed is that it is a probiotic that helps diversify our gut microbiome. There are numerous fungal and bacterial species found in the kombucha microbial community, with the two most prevalent species being yeast (Saccharomyces cerevisiae), the fungal species responsible for brewing soda, beer, mead, and wine, and acetic acid bacteria (Acetobacter), which are responsible for fermenting vinegar. This combination is relatively unsurprising; if I had to explain to someone what kombucha tastes like, "vinegar soda" might be the phrase I'd use. These species exist in symbiosis in a SCOBY that is unique to kombucha and known as a "kombucha mother" or "kombucha mushroom." Much like the vinegar mother, the kombucha SCOBY is a disc-shaped, gelatinous biofilm composed of cellulose, with the only distinguishing difference being the microbial composition of each.

You can either obtain a healthy SCOBY from an external source (via the internet, homebrew store, or a kombucha-brewing friend), or you can grow one spontaneously by pouring a bottle of unpasteurized kombucha into a vat of sweetened tea. Cover with cheesecloth, a tea towel, or other non-airtight lid and wait about 1 week for a new SCOBY to appear. Over time, your SCOBY will grow thicker, giving birth to new layers in the process, which can then be split off and used to ferment new batches of kombucha. I usually like to keep one crock fermenting continuously (meaning I never expect to bottle it) that will grow multiple SCOBYs. This little SCOBY factory is typically referred to as a "SCOBY hotel." To keep it healthy, I top it off with sweetened tea (three parts tea to one part simple syrup, page 25) every month or so, making sure to never let it dry out.

Though the preferred medium of kombucha fermentation has traditionally been sweetened black tea, it is also possible to brew it using green tea sweetened with honey (known as jun), as well as other teas, tisanes (herbal teas), or sweetened fruit or vegetable juice. To make kombucha of any type, simply add 2 cups/475 ml kombucha from a previous batch or a store-bought unpasteurized brand into a food-safe vessel, followed by a mix of 3 quarts/2.8 L tea or juice and 1 quart/950 ml simple syrup and top with a SCOBY (or wait until a new one forms if you don't have a SCOBY). Loosely cover with cheesecloth or a tea towel secured with a rubber band or other non-airtight lid, and let sit at room temperature for a week before bottling.

One of my favorite aspects of kombucha fermentation at this stage is that it is an opportunity to watch evolution play out in real time. For example, if you are using a SCOBY from a previous batch, you will watch as the introduced SCOBY dies, sinks to the bottom, and a new one forms on top of the brew that is better equipped to survive in the new environment. It will also change shape to form a protective umbrella that covers the brew beneath it from the external environment in a way that gives the phrase "kombucha mother" a whole new meaning. As the newly formed SCOBY begins to work its microbial magic in the primary fermentation, a symbiotic relationship plays out as yeast converts sugar to alcohol and carbon dioxide while AAB simultaneously convert the alcohol into vinegar. Since the AAB work rapidly to convert the alcohol to acetic acid, the alcohol level of kombucha will never be high, but it also won't be zero, with alcohol levels in kombucha typically hovering between 0.5 and 1%, though it is possible that they can sometimes go as high as 3%, especially if there is a high level of fruit juice. If left to ferment completely, nearly all the alcohol would be converted to acetic acid and result in a final product that is essentially vinegar.

The goal (for me at least) is to stop this primary fermentation when the brew has a nice balance of sweetness and acidity. It can then be bottled and moved to the refrigerator as is, or left in the sealed bottles at room temperature with an additional Tbsp of simple syrup to ferment further, carbonating itself during a secondary fermentation in the process. I usually prefer the latter approach for an effervescent kombucha to be enjoyed on its own, or used to add bubbles and acidity to Highballs, Collinses, and Spritzes. Once sufficiently bubbly, move your bottles of kombucha to the refrigerator, where they will keep for months as fermentation slows to a crawl and flavors continue to meld and change over time. I've had various bottles of kombucha that were over a year old that were absolutely incredible in terms of flavor and carbonation. Follow this outlined recipe, and over time you will develop your own tastes, preferences, and tricks for brewing kombucha best suited to your environment and needs.

KOMBUCHA MASTER RECIPE

Makes approximately six 750 ml bottles

---

3 qt/2.8 L tea, tisane, fruit or vegetable juice

1 qt/950 ml Simple Syrup or 3:1 honey syrup (see page 25, to make *jun*), plus 1 Tbsp per bottle for priming (see page 43)

2 c/475 ml kombucha from a previous batch or unpasteurized, store-bought kombucha

1 SCOBY (preferable, but if you don't have a SCOBY one should form on its own)

DIRECTIONS

Combine the tea, 1 qt simple syrup, the kombucha, and SCOBY in a ceramic fermentation crock, glass jar, or food-safe plastic container and cover with a tea towel or cheesecloth bound with a rubber band or other non-airtight lid, and let ferment at room temperature for approximately 1 week (longer if you prefer a more sour brew), tasting frequently until you're happy with the balance of sweetness and acidity. If you don't have a SCOBY, one should form within a week or two.

Remove the SCOBY from the top of the brew and put it in another batch of kombucha, or discard it (especially if you have an abundance of kombucha mothers from your SCOBY hotel). Pass the liquid through a fine-mesh strainer and decant into 750 ml swing-cap bottles primed with the remaining 1 Tbsp simple syrup. Let sit for roughly 1 week more at room temperature, making sure to burp the bottles periodically to make sure they haven't overcarbonated. Once the brew is sufficiently bubbly, move it to the refrigerator. The kombucha will keep for 3 months or more.

ALCOHOLIC PRESERVATION

Infusing high-proof alcohol with any number of botanical products has been one of the easiest and most effective ways of capturing an ingredient's flavor, aroma, and color since the invention of distillation many centuries ago. Alcoholic preservation can be accomplished in two ways: through distilling it—either from a fermented alcoholic base made with the ingredient, or by adding the ingredient directly to the still with another fermented product—or by steeping an ingredient in a highly potent alcoholic solvent in a process known as *maceration*.

Unfortunately, home distillation of alcohol is illegal here in the United States. Lucky for us, though, maceration is completely legal and, although it isn't quite as refined as distilling, it is a much easier and safer method of preservation. In addition to being easy to prepare, alcoholic infusions are shelf-stable and can be kept indefinitely as long as the alcohol content is high enough, though their color, flavor, and aroma will change gradually over time.

In the simplest terms, maceration requires simply submerging a botanical ingredient in alcohol in a food-safe vessel such as a wide-mouth mason jar, letting it infuse at room temperature for a period, and then straining out the solids to create an extract or tincture. From there, you can adjust alcohol proof, type, number of ingredients, and sweetness to create ingredients as different as liqueurs, bitters, amari, vermouth, and more.

In the flowchart (opposite), you can see how many directions you can go in with a single ingredient. The main takeaway is that there is no one right way to treat any ingredient, but rather an infinite world of possibilities.

ALCOHOLIC PRESERVA[TION]

SPIRIT

VODKA
151 PROOF

COCKTAIL
PRESERVES

TINCTURE

INFUSION

WATER, BITTER
INGREDIENTS

SUGAR
WINE

SU[GAR]

BITTERS

VERMOUTH /
AROMATIZED WINE

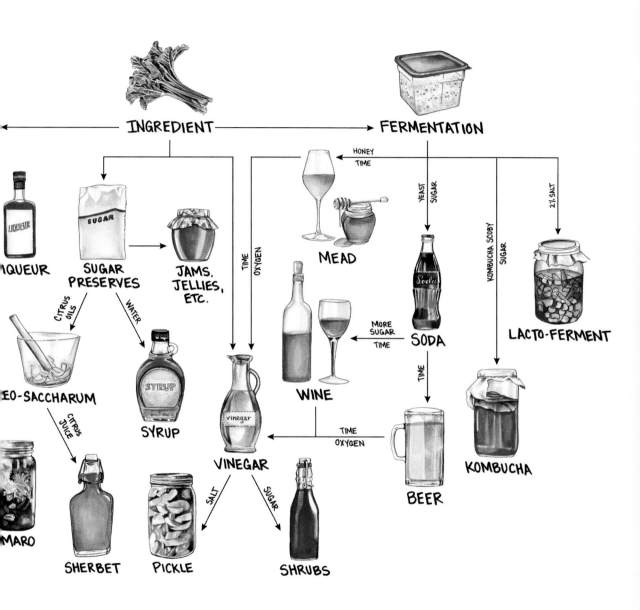

INGREDIENT → FERMENTATION

LIQUEUR

SUGAR PRESERVES

JAMS, JELLIES, ETC.

CITRUS OILS

WATER

EO-SACCHARUM

CITRUS JUICE

SYRUP

MARO

SHERBET

PICKLE

SALT

VINEGAR

vinegar

SUGAR

SHRUBS

TIME
OXYGEN

HONEY
TIME

MEAD

WINE

MORE SUGAR
TIME

TIME
OXYGEN

TIME

BEER

YEAST
SUGAR

Soda

SODA

TIME

KOMBUCHA

KOMBUCHA SCOBY
SUGAR

2% SALT

LACTO-FERMENT

Infusions and Tinctures

Tinctures and infusions differ only in proof and type of spirit used. Tinctures refer to an ingredient that is macerated in high-proof, neutral grain alcohol ("neutral" meaning colorless, odorless, and flavorless). Infusions, on the other hand, can be done with nearly any spirit—vodka, gin, whiskey, tequila, brandy, and so on—all of which are typically bottled at between 35 to 45% alcohol by volume (ABV). Infusions can also be achieved with lower-alcohol ingredients such as wine and vermouth, but will require more time to extract the flavors.

Infusions are wonderful in that the finished product is ready to mix, no further dilution or sweetening needed. Just cover an ingredient in the spirit of your choosing and let it sit, tasting frequently as you go until you are happy with the result. When deciding which spirit to pair with a particular ingredient, keep in mind complementary and clashing flavors. For instance, you probably don't want to infuse a peaty Scotch with a tender herb, as the herb's flavor will likely get lost in the smoke and oak imparted from the Scotch. Instead, go for something more neutral like vodka, unaged brandy, or even tequila.

When infusing most fruits, delicate herbs, and vegetables, I like to mix them at roughly one part ingredient to one part spirit (by volume) for the best results, slicing them to expose more surface area and extract more flavor. When it comes to stronger, more concentrated ingredients such as spices, strongly flavored herbs, and teas, it's impossible to give a general ratio. Instead, I recommend taking each into careful consideration before infusing. For instance, one or two hot peppers may be enough to infuse in a bottle of tequila depending on your taste, ¼ cup/60 ml dried chamomile per 1 liter of rye, and a stick or two of cinnamon per bottle of rum may all prove more than enough to impart their essence. Boldly flavored ingredients like this can either be chopped or crushed to help release their flavor faster or be infused whole for a longer time.

As for timing, strongly flavored ingredients such as teas, herbs, and spices can be infused for relatively short periods of time, from as little as a few hours to a few days, whereas fruits and vegetables benefit from a longer maceration time, usually anywhere from a few days to a few weeks. These ranges may seem a bit intimidating when starting on your own infusions, but just remember to taste frequently and trust your palate.

I find the tincture-making process to be forgiving. The goal is to have a highly concentrated flavor using a neutral alcohol solvent, so I usually opt for roughly one part ingredient to two parts spirit, and allow it to macerate for a minimum of a few weeks and upwards of six months. You can do this with a single ingredient, or you can do it with a blend of ingredients as you'll see with bitters and amari. Sometimes I'll do a more concentrated 1:1 infusion to extract more flavor, especially if I'm planning on diluting and sweetening it into a liqueur, such as with the Walnut Nocino on page 151. In either case, once the solids have been strained out, you have a perfect encapsulation of an essence that can be added to your liquid pantry to add florality, bitterness, spice, umami, or any other number of complex flavors to a drink.

When it comes to choosing which alcohol to use in your tincture, keep in mind that the higher the alcohol percentage, the better its ability to extract flavor. Many commercial tinctures use an alcoholic solvent that is close to 100% pure ethanol. The closest you can get to this here in the United States is Everclear at 190 proof (95% alcohol by volume), however it is illegal in many US states. Luckily, Everclear also makes a 151-proof option that is available to purchase everywhere and still works wonderfully as an extractant. It's worth noting that there are many locally produced 151-proof options. I use New Jersey–made Devil's Springs 151-proof vodka, but any brand will do as long as it is of suitable quality.

Tinctures can be used on their own, added to a cocktail by the drop or dash, or atomized over top of a finished beverage to lend their aroma. Additionally, they can be tasted on their own as a bracing reminder of how an ingredient tastes in its most concentrated form. However, I wouldn't recommend tasting tinctures at more than an eyedropper's worth at a time, as consuming something with such high alcohol levels can be harmful.

TINCTURE MASTER RECIPE

Makes approximately 2 to 4 c/475 to 950 ml

2 c/475 ml ingredient, such as spices, herbs, fruits, vegetable, etc.

2 to 4 c/475 to 950 ml 151-proof neutral grain spirit (to cover ingredient)

DIRECTIONS

Add all ingredients to a 1 qt/1 L mason jar and let sit for a minimum of 2 to 4 weeks and up to 6 months or a year. Once pleased with the final flavor, strain out the solids and store the liquid in an airtight bottle or jar. Will keep indefinitely, though the flavors and colors will gradually change with time.

Liqueurs

Liqueurs are the generic name given to botanically flavored alcoholic beverages that are bottled with added sugar. Their name comes from the Latin word *liquifacere*, meaning "to liquefy," as these are essentially liquefied versions of the solids used to create them. They can be made with distilled ingredients, or they can be made with a macerated tincture or extract that is diluted and sweetened. Liqueurs have a wide array of possible ingredients including fruits, vegetables, flowers, nuts, spices, and herbs, and with alcohol percentages ranging from 15% to 55%. Within this category you have fruit and vegetable liqueurs, cream-based liqueurs, nut liqueurs (like the Walnut Nocino, page 151), the extra-sweet crème liqueurs, flower liqueurs (like the Elderflower Liqueur, page 158), and herbal liqueurs including amari.

You can make your own liqueur out of pretty much any botanical ingredient, assuming it's safe to consume. All that's needed is to macerate it in 151-proof neutral grain spirit for a minimum of 2 to 4 weeks (or upwards of 6 months or more if you think it would benefit from a longer infusion). Next, strain out the solids, dilute, and sweeten to your liking. You now have a shelf-stable, sippable expression of that ingredient.

As a rule of thumb, diluting any volume of alcohol with an equal amount of water and sweetener will cut the proof in half. For example, if you strain out your solids, resulting in 4 cups/950 ml of 151-proof spirit, adding 2 cups/475 ml water and 2 cups/475 ml simple syrup (4 cups/950 ml total) will yield a final product that is approximately 38% ABV, which is half the original percentage. Obtaining an alcohol percentage that is a quarter of the original can be achieved by adding three times the original volume of the alcohol. This means that if you start with 4 cups/950 ml of 151-proof spirit, it can be diluted to roughly 19% ABV by diluting with 6 cups/1.4 L water and 6 cups/1.4 L simple syrup for a total of 12 cups/2.8 L. Although you may find that this 1:1 mix of simple syrup to water results in a product that's too sweet, dry, diluted, or otherwise imbalanced, having it as a benchmark will prove useful as you begin to craft your own liqueurs suited to your personal preferences.

When I'm diluting and sweetening my homemade liqueurs, I tend to do so to taste, rather than to achieve a certain ABV, with the goal of finding the perfect balance between the flavor of the ingredient, sweetness, and alcohol level. Once that is achieved, the liqueur can then be stored in a bottle or mason jar at room temperature indefinitely. It's important to use the master recipe below not as an unwavering recipe, but rather as a rough guideline since the flavors of individual ingredients will need to be accounted for. Making a strawberry liqueur will require less sugar than sweetening an amaro with a lot of bittering agents. Something else to keep in mind is that you can dilute with wine or fruit juice and sweeten with other sources of sugar such as honey and maple syrup, but you will have to adjust your levels of dilution and sweetness accordingly. Make sure to take notes as you go for reference.

A note on clarity: You will notice that after you add water and sweetener to your tincture, the color will change and the mixture will turn opaque. This is due to a process known as "louching," which is what happens when you add water to absinthe or pastis and it turns cloudy (this is the whole point of the absinthe "drip"). It's caused by the precipitation of oils in the solution when they come in contact with water. There is nothing inherently wrong with this, but it's not something you'll usually see with commercial brands. If it bothers you, you can let gravity settle the precipitate to the bottom and rack it (exactly like you would with beer, see page 51), or you can purchase clarifying agents including pectin enzyme, bentonite, and Sparkolloid. Personally, this doesn't really bother me when using liqueurs in cocktails, but if I plan on serving them neat, I'll let gravity settle them and serve the racked clarified liquid.

LIQUEUR MASTER RECIPE

This is an approximation, not a one-size-fits-all approach. You may find that these proportions need to be adjusted based on the flavor of the tincture, as well as personal taste. Following these proportions will result in a liqueur that is roughly 37.75% ABV.

Makes 1 qt/950 ml

---

2 c/475 ml 151-proof tincture   1 c/240 ml simple syrup (see page 25)
1 c/240 ml water

DIRECTIONS

Make a single- or multiple-ingredient tincture following the recipe on page 73. Add the water and simple syrup using the above proportions as a guide, tasting as you go until the desired dilution and sweetness are achieved. When you're happy with the flavor, put it in an airtight container and store at room temperature. It will keep indefinitely.

Bitters

In the simplest definition, bitters are aromatic flavoring agents made from infusing botanical ingredients in high-proof spirit. Their use in cocktails is a more recent development; they were originally made as cure-all medicines. While many of the claims touted by these old bitters companies were bogus, they do aid in digestion. Like many mammals, humans are programmed to avoid bitter flavors, as they often signal the presence of poison. As a result, when they are consumed, the body increases the production of saliva, digestive acids, and enzymes, which speed up digestion. Although bitter flavors are largely absent in the American diet (minus coffee and chocolate), they are integral in many culture's cuisines, notably Italy's.

Bitters can fall into two main categories: nonpotable bitters meant to be used by the dash or drop, such as Angostura and Peychaud's, and potable bitters (a.k.a. amaro, from the Italian "bitter"), meant to be consumed on their own or mixed into cocktails. Nonpotable bitters typically have a more concentrated flavor and contain far less sugar than amari, if they contain any sugar at all. You can make your own bitters by first making separate tinctures and then adding them in specific amounts, or by making a single tincture out of numerous ingredients at the same time, which is what I do.

The options are limitless when choosing exactly which botanical elements to infuse in your bitters—roots, barks, seeds, citrus peel, herbs, flowers, fruit, and vegetables have all made their way into bitters throughout the ages—however, the presence of a bittering agent is of paramount importance. The most common bittering agents for nonpotable bitters include gentian, cinchona, dandelion, burdock, bitter orange peel, and quassia, to name a few. The ingredients are left to infuse for around 1 month before they are strained out. From there, they are often diluted to between 35 and 45% ABV. Even with that dilution, their botanical flavor is still very concentrated and is intended to be used in only very small amounts.

Despite their name, bitters add much more than bitterness to drinks. They help balance out sweet and sour flavors, adding complexity, in the form of spice, brightness, acidity, and herbaceousness. Today, there are an endless number of bitters on the market, but the commercial brands I always make sure to have stocked in my home bar are Angostura, Peychaud's, orange, chocolate, and celery bitters, in addition to numerous homemade varieties.

BITTERS MASTER RECIPE

Makes 1 qt/950 ml bitters at 37.75% ABV

2 c/475 ml 151-proof tincture (see page 73)

About 2 c/475 ml water

Sweetener such as sugar, honey, or maple syrup (optional)

DIRECTIONS

Make a tincture following the recipe on page 73. Add water to your tincture until the desired dilution is achieved and sweeten, if desired. When you're happy with the flavor, put it in an airtight container and store at room temperature. It will keep indefinitely.

Amaro

Potable bitters, known in Italy as *amaro* and in France as *amers*, can be further divided into the appetite-stimulating category of *aperitifs*, coming from the Latin verb *aperire*, meaning "to open," and *digestivi* or *digestifs*, for digestion. The most common aperitifs are the citrusy, red-hued bitters such as Campari, Aperol, and Cappelletti Aperitivo. This style of amaro is rarely drunk alone, but instead mixed with club soda, sparkling wine, or tonic and consumed before a meal.

The digestifs, on the other hand, are consumed after a meal. This category is broad and can be broken down into even further specialized categories. Some of these are defined by their principle bittering agent, such as *carciofo* (artichoke), *rabarbaro* (rhubarb), *génépy* (wormwood), and *tartufo* (black truffle), whereas others are categorized by their style. These include fernet (bitter and high in alcohol), alpine (made from mountain botanicals), light (citrus-forward), medium (darker color and balanced between bitter, sweet, and citrus). Then there are the other "herbal liqueurs" such as Chartreuse and German Kräuterlikör. Each of these styles of digestivi are traditionally consumed on their own, however they have been making waves over the last decade for their ability to add dimension and depth to cocktails.

When I make bitters and amari, I am a little obsessive about using only ingredients that grow around me. This is the spirit in which they were originally crafted centuries ago. For me, the greatest joy in this practice is making a liqueur that acts as a snapshot of a certain time and place. I typically use mostly fresh ingredients, although sometimes roots, flowers, barks, or other things I've collected and dehydrated throughout the year make their way into the infusion.

You may be wondering how I know exactly what the final product is going to taste like when I'm just adding various ingredients into a jar and covering them with booze, and the answer is, I don't! Nature changes all the time, and I want my bitters and amari to be an expression of that spontaneity. This uncertainty doesn't matter so much when making bitters, since they are only used by the drop or dash. However, when it comes to amari, the goal is to have something that can be sipped on its own or mixed into a cocktail without overpowering the other ingredients.

To achieve this, I have developed a way to approximate a final product that is balanced and well-rounded: I break the ingredients down by flavor profile (bitterness, sweetness, acidity, florality, spice, herbaceousness, and depth of flavor) and then choose ingredients that fall in each of these categories (see Botanical Flavoring Agents page 26). From there, I rely on dilution and sweetening to help correct any overpowering flavors. I'm happy to say that I've made an amaro for each season for the last six years, and I've been happy with how they have all turned out. I still make sure to write down amounts for each ingredient used; this way if I find that one of my ingredients was too prominent or not pronounced enough, I have a benchmark from which to start the following year.

After deciding which ingredients you'll include in your amaro, you'll need to decide which type of spirit you want to use to extract the flavors. The alcohol needs to be at least 100 proof (50% ABV), but the higher the proof, the better the flavor extraction. I use 151-proof vodka for most of the recipes in this book; however, for the fall amaro, I opt for a 100-proof bottle of unaged Laird's apple brandy known as "Jersey Lightning." Overproof whiskey, rum, or another base spirit will also work, though they won't have the same neutral flavor profile as vodka.

Bitter

Acidic

Herbaceous

Floral

AMARO

Sweet

Depth

Spice

Next comes the process of maceration, wherein the botanical ingredients are added to a mason jar and left to infuse in the alcohol over the next 5 weeks before the botanical elements are strained out. While I may opt for a longer infusion when making liqueurs, I'm pretty strict about this 5-week infusing period for amari and bitters due to the variation in ingredients. After this period is over, strain out the solids, and then move to a barrel to age or skip ahead to dilution and sweetening. Just like making other types of liqueurs, you can dilute with wine or fruit juice and sweeten with other sources of sugar, such as honey and maple syrup, but you will have to adjust your levels of dilution and sweetness accordingly.

You can see this practice executed in more detail at the end of each of the seasonal chapters later in the book, but my best advice when making an amaro is to embrace the unknown element of it. Chances are, you're not going to re-create Averna, Campari, or one of the other commercial amari brands on your first shot. Instead, start with ingredients that excite you, write down your recipes, and enjoy the journey of tweaking and refining.

AMARO MASTER RECIPE

Makes 1 qt/950 ml amaro at 37.75% ABV

2 c/475 ml tincture
(see Tincture Master Recipe page 73)
1 c/240 ml water

1 c/240 ml simple syrup
(page 25)

DIRECTIONS

Make a tincture following the recipe on page 73. Add water and simple syrup, tasting as you go until the desired dilution and sweetness are achieved. When you're happy with the flavor, put it in an airtight container and store at room temperature. It will keep indefinitely.

Aromatized Wines

There are quite a few popular examples of aromatized wine, including wormwood-infused vermouth, cinchona-spiked quinquina and Barolo Chinato, and Americano Amaro (from *amaricante*, meaning "bittered" in Italian), whose bitterness comes from gentian root. Aromatized wines have lower alcohol levels, so are more prone to spoiling. Once opened, these wines will begin to oxidize and lose their character and complexity within a matter of a few weeks. Storing them in the refrigerator will help delay this process.

Aromatized wines are sometimes made by infusing a base wine with fruit, spices, and herbs, before sweetening and fortifying with a neutral alcohol, such as vodka or unaged brandy. Alternatively, you can also add alcoholic tinctures to a wine base, which will fortify the wine as well as impart it with flavor.

AROMATIZED WINE/VERMOUTH MASTER RECIPE

Makes 1½ cups/395 ml

2½ c/590 ml red wine, white wine, or mead at roughly 14% alcohol

½ c/120 ml homemade amaro or bitters, or 3 Tbsp/45 ml 151-proof tincture(s)

simple syrup (see page 25)

DIRECTIONS

To the wine of your choosing, add your homemade amaro, bitters, or tincture and stir. Taste and adjust the sweetness as desired. For each 1 Tbsp simple syrup added, you will need to add an additional 1 Tbsp 37.75% ABV amaro or bitters or 1 tsp 75.5% ABV tincture.

Store in a swing-cap bottle or mason jar in the refrigerator. It will keep for a month or two before the flavors start to oxidize and change.

As a rule of thumb, one part of any one of the amari recipes added to five parts of 14% wine will yield a fortified wine or vermouth that is around 18%. You can leave it as is, or add additional sugar syrup to make it sweeter. If adding simple syrup, fortify with 1 Tbsp bitters or amari per 1 Tbsp simple syrup, or 1 tsp 151-proof tincture to maintain the desired 18% ABV.

Cocktail Preserves

The idea for making cocktail preserves came to me after years of working at events where I'd have leftover batched cocktails that I wasn't sure what to do with. I remember one day reading about how colonial British navy ships would carry massive batches of punch as a way to preserve citrus juice to prevent scurvy. I thought that if punch, with its mix of alcohol, sugar, citrus, spice, and tea or water, could survive these trips, why couldn't the same principles be applied to batches of cocktails that are prepared the same way?

I can now confirm that cocktails will store in a sealed jar or bottle in the refrigerator for years. Sure, their flavors gradually change, mellowing and softening over time, but something magical happens as the burn of alcohol seemingly disappears as the months pass. Aged cocktails become something totally unique, arguably getting better with time like a fine wine. Although the process doesn't work with soda-spiked drinks like Mules or Highballs, any Sour, Flip, Punch, Negroni, Manhattan, Martini, or Old Fashioned is a perfect candidate for batching ahead of time and sticking in your refrigerator.

So why age a cocktail? Besides the experimental element of tasting how the cocktail morphs and changes, it's also very convenient to have a batched cocktail on hand to pull out when friends come over. Additionally, say you make a syrup that you want to use in cocktails, but the shelf life of the syrup is only a few weeks or a month; you can just mix the whole syrup into a batched cocktail, and extend its life by years. It's an incredibly easy technique and one that I don't think gets nearly the attention it deserves.

As for how long they can age, I have a few cocktails coming up on three years of aging now that show no signs of spoiling in any way. I've heard of well-respected bartenders in New York serving aged Whiskey Sours, people aging eggnog for upwards of seven years, and Charles Dickens's aged Milk Punch being discovered in his wine cellar after his death that was still in exceptional condition years after being made.

To batch cocktails, I multiply everything by 32 to translate from ounces to quarts. Here is an example:

Individual Whiskey Sour:

2 oz/60 ml bourbon
¾ oz freshly squeezed lemon juice
¾ oz simple syrup
2 dashes of bitters

Batched Whiskey Sour:

2 qt/1.9 L bourbon
3 c/720 ml freshly squeezed lemon juice
3 c/720 ml qt simple syrup (see page 25)
64 dashes of bitters

Once batched, store in the refrigerator in an airtight container such as a mason jar. It will keep for years.

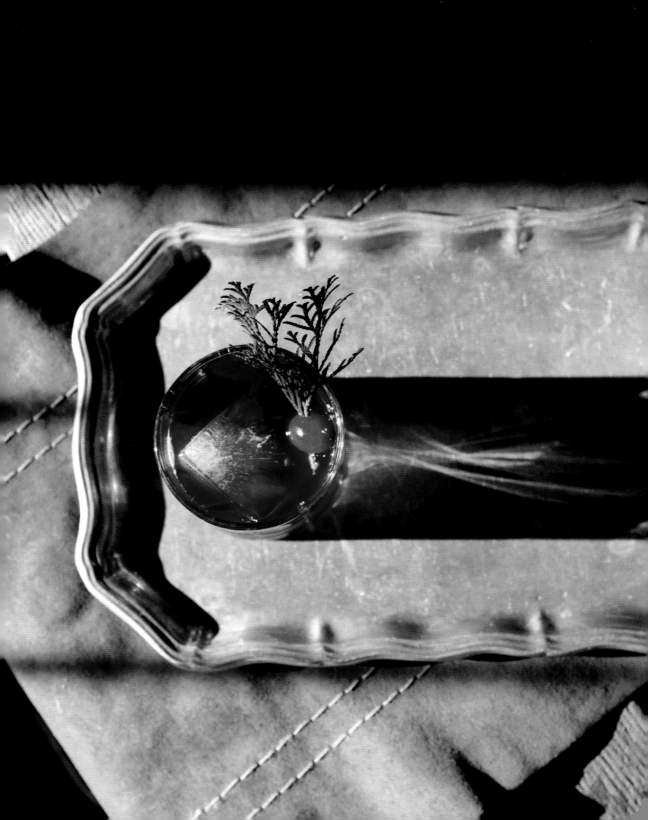

SUGAR PRESERVES

Sugar inhibits the growth of microorganisms by drawing out water, thereby dehydrating and killing the microorganisms in the process. Sugar can be used on its own to dehydrate ingredients in a process known as "sugaring," such as with candied ginger and citrus peel. And it can be used in fermentation to facilitate the production of ethanol (alcoholic fermentation) and lactic acid (lacto-fermentation).

However, the sugar preserves we'll explore here are simple syrups, citrus oil syrups known as oleo-saccharum (plural: oleo-sacchara), and pantry staple fruit preserves like jams and jellies. As commonplace as each of these are, they are also imperfect because they will spoil relatively quickly on their own if they're not used in conjunction with another type of preservation method.

Fruit preserves will last longer than syrups when refrigerated; however, you must jar and process them for long-term storage. In the case of syrups and oleo-sacchara, their shelf life can be extended by refrigeration or by mixing them into batched cocktails. Syrups also have the added benefit that they can be used to make kombucha, soda, beer, mead, or wine, which can then all be left to further ferment into vinegar. Oleo-sacchara cannot be used in fermentation due to the antimicrobial properties of the citrus oils.

Simple Syrups

Syrups are possibly the most ubiquitous of nonalcoholic cocktail ingredients for their ability to simultaneously add sweetness, body, and texture to drinks. The easiest and most neutral flavored of all is simple syrup, made with equal parts granulated sugar and water. This can be an exact measurement by weight, or it can be an approximation by volume. Swapping out white granulated sugar for less-refined demerara, dark brown, light brown, or raw sugar can add complexity and depth. Syrups can also be made with honey, agave, and maple (each of these are explored on page 25), as well as other liquid mediums such as teas and juices.

The one drawback of simple syrups is that they are not a long-term preservation solution. As a rule of thumb, simple syrups should be kept for only 1 month, and flavored syrups for around 2 weeks. Check any syrup older than 2 weeks for cloudiness, mold, or an off smell or taste. Increasing the amount of sugar will increase the shelf life (2:1 simple syrup will last for 6 months); adding 1 Tbsp high-proof vodka per cup/240 ml of 1:1 syrup will extend its life to 3 months; and mixing it into the cocktail will preserve it indefinitely (see page 82). You can also freeze syrups and use them later.

Ingredients can be incorporated into syrups in two main ways. They can be blended directly into an already prepared syrup, or in the case of more strongly flavored ingredients such as teas and spices, they can be infused into hot water and then mixed with an equal amount of sugar. Heating ingredients, rather than using them fresh, will change the flavor and texture of the syrup, which isn't necessarily a bad thing, just something to consider.

Something else to consider is strength of flavor and size of ingredient when making syrups. For fruits and vegetables, I'll usually start with an equal amount of a chopped ingredient to water and sugar by volume, and if it doesn't taste strong enough, I'll increase the ratio to two parts ingredients to one part each sugar and water and go up from there. For herbs, I'll usually do equal parts by volume with sugar and water. And with strongly flavored spices and teas, I'll usually brew an infusion before straining out and discarding the solids, adding the sugar, and stirring to incorporate.

FLAVORED SIMPLE SYRUP MASTER RECIPE

Makes approximately 2 cups/475 ml

1 c/240 ml water

1 c/240 ml sugar

1 c/240 ml chopped fruit, vegetable, or herb

DIRECTIONS

To a medium saucepan over medium-low heat, add the water and sugar and stir frequently, until the sugar dissolves. Move to the refrigerator and let cool.

Once cool, pour the syrup into a blender with the chopped ingredient and blend on high for 15 seconds. Strain out and discard the solids and pour the syrup into a sealable container. Move to the refrigerator and use within 2 weeks.

Fruit Preserves

Most of us are well-acquainted with using fruit preserves with food, but the idea of using them in drinks may seem unfamiliar. However, fruit preserves are a wonderful way to add body, sweetness, and acidity to beverages. Despite this, they remain widely underutilized, with the most famous example of a jam cocktail being the Breakfast Martini, a mix of orange marmalade, gin, Cointreau, and freshly squeezed lemon juice, which most people have never even heard of, let alone tried. I was admittedly one of these people, but that all changed when I first created the Pine Barrens cocktail on page 245, which opened up my eyes to the possibility of using fruit preserves in drinks.

There are many books available that go into great detail on the hows and whys of preserving specific types of fruit. However, having an easy recipe to turn to during peak fruit season is an invaluable tool. For me, that's the Any Fruit Jam that follows. I've made it with a number of different fruits through the years, and I can attest that the jams made from it are as great smeared on a piece of toast as they are in a Whiskey Sour.

Sugar preserves can be canned for long-term storage, or you can pour them into sterilized jars and store them in the refrigerator to be eaten within a few weeks or a couple of months, depending on the fruit.

ANY FRUIT JAM MASTER RECIPE

Makes approximately 2 cups/475 ml

---

2 lb/900 g fruit, pitted and chopped if necessary

1½ c/300 g sugar

¼ c/60 ml freshly squeezed citrus juice and/or vinegar

1 Tbsp grated lemon zest

DIRECTIONS

Add the fruit and sugar to a medium saucepan and let macerate overnight at room temperature to draw out the fruit juices. The next day, add a plate to the freezer to use later. Place the sugar and fruit over medium heat and cook until it starts to boil, about 10 minutes. You'll need to stir occasionally when the liquid boils rapidly, gradually increasing the frequency to a constant stir to prevent scorching as the boiling slows and thickens.

Once the jam reaches a thick boil, add the citrus juice and cook until thick again (another few minutes), stirring constantly. Remove from the heat and add in the lemon zest. Stir to incorporate.

Pull your plate out of the freezer, place a bit of jam on it, and wait 30 seconds. Push your spoon through it. If it wrinkles up, it has reached its setting point. If it hasn't, keep cooking and conducting the same test every few minutes until it reaches a jam-like consistency.

Funnel into a clean 1 pt/475 ml mason jar, filling to just under the glass threading. Process the jam in a boiling water bath for long-term storage or move to the refrigerator and consume within a few months.

Oleo-Saccharum & Sherbet

Like many, my introduction to the magic of the oleo-saccharum came from Dave Wondrich's canonical book *Punch: The Delights (and Dangers) of the Flowing Bowl*. In it, Wondrich quotes Jerry Thomas, the father of mixology, as saying "to make punch of any sort in perfection, the ambrosial essence of the lemon must be extracted." What Thomas was referencing was the oleo-saccharum, Latin for "oil-sugar," which refers to extracting the oils present in citrus peels and capturing them in sugar. To do this, citrus zest must be peeled from the fruit taking with it as little of the bitter white pith as possible. Next, the peels are covered with sugar and firmly muddled. I like to add spices prior to muddling. Over the course of the next few hours (or preferably overnight), the oils will be drawn from the peels and spices to be suspended in a sweet slurry that smells like the ambrosia of the gods, as Thomas stated.

The next step in crafting a quality punch is adding citrus juice, another fruit's juice, or water to the oleo-saccharum to create what was traditionally known as a *sherbet* or *shrub*. I refer to them as *sherbets* to avoid confusion with vinegar shrubs. At this stage, the sugar, peels, spices, and citrus juice are gently heated to dissolve the sugar before straining out the solids. You can also add other fruit during this stage to create a flavored sherbet.

Sherbets will keep for a month or two as long as they are stored in a clean sealed jar in the refrigerator. If another type of fruit is added, they should be consumed sooner.

Punches are the obvious route to go with sherbets; however, I also use them in nonalcoholic drinks, to which they add a velvety texture—a great stand-in for the viscosity of whiskeys, rums, and other pot-stilled spirits. I always have a sherbet or two on hand in my home refrigerator to make delicious nonalcoholic drinks for the whole family to enjoy.

OLEO-SACCHARUM & SHERBET MASTER RECIPE

Makes approximately 1½ cups/360 ml

---

4 lemons, 2 oranges, or 6 limes, plus more as needed

1 c/200 g sugar

1 c/240 ml freshly squeezed lemon, orange, or lime juice

DIRECTIONS

To make the oleo-saccharum, peel the citrus and top with the sugar in a food-safe container. Muddle the peels to release their oils. Cover and let sit overnight at room temperature. Meanwhile, juice the peeled citruses until 1 cup/240 ml of juice is yielded (you may need to supplement with additional fruit). Refrigerate in an airtight container.

The next day, add the citrus juice and oleo-saccharum to a medium saucepan and gently heat until all the sugar dissolves. Pass through a fine-mesh strainer into a large bowl, being sure to squeeze as much liquid from the peels as possible. You now have a sherbet. Discard the solids after straining and store the sherbet in the refrigerator for up to 1 month.

CHAPTER 3

SPRING

Dandelions | Ramps | Rhubarb | Spruce | Sassafras | Strawberries Mulberries | Cherries | Spring "Rabarbaro" Amaro

---

I remember the chef at the Farm and Fisherman once saying that March was the hardest month to be a farm-to-table restaurant. All the storage crops have pretty much run out, and the days in the Northeast are still too short and cold for anything to grow. Come April, though, signs of life start to appear. The forsythia blooms, ramps begin to emerge from the blanket of leaves on the forest floor, and dandelion blooms abound. In the garden, the perennial herbs return one by one; rhubarb stalks reappear, and clusters of green strawberries start to bunch along the ground. Flower buds begin to open, and, before you know it, nature is once again awake and abloom.

This is the most hopeful, optimistic part of the year. Green is returning to the landscape, fresh ingredients come back into the kitchen, and the prospective projects lined up for the year ahead fill me with joy. The first few weeks of the season are a leisurely re-entrance into the growing cycle, but come late May and the beginning of June, I find myself in a mad dash of preserving that will continue well into the fall. Spring ingredients, perhaps more than any other season, are brief and ephemeral. One day honeysuckle is everywhere you look, the next it is nowhere to be found. Cherry trees so full it seems possible to pick them for weeks are suddenly bare.

In a season with so much to choose from, it is sometimes hard to decide exactly what to focus on. The following is what I feel is the best course of action for navigating spring's bounty. We will start the season with the roots and shoots—dandelion, ramps, and rhubarb—before moving on to trees, including spruce tips and sassafras. Finally, we'll get into the beginning of fruit and berry season, with strawberries, mulberries, and sour cherries being the first to emerge. Just before the summer equinox, we will combine many of the spring ephemerals into an amaro that, when it is ready in the fall or winter, will bring us back to the bright, hopeful days of spring.

DANDELIONS | *Taraxacum* spp.

The idea of a spring tonic is one that spans many cultures throughout time. It was born partially out of necessity, since people needed something nutritious—be it food, drink, or medicine—to restore strength after living off preserves and storage crops all winter.

However, part of the appeal of a spring tonic is also symbolic. Consuming freshly harvested ingredients for the first time each spring is invigorating. Even the act of watching them grow is revitalizing. And while we don't rely as heavily on the larder as our ancestors once did, the symbolic consumption of a spring tonic is still an essential rite of spring observed by many. For me, there is no plant that embodies this spirit more than the dandelion, which despite its inherent beauty and millennia-long importance, is still one of the most highly contentious plants today.

The dandelion genus, *Taraxacum*, is composed of roughly sixty species that can be found growing in nearly every corner of the globe. Its name comes from the jagged young leaves that look like lion's teeth (*dent de lion* in French). Dandelion roots, flowers, and leaves have been used both culinarily and medicinally for hundreds of years, if not longer.

Recent scientific studies have corroborated their therapeutic potential by showing that, in addition to high levels of vitamins and minerals, they possess diuretic properties that aid in liver and kidney function, as well as bitter compounds that assist with digestion and appetite stimulation.

European cultures have a longstanding tradition of making alcoholic beverages with dandelions. Prior to the widespread availability of hops, dandelion was a common bittering agent used to flavor herbal beers known as *gruit*, and dandelion wine was so common it was referred to as the poor man's wine because anyone and everyone could—and did—make it. When European colonists came to America in the mid-1600s, they brought the seeds of the common dandelion, *T. officinale*, with them as a taste of home in their New World. Of course, this would have unforeseen consequences.

Dandelions are aggressively invasive and have since spread across the entirety of this continent and others, rightfully earning their reputation as one of the most prolific weeds in the world. Part of their success is due to their puffball heads, known in botanical lingo as a pappus, which contain seeds that can be carried by the wind as far as five miles from their origin. Another contributing factor is their deep taproot, which, despite the best efforts of gardeners, will sprout new growth if even only a small piece is left behind.

CONTINUED

While its tenacity is what villainizes the plant for some people, I view the dandelion as a welcome part of my backyard lawnscape, as it's one of my favorite ingredients of the year. I use the dandelion's young greens raw in salads, and as they get older and more bitter, they are great cooked in soups and braises. The roots make a great addition to my homemade spring amaro and can be roasted and ground to use as a decaffeinated coffee substitute, like its close botanical relative, the chicories (see page 266). My favorite part of the dandelion, however, is the flower heads, which are full of wild yeast making them perfect for fermenting into wild sodas, beer, wine, or mead.

In researching the subject, my wife Katie and I have learned that there was a history of making dandelion wine in both of our families until just a few generations ago. A video recently circulated in my family of a distant aunt talking about how her mother (my great-great-great-grandmother) who immigrated from Lithuania used to make dandelion wine each spring and how the whole family (including the kids) would drink it. On Katie's side, her great-grandfather, who lived in Hanover, Pennsylvania, located in the heart of Pennsylvania Dutch country, learned of the practice of making dandelion wine from his German immigrant ancestors and continued to make it well into old age.

This recipe is adapted from Katie's great-grandfather's original recipe, but I've taken the liberty of substituting honey for sugar since the floral notes of honey pair perfectly with dandelion flowers. Once complete, I use this dandelion mead to add florality and sweetness to a cocktail I've befittingly named the Spring Tonic. Along with the dandelion mead, I add roasted dandelion root- and flower-infused gin, Yellow Chartreuse, freshly squeezed lemon juice, and good tonic water, such as Fever Tree's Premium Indian Tonic Water. This cocktail is best enjoyed on a blanket in the grass on a warm spring day, preferably nestled among dandelion blooms.

Foraging Advice: The good thing about foraging for dandelions is that you don't have to travel far to find them, as they are likely growing on your lawn or not far from it. Dandelions are relatively easy to identify with their toothed leaves and yellow flowers, but do have some lookalikes, which are luckily nontoxic, including cat's ear (*Hypochaeris radicata*) and sow thistle (*Sonchus* sp.).

Regional Substitutes: Dandelions can be found growing on every continent except Antarctica. Any of the more than sixty varieties worldwide can be used in the recipes below.

N/A Alternative: The fermentation time in this dandelion mead recipe can be shortened to make a delightfully tart, floral nonalcoholic soda by following the Ginger Beer Master Recipe (see page 43).

DANDELION MEAD

Pick the dandelion flowers from the plant, making sure to get the yellowest, healthiest looking flowers. If making your own dandelion mead seems daunting to you, fret not. Dandelion wines and meads are part of a growing trend of alt-wines being produced by small purveyors across the country, including Brooklyn's Enlightenment Wines Memento Mori, which ships nationwide.

This recipe is based on the Mead Master Recipe, page 55

Makes approximately seven 750 ml bottles

---

1 qt/950 ml packed, freshly picked dandelion flowers (should weigh approximately 6 oz/170 g)

1 qt/950 ml of honey

1 gal/3.8 ml water

½ c/120 ml Ginger Bug, liquid only (see page 39)

3 oz/89 ml freshly squeezed lemon juice

DIRECTIONS

To reduce bitterness, remove as much of the calyx (green part) from under the flower head as you can. Personally, I think it adds a nice component to the brew, so I don't sweat it too much. This is also why I opt to leave my dandelion flowers in for the entirety of the fermentation. If you want to reduce bitterness, follow the steps below and strain the flowers out once signs of fermentation appear.

Add the dandelions and honey to a 6 qt/5.7 L heatproof food-safe container. In a pot, bring the water to a boil, let cool for a few minutes, then pour over the dandelions and honey. Stir well to loosen the honey. Allow to sit at room temperature until cool. Once cool, add the ginger bug and lemon juice, stirring well to incorporate. After a few days, signs of active fermentation should appear.

You can leave the dandelion mead to ferment in the 6 qt/5.7 L container covered with cheesecloth or a tea towel secured with a rubber band or other non-airtight lid, or transfer it to a carboy or fermentation bucket outfitted with an airlock to play it safe. If using an airlock, fill it with water and a splash of vodka (vodka prevents mold from growing in the water) to the designated lines and place it into the container opening.

CONTINUED

Once fermentation has slowed, usually after 4 to 6 weeks, carefully rack the mead into a new container (see page 51), being careful not to disturb the yeast on the bottom. Pour the racked mead into 750 ml swing-cap bottles. Drink immediately, or let it rest for the flavors to mellow and change. It will keep for 1 year or more stored at room temperature, or longer if stored in the refrigerator.

*This mead is also great sparkling. Simply add 1 Tbsp 3:1 honey syrup (see page 25) per bottle and let sit in a cool, dark place until sufficiently carbonated, anywhere from 1 to 4 weeks.

ROASTED, GROUND DANDELION ROOT
The dandelion root can be roasted and ground following the same process as for chicory root (see page 266), its closely related cousin in the *Asteraceae* family. Dandelion root tea bags can also be easily found at health food stores or online retailers.

DANDELION-INFUSED GIN

This recipe is based on Infusions and Tinctures, page 72.

Makes approximately 2 cups/475 ml

---

2 c/475 ml London dry gin

½ c/120 ml dandelion flowers

½ tsp ground dandelion root, roasted

DIRECTIONS

Add all the ingredients in a 1 qt/950 ml jar and allow to infuse for 2 hours (or longer for stronger taste). Strain the liquid through a fine-mesh strainer and discard the solids. It will keep indefinitely at room temperature.

SPRING TONIC

Makes 1 cocktail

1½ oz/44 ml Dandelion-Infused Gin (see page 96)

1 oz/30 ml Dandelion Mead (see page 95)

½ oz/15 ml Yellow Chartreuse (Strega also works as a cheaper alternative)

½ oz/15 ml freshly squeezed lemon juice

Tonic water, for topping (I like Fever Tree Premium Indian Tonic Water)

Dandelion flower, for garnish

DIRECTIONS

Fill a Collins glass with ice and add the gin, mead, Chartreuse, and lemon juice and top with tonic water. Garnish with a freshly picked dandelion leaf or flower.

RAMPS | *Allium tricoccum*

In the early days of spring, out of the detritus of the forest floor emerge vibrant green ramp leaves like beacons of culinary hope. Their flavor is unparalleled: sweet, pungent, and spicy, nature's remedy to the doldrums of winter. Although we have recently grown accustomed to seeing them on restaurant menus each year as a harbinger of spring, many still don't know what they are, let alone where to find them.

North American ramps (*Allium tricoccum*), also known by their common names, wild leeks, wild garlic, and spring onions, are just one of more than 250 species in the Allium family, including onions, leeks, garlic, and shallots. Ramps grow in rich, moist deciduous forests from Georgia to southern Canada and as far west as the Plains. They were widely consumed in both fresh and dried form by many different Native American groups, including the Cherokee, Iroquois, Ojibwa, and Potawatomi. In Europe and Western Asia, their close cousin "ramsons" (*Allium ursinum*) are equally coveted. Because they take almost a decade to reach maturity, ramps and ramsons are rarely grown commercially, instead they must be

sought out in the wild and are found only on hilly slopes in densely forested areas, usually with a water source in the vicinity.

Ramps have been revered for hundreds of years as a traditional food and medicinal plant, but it is only within the last twenty years that they have become an obsession of chefs and gastronomes across the world. Due to their high demand and low supply, ramps fetch quite a high price. That is, of course, unless you know where to find them. I've picked from a few spots over the years, but the most promising came a few springs ago when I received a call from my grandfather that he'd stumbled upon "ramp heaven."

My grandfather is an avid birder, citizen scientist, and an all-around naturalist in the truest sense of the word. Knowing that he lives in a part of Pennsylvania where ramps are, well, rampant, I have been asking him for years to keep his eye out for them, and that year he finally hit the jackpot. We went out to his spot together and after wandering through rolling meadows and pasture, came to a wooded hill next to a stream that was covered with a sea of green ramp leaves, mixed with stinging nettles, fiddlehead ferns, and mayapple.

After my grandfather and I harvested just enough for ourselves, I brought them home to begin the work of processing them. My favorite way to use them in the kitchen is to vinegar pickle them and use the delicious brine to make a Dirty Gibson, a close cousin of the Martini that

CONTINUED

is traditionally served with a pickled cocktail onion. I don't find bar guests asking for Gibsons often, but for those who do, I love talking them into trying a Dirty Ramp Gibson instead and watching their expression as they experience this wild, unique flavor for the first time.

While it is easy to become overtaken with ramp fever, their recent surge in popularity and the long time they take to establish themselves in patches have placed them in danger of being overharvested. For this reason, there is a common code of conduct among responsible foragers to harvest sustainably: If you are taking leaves, the general rule is one leaf per group of three, and if you are harvesting bulbs, you should take less than 5% of the patch every other year to keep the population healthy and thriving.

That being said, many foragers recommend we stop harvesting ramp bulbs altogether due to their threatened species status, instead suggesting people only sparingly harvest the leaves above the soil line to preserve them for generations to come. I've converted to this school in recent years, trading my jar of pickled bulbs for pickled ramp greens, and I am happy to report that I actually prefer the brine from the ramp greens in my Gibson, as the herbaceous, spicy flavor really complements the vodka and vermouth. Cheers to growing and learning a bit more each year.

Foraging Tips: Make sure you are able to spot the difference between ramps and the poisonous lily of the valley, as they bloom around the same time and have similar leaves and coloration. The oniony smell of ramps is a good sign that you have found what you are looking for, whereas lily of the valley is relatively odorless. Another way to differentiate

the two is that ramps have two leaves that emerge from the ground, whereas lily of the valley has a single stem with leaves that wrap around the center. As always with foraging, it is important to be certain you are harvesting the desired plant and not something that could harm you or anyone else. Consult a guidebook or an experienced forager in your area.

Regional Substitutes: There are wild and cultivated onion varietals all over the world that can be substituted for ramps, especially if utilizing the greens. In the arid southwestern parts of the United States, you can use i'itoi onions (*A. cepa*), and in Northern California and the Pacific Northwest, keep your eye out for the invasive three-cornered leek (*A. triquetrum*). In temperate Europe and western Asia, you can easily swap in ramsons (*A. ursinum*) in place of ramps, as they are nearly identical to one another, or one of the countless other alliums from this region. In eastern Asia, you can find the closely related species *A. ochotense* growing in China, Japan, Korea, and Siberia where they have been utilized for thousands of years.

As you move to the southern hemisphere, wild allium options are much more scarce, although there are some. In South America you can find *A. juncifolium* in the western part of the continent and *A. sellovianum* in the east. In sub-Saharan Africa you can find *A. dregeanum*, and in North Africa there are quite a few native wild species that are also widespread throughout southern Europe and western Asia. Despite having no endemic native species, Australia has a few alliums that have naturalized after their introduction, including crow garlic (*A. vineale*) and the three-cornered leek (*A. triquetrum*).

PICKLED RAMP LEAVES

This recipe is based on the Basic Pickle Brine recipe, page 65.

Makes approximately 1 pt/475 ml

¾ c/175 ml water

6 Tbsp/90 ml distilled white vinegar

6 Tbsp/90 ml white balsamic vinegar (if you can't find it, white wine vinegar works)

1½ Tbsp/20 ml sugar

2¼ tsp kosher salt

Three 2 in/5 cm thyme sprigs

½ tsp black peppercorns

½ tsp fermented red chile flakes (optional, see page 187)

1 bay leaf

60 ramp leaves

DIRECTIONS

To prepare your brine, add the water, white vinegar, balsamic vinegar, sugar, and salt to a medium saucepan and bring to a roaring boil. Meanwhile, add the thyme, peppercorns, chile flakes, and bay leaf to a 1 pt/475 ml mason jar, followed by the ramp leaves, being sure to pack them in tightly.

Pour the boiling brine into the jar and immediately cap tightly. These can be quick pickled and consumed within 1 or 2 months or water-bath processed for long-term storage.

DIRTY RAMP MARTINI

People tend to have very strong opinions when it comes to how they like their Martinis. Feel free to adjust the recipe by swapping in gin, or making it more stiff or dirty to make it to your liking.

Makes 1 cocktail

---

2 oz/60 ml vodka

½ oz/15 ml ramp brine from Pickled Ramp Leaves (see page 103)

½ oz/15 ml dry vermouth

Chive blossom, for garnish

DIRECTIONS

Fill a cocktail shaker with ice and add the vodka, brine, and vermouth. Shake, double strain into a chilled Martini coupe, and garnish with a chive blossom.

RHUBARB | *Rheum rhabarbarum*

My first encounter with a rhubarb patch came while I was working on Plowshare Farms in Bucks County, Pennsylvania, and we had to take the tractor up the road for repairs. The mechanic, who worked out of a barn, came from a large farming family. His father had once farmed a huge swath of land but had since gone into semi-retirement. These days, his only crop is rhubarb, which he grows in a giant patch next to the repair shed and sells at a roadside stand.

I found the whole operation fascinating. The family patriarch relinquishing all farming activities except for . . . rhubarb? Was it his favorite crop? Or a best-seller?

I started to talk to people in the area about rhubarb and heard many vivid stories and memories. Picking rhubarb from Grandma's garden first thing every spring to make pie, sauce, jam, pandowdy, or pudding. Our chef at the Farm and Fisherman, Todd Fuller, told me how he would sit with his siblings in the kitchen and dip raw rhubarb into sugar to cut the acidity before chomping it down. I also heard stories of kids having sword fights with the stalks in the garden when the adults weren't looking.

Perhaps the reason for the prominence of these memories is that rhubarb is the first thing in the garden to ripen in the spring. However, I also think it's a generational memory, passed down

through families here in the Delaware Valley, where rhubarb was first successfully grown in the United States. It was cultivated by John Bartram of Philadelphia in the 1730s. Bartram was a Quaker farmer and botanist who had an interest in medicinal plants. He was sent rhubarb seeds from an English colleague who noted that the Chinese had been using the plant as medicine for thousands of years. These pharmaceutical applications caused Marco Polo to bring it back to Venice with him after his journeys through China, sparking a European market for medicinal rhubarb.

To help the medicine go down, so to speak, Italians infused it in alcohol along with other medicinal herbs, sugar, and spices to make what we now call an amaro. Rhubarb-based amari became so common that they were given their own subcategory: rabarbaro.

Here, tequila, rhubarb-hibiscus ginger beer, and rabarbaro amaro come together in a drink I've dubbed the "Mexican Rhubarb Mule." My wife, Katie, and I enjoy this drink so much we served it at our wedding five years ago and have tried to share one each year since on our May 5 anniversary.

N/A Alternative: The ginger beer that follows is not beer at all, but rather a spicy, tart, nonalcoholic soda that can be easily enjoyed on its own. Rhubarb also makes wonderful shrubs, kombuchas, and, of course, desserts.

Safety: The following recipes all include hibiscus, which is not recommended for consumption during pregnancy. Rhubarb leaves are poisonous due to high levels of oaxalic acid.

RHUBARB-HIBISCUS SYRUP

This recipe is based on the Flavored Simple Syrup recipe, page 85.

Makes approximately 1 qt/950 ml

---

4 c/488 g chopped rhubarb stems
(1 in /2.5 cm pieces)
2 c/400 g sugar

2 c/475 ml water
⅓ c/80 ml dried hibiscus flowers

DIRECTIONS

In a medium pot, combine all the ingredients and bring to a boil, stirring occasionally. Remove from the heat, and allow to steep for 30 minutes. Strain the liquid through a fine-mesh strainer, pressing the solids to extract as much syrup as possible. Will keep for 2 weeks in the refrigerator.

RHUBARB GINGER BEER

This recipe is based on the Ginger Beer Master Recipe, page 43.

Makes approximately six 750 ml bottles

---

3 qt/2.8 L water
1 qt/950 ml Rhubarb-Hibiscus Syrup (see above)
2½ c/590 ml freshly squeezed lime juice

1¼ c/120 g grated fresh ginger
½ c/120 ml Ginger Bug (see page 39)
1 Tbsp simple syrup for priming (see page 43)

DIRECTIONS

Add all the ingredients in a food-grade plastic container. Cover with cheesecloth or a tea towel secured with a rubber band or other non-airtight lid, and allow to sit at room temperature for 2 days to ferment.

Pass your soda wort through a fine-mesh strainer to remove the solids and decant the strained ginger beer into 750 ml swing-top bottles primed with simple syrup (see page 43).

Ferment at room temperature for 1 to 2 days more (or longer if needed). Once carbonated, move it to the refrigerator before consuming. It will keep for a few months or more.

MEXICAN RHUBARB MULE

Makes 1 cocktail

1½ oz/45 ml blanco tequila

¾ oz/22 ml rabarbaro amaro, such as smoky Zucca Rabarbaro or the spiced Mexican-made Amargo-Vallet Cortezas de Angostura

Rhubarb Ginger Beer (see page 108), for topping

Rhubarb ribbon (for garnish)

DIRECTIONS

Fill a Collins glass with ice, add the tequila and amaro, and top with Rhubarb Ginger Beer. Garnish with a rhubarb ribbon.

SPRUCE | *Picea*

With all the exciting ingredients that come back to life each spring, spruce trees are probably the last thing on people's minds. There seems nothing novel about them during this season, as they are available year-round, but what many people don't know is that there is a brief window each spring when new, flavor-packed green growth emerges from the ends of their branches. The flavor, which is akin to citrus, is markedly different from the bitter older needles on the same tree and unique among evergreens. They offer a level of brightness to rival any other spring ingredient and are perfect to use in drinks, adding acidity, floral notes, and astringency.

Spruce beverages are not a new trend, however. Tea made from the needles of various spruce species were consumed by Indigenous American groups like the Chippewa, Mi'kmaq Iroquois, and Cherokee, both for its flavor and as an effective remedy to ward off a number of ailments, including scurvy. Scurvy is caused by a deficiency in vitamin C, but this wasn't fully understood by Western medicine until the 1930s. Different cultures developed folk remedies that were effective in its treatment, but when European colonists found themselves in unfamiliar lands where they lacked knowledge of local flora, they often suffered harrowing bouts of the disease.

This is exactly what happened to the French explorer Jacques Cartier and his crew when they arrived in present-day Quebec in the winter of 1535. Cartier began to see the symptoms take hold of his men, including bloody gums, swollen legs, extreme fatigue, and bruising. With nothing growing around him and his ships' stores depleted, he had no way of treating them. Luckily, upon making contact with the St. Lawrence Iroquois tribe, they showed him how to treat the illness by boiling evergreen needles and brewing a tea with them.

The practice of drinking evergreen tea was soon adopted by the British Navy and eventually gained popularity in both England and mainland Europe. Given the longstanding beer-brewing tradition in England, it wasn't long before people started brewing with evergreen needles, and soon spruce beers became their own category intended for everyday consumption to keep scurvy at bay. Captain James Cook had designated spruce beer brewers on board for his journey to New Zealand and Australia, Jane Austen wrote of it in the pages of *Emma*, and Benjamin Franklin brewed his own proprietary spruce beer in the United States. This practice has continued into modern times with dozens of commercially marketed spruce beers on the market today, including Yards' Poor Richard's Spruce Ale, modeled after fellow Philadelphia native Ben Franklin's original recipe.

Brewing spruce beer is a ritual that anyone can embrace. The bright green spruce tips are very easy to identify when they pop through in the spring. Plus, they are loaded with ambient yeast that should make fermentation an easy task. After carbonation is complete, spruce beer is incredible on its own, however if you want a lower ABV treat that lessens the "spruciness" of the brew, try it in a Spruce

Shandy (see page 114) with lemon, simple syrup, and sparkling water.

Foraging Advice: Many species of spruce trees grow across the temperate and boreal regions of the United States and Canada, as well as northern and central Europe and Asia. If spruce cannot be found, try using pine, cedar, or fir tips in its place, although the flavor of each will vary. When foraging for evergreens, be sure not to confuse them with yew. Yew can be easily identified with their bright orange "berries," which ripen from June through September, but remain dried on the trees for the rest of the year. Another distinguishing feature of yew is their flat, shiny needles arranged in lateral rows along the branch. As always with foraging, it is important to be certain you are harvesting the desired plant and not something that could harm you or anyone else. Consult a guidebook or an experienced forager in your area.

N/A Alternatives: Spruce tips can be brewed into a delicious tea that's great on its own or sweetened to make a quick-fermented nonalcoholic soda (see Ginger Beer Master recipe, page 43). Alternatively, spruce tips can be macerated in sugar to extract the oils into an oleo-saccharum (see page 89) that is great when mixed with citrus and topped with sparkling water.

SPRUCE BEER

I find the delicate flavors of spruce tips are best extracted through an extended infusion using the cold-brew method outlined on page 50. Since we won't be killing off any yeast with hot water, we can allow the spruce tips to undergo a true "wild fermentation" with nothing except the ambient yeast present on their needles. Feel free to add some of your ginger bug for peace of mind or if your fermentation isn't becoming active.

This recipe is based on the Beer Master Recipe, page 43.

Makes approximately seven 750 ml bottles

---

1 gal/3.8 L water

1 qt/950 ml simple syrup (see page 25) made with light brown sugar, plus 1 Tbsp syrup per bottle for priming (see page 43)

1 qt/950 ml roughly chopped spruce tips

3 oz/89 ml freshly squeezed lime juice

DIRECTIONS

Pour everything into a large food-safe container and stir well to incorporate. For a more rudimentary setup, leave the wort to ferment in the container covered with cheesecloth or a tea towel bound with a rubber band or other non-airtight lid, or transfer it to a carboy or fermentation bucket equipped with an airlock to play it safe. If using an airlock, fill it with water and a splash of vodka (vodka helps prevent mold from forming in the water) to the designated lines and place it into the container opening. Stir once or twice a day for 2 to 3 days to help jump-start the fermentation process.

Once the primary fermentation has finished (4 to 6 weeks) and the bubbling subsides, strain out the spruce tips and bottle the beer in 750 ml swing-top bottles primed with 1 Tbsp brown sugar syrup. Close the lid, shake to incorporate, and store in a cool, dark place. Wait 1 to 4 weeks for the beer to carbonate, checking every few days by "burping" the bottles to make sure they haven't overcarbonated. Once sufficiently carbonated, move to the refrigerator. It will keep for a year or more and will continue to change and evolve with time.

SPRUCE SHANDY

Whether you're drinking a British shandy, German *radler*, Spanish *clara*, or French *bière panaché*, all refer to a beer made more sessionable with the addition of a soft drink (most commonly lemon soda). The result is a lower-alcohol, sweet and sour beer, or a slightly boozy soft drink depending on how you look at it. In either case, it's extremely refreshing.

Makes 1 cocktail

---

6 oz/177 ml Spruce Beer (see page 113)

3 oz/89 ml sparkling water

1½ oz/45 ml freshly squeezed lemon juice

1½ oz/45 ml simple syrup (see page 25)

DIRECTIONS

Add all the ingredients in a pilsner glass and enjoy without a garnish.

SASSAFRAS | *Sassafras albidum*

It's hard to imagine that not long ago, the sassafras tree was one of the most coveted plants in the United States and the nation's second largest export after tobacco. It was revered by many Native Americans as a cure-all, with groups such as the Cherokee and Lenape who used it as a blood purifier and overall health tonic. Culinary uses of sassafras, which was originally known to mid-Atlantic tribes as *winauk*, included boiling the roots to make tea and adding the ground leaves to thicken stews, a practice that originated with the Choctaw and still continues today in traditional Louisiana gumbo with sassafras filé.

However, it was in my home state of New Jersey where sassafras was transformed from a folk medicine and foodstuff into a commercial drink marketed to the masses. In the 1800s a business-savvy Quaker pharmacist named Charles Hires decided to cash in on the budding American soda business. He traveled to the Centennial Exposition in Philadelphia in 1876 and unveiled his sassafras root beer, a nonalcoholic temperance drink that he marketed as "the greatest health-giving beverage in the world." It was Hires's basic flavor and formula that would become the benchmark for all commercially produced root beer.

How is it possible for a plant to experience such a meteoric fall from grace, such that most modern Americans have virtually no idea what it is? Part of the answer is that in the 1950s, sassafras became blacklisted due to the drug paranoia that gripped the nation. This stemmed from the discovery that you could synthesize the hallucinogenic compound MDMA from

a chemical in the plant known as safrole. The concern intensified when a scientific study several years later injected incredibly high levels of safrole into lab rats for an extended period, which caused the rats to grow tumors. And although this was never seen in humans, in 1960 the FDA labeled safrole carcinogenic and subsequently banned the use of sassafras in commercially sold foods, drinks, and drugs, and it remains banned to this day.

When I first heard about the potential dangers associated with sassafras, I started to research the case. What I've discovered is that the consensus in the foraging community is that it is safe in moderation, and the more I read, the more I was convinced that the occasional consumption of sassafras soda was no more dangerous than moderately consuming alcohol or eating cured meats. One estimate I came across was that you would have to drink approximately 24 gallons/90 liters of root beer per day for an extended period to ingest the level of safrole given to the rats in the lab study. Taking all this into consideration, I decided that I wanted to try my hand at making my own root beer.

CONTINUED

First, I had to find sassafras. One spring day at the dog park, I noticed a grove of saplings with the telltale mitten-shaped leaves. I bent down and grabbed one by the base, pulled it up with all my might to unearth the sassafras tuber, and filled the air with the smell of root beer. I continued doing so until I had a good haul, and when I got home, I scrubbed all the dirt off the roots and boiled them to make a concentrated tea, the first step of making root beer. I then sweetened the wort, added a bit of lemon juice to acidify, and inoculated it with beneficial yeast and bacteria from the ginger bug.

The result from this first attempt was better than I could have ever hoped. It had a creamy sudsiness, lingering herbaceousness, and earthy flavor from the fermentation. A few months later, my great-uncle came into the restaurant and tried some of the root beer. He told me how my great-grandfather also made his own sassafras root beer the same way. He would send all the grandkids out into the woods near the house to collect the roots for him. It was a surreal feeling to learn that in rediscovering a culinary practice from this region, I was also resurrecting an old family tradition.

Over the years, I've tried mixing sassafras root beer with whiskey, rum, and every other imaginable spirit, but always struggled with overpowering its delicate, herbaceous flavor. One day, a bartender friend suggested spiking it with Fernet-Branca, to make a Highball similar to a traditional Fernet and Coke. Rather than overpower the sassafras, the herbaceous notes of the root beer were fortified with the congruous flavors of the fernet. Shortly after, I added it to the cocktail menu as the "Bartender's Handshake," both as a nod to my friend's stroke of genius, as well as the hospitality vernacular used when one bartender orders a shot of Fernet-Branca from another bartender.

Foraging Advice: Sassafras grows in forests from Florida to southern Ontario and west to the Plains. It is so tenacious it is considered by many to be a weed and is in no danger of being overharvested. It is easily identified from spring through fall with its characteristic two- and three-lobed mitten-shaped leaves. If you are unsure if the plant you are harvesting is sassafras, pull the plant up by the root and you should be met with the unmistakable scent of root beer. If you don't live in an area where sassafras grows, check your local herb shop or an online herb store for sassafras root bark and substitute 3 cups/720 ml sassafras root bark in place of the sassafras roots in the sassafras root tea recipe.

N/A Alternative: This recipe for root beer is nonalcoholic, and the resulting root beer is delicious on its own. It's also great with a scoop of vanilla ice cream for an old-fashioned root beer float.

Safety: Don't consume sassafras if you are pregnant or breastfeeding. Also, safrole is more soluble in alcohol than water, so I don't recommend using it in alcoholic infusions.

SASSAFRAS ROOT TEA

Makes approximately 3 qt/2.8 L

---

2 lb/900 g sassafras roots,
cut into 8 in/20 cm segments

6 qt/5.7 L water

DIRECTIONS

Fill a large stockpot with the sassafras roots and cover with the water. Bring to a boil and let it reduce by half. Strain out the solids. Will keep in the fridge for about a week.

ROOT BEER

This recipe is based on the Ginger Beer Master Recipe on page 43.

Makes approximately five 750 ml bottles

---

3 qt/2.8 L Sassafras Root Tea (see above)

3 c/720 ml rich demerara syrup
(see page 25) plus 1 Tbsp syrup per bottle
for priming (see page 43)

¼ c/60 ml freshly squeezed lemon juice

½ c/60 ml Ginger Bug (see page 39)

1½ tsp molasses

DIRECTIONS

Add all the ingredients to a food-grade plastic container. Cover with cheesecloth or a tea towel secured with a rubber band or other non-airtight lid, and allow it to sit at room temperature for 2 days to ferment.

Pass your soda wort through a fine-mesh strainer to remove the solids and decant the strained root beer into 750 ml swing-top bottles primed with 1 Tbsp demerara simple syrup.

Shake the bottles to incorporate and allow it to ferment at room temperature for 1 to 2 days more (or longer, if needed). Once carbonated, chill it in the refrigerator before consuming. Burp before opening to make sure that too much pressure hasn't built up. It will keep for a few months or more.

BARTENDER'S HANDSHAKE

Makes 1 cocktail

---

2 oz/60 ml Fernet-Branca

Root Beer (see page 119), for topping

Sassafras leaf, for garnish

DIRECTIONS

Fill a Collins glass with ice, pour in the Fernet-Branca, top with the Root Beer, and garnish with a sassafras leaf.

STRAWBERRIES | *Fragaria*

For me, the official start to fruit season begins the moment I sink my teeth into my first sun-ripened strawberry that's so juicy and sweet, it feels like eating nature's equivalent of candy. Although they can be purchased year-round in the grocery store, tasting them at peak ripeness is a revelation that will make you never want to eat off-season strawberries again. Equally as enjoyable during this period is the act of eating wild strawberries on walks through the woods. Although the flavor and aroma of wild strawberries are often more intense than cultivated varieties, their biggest drawback is that I can't devour them as quickly due to their small size and sparsity on the vine. Whenever I find myself feeling annoyed about this, I remind myself that this is exactly how people have known strawberries for thousands of years: wild, small, and scant.

People began to try and change this as early as the fourteenth century when Europeans attempted to cultivate a better strawberry from their endemic wild varieties, the wild Alpine strawberry (*F. vesca*), the creamy strawberry (*F. viridis*), and musk strawberry (*F. moschata*), to little avail. Their solution, instead, was to plant them en masse in order to get a substantial haul (Charles V is said to have had over five thousand strawberry plants in his gardens at the Louvre!). When Europeans began sending expeditions to the Americas, some of the first plants they brought back were the equally small wild Virginia strawberries, *F. virginiana*, in hopes of breeding a new variety of strawberry with the native European species. However, these North American strawberries wouldn't hybridize with European varietals. While the American berries provided a novel variety for European palates, they exhibited more of the same in terms of size and abundance.

So how did we go from the tiny wild types to the plump strawberries we've grown accustomed to eating today? The answer can be traced back to the early 1700s when a French spy named Amedée-François Frézier traveled to Chile to collect intelligence on the then-Spanish colony. While in the port city of Concepción, Frézier was surprised to discover strawberries much different from those he was accustomed to seeing in Europe in that they were large and, even more remarkably, entirely white! This variety is the Chilean white strawberry (*F. chiloensis*), known locally as the *frutilla blanca*, which has been cultivated by the indigenous Mapuche people in the region since long before the Spanish arrived.

Frézier brought five of these plants on his return voyage to France, keeping one for himself and gifting the rest. One of the recipients was Antoine de Jussieu, the head of the Royal Gardens in Paris, who distributed clones of Frézier's specimens to his colleagues. However, they came to find out that Frézier brought only male plants, which didn't bear any fruit.

CONTINUED

It wasn't until decades later, when Frézier's Chilean strawberry was planted alongside its distant relative, the Virginia strawberry, that they crossed and produced the hybrid we now know as the common strawberry, *Fragraria ananassa*. It inherited the large size from its Chilean side, red color from its North American heritage, and ended up creating a hybrid with the flavor of pineapples, hence its species name *ananassa*, meaning "pineapple" in Latin. Every strawberry you've ever seen on a dessert, purchased at the supermarket, or harvested from a U-pick farm is a descendent of this hybridization.

One of the easiest ways to preserve peak-season strawberries is by simply submerging them in alcohol. This practice is widespread throughout Europe and goes by many names including the English *bachelor's jam*, German *rumtopf* (rum pot), French *confiture de vieux garçons* (old boys' jam). While these versions may contain a plethora of fruits, in Mexico they follow the same principle to solely preserve strawberries in tequila and refer to it with the charming name of *tequila por mi amante* (tequila for my lover). A few years back, I decided to take the same approach using pisco, a white grape brandy that's the national spirit of Chile, for an infusion I've befittingly dubbed *pisco por mi amante*.

When deciding how to best utilize my *pisco por mi amante*, I looked to inspiration from the relatively short list of famous pisco cocktails throughout history and settled on the oldest recipe in the canon, the Pisco Punch, which originated in San Francisco during the 1850s Gold Rush. The drink's creator, Duncan Nicol, served many a thirsty '49er with his proprietary mix of pisco, pineapple, lemon, and gum

(a.k.a. "gomme") syrup, which attains a rich texture and mouthfeel thanks to the addition of gum arabic, made from the crystallized sap of a species of acacia tree. It's also rumored that Nicol's version contained cocaine, but that's neither here nor there. In my version, I omit pineapple completely, instead relying on the pineapple flavor imparted by the strawberries. Although regular simple syrup could be swapped in place of the gum syrup here, it's worth the extra bit of time and effort to make a truly exceptional drink.

I like to use these pisco-laden strawberries as the first layer of my bachelor's jam for the rest of the fruit season. From now through the end of autumn, I will continue to add layers of ripe (and overripe) fruit and top with brandy for an easy preserve that lives in a crock on my counter. A lot of people use this alcohol-soaked fruit around Christmas to bake boozy fruit cakes, but the true treasure for me is the brandy, which makes a great addition to Sangria.

N/A Alternatives: Strawberries are excellent in kombucha, jams, sodas, and shrubs with balsamic vinegar.

PISCO POR MI AMANTE

This recipe is based on Infusions and Tinctures, page 72.

Makes approximately 1 qt/950 ml

_____

2 qt /1.2 kg cultivated or
wild strawberries, halved

1 qt/950 ml Chilean pisco
(Peruvian works fine as well)

DIRECTIONS

Add the strawberries and pisco to a 2 qt/2 L jar and let infuse for 3 weeks. After infusing, strain the strawberries out of liquid and reserve the liquid. Store in an airtight container. It will keep at room temperature indefinitely.

GUM (GOMME) SYRUP

Makes approximately 3 c/720 ml

_____

4 oz/115 g gum arabic powder
1½ c/360 ml water

1 lb/450 g sugar

DIRECTIONS

In a bowl, combine the gum arabic powder and ½ c/120 ml of the water and allow to soak for 1 day. The following day, add the sugar and remaining 1 c/240 ml of water to a medium saucepan and bring to a boil. Using a rubber spatula, fold the gum solution into the boiling syrup, stir well, and turn off the heat. As the gum syrup is cooling, skim off the foam. Once cool, strain through a fine-mesh strainer lined with cheesecloth or tea towels. It will keep in the refrigerator for 1 month.

STRAWBERRY PISCO PUNCH

Makes 1 cocktail

---

2 oz/60 ml Pisco Por Mi Amante
(see page 125)

¾ oz/22 ml Gum (Gomme) Syrup
(see page 125)

¾ oz/22 ml freshly squeezed lemon juice

1 strawberry, for garnish

DIRECTIONS

Fill a cocktail shaker with ice and add the pisco, gum syrup, and lemon juice. Shake vigorously and strain over small cubes in a rocks glass. Garnish with a strawberry on the rim of the glass.

MULBERRIES | *Morus*

When we bought our house four years ago, the branches from a tree on our neighbor's property hung down into our yard. Unable to identify it in the winter, I watched the following spring as the tree erupted in so many mulberries that the branches touched the ground under their weight. From that year on, I made a ritual out of laying a tarp on the ground, climbing into the tree, hanging from the branches, and shaking them as hard as I could to make the fruit drop. The tree was so large it provided us with close to 10 pounds/4.5 kg of fruit each year that we used to make all kinds of delicious treats. You can imagine my sadness last fall when I went outside to find my neighbors had hired tree surgeons who had reduced the mighty mulberry to little more than a stump.

"What are you doing to the mulberry tree!?" I yelled over the buzzing chainsaws.

"You don't want this tree. It's a weed," he responded coldly from behind his sunglasses.

What he didn't know was that mulberries are for me what a tea-soaked madeleine was for Marcel Proust: a profound trigger of a memory from my distant past. Each June, when the smell of overripe fruit fills the air, it immediately brings me back to my first day at a new school when I was just four years old. I could see the whole scene as clear as day. I remember looking around and not knowing anybody and feeling shy and scared. I retreated behind the swing set to the fence that was lined with honeysuckles and low-hanging mulberry fruit. The teacher came over and showed me how

you could pick the honeysuckle and pluck the stem of the flower to expose the nectar. She also showed me how to pick mulberries and how to tell when they were ripe. As we ate the berries, I remember feeling an overwhelming sense of relief. Perhaps it was the teacher showing me kindness, or maybe it was the deliciously sweet morsel of fruit itself, but this moment was more impactful than I realized, and I would have never known this if not for encountering the same fermenting mulberry aroma so many years later. In addition to losing a source of fruit in our backyard, I also lost a connection to my past.

There are over fifty species of mulberry in the world. The majority of them grow wild in temperate regions, whereas others have been selectively bred into commercially grown varieties. The fruit comes in all different shapes and sizes; some are round and squat, others can grow up to 5 inches/13 cm long. There are three main colors of mulberry: red, which is native to the eastern United States; black, native to the Middle East and northern Africa; and white, which is originally from south Asia, but has since spread to the United States and Brazil where it is now considered invasive.

CONTINUED

Here in the United States, mulberries are not finicky about where they grow, and various species can be found in all the lower forty-eight states where they have been used by indigenous groups for food, beverage, and medicine since pre-Columbian times. Today, mulberries are as at home growing along the borders of parking lots as they are in parks and forests. If you are looking for them near you, it is as helpful to use your sense of smell as your eyes. Once they fall on the ground and their sugars begin to ferment, they create a very strong aroma—sweet and floral, but also slightly sour and alcoholic.

Although I have used mulberries to make wine and vinegar in recent years, my favorite application these days is to make them into a jam. It's great spread on toast with butter, and shines with mint and bourbon in a jammy whiskey smash.

N/A Alternatives: The mulberry jam recipe is as good on a scone as it is shaken with some lemon juice and topped with sparkling water. Mulberries are also great candidates for fermented nonalcoholic sodas, kombuchas, vinegars, or shrubs.

MULBERRY JAM

This recipe is based on the Any Fruit Jam recipe found on page 87.

Makes approximately two 8 oz/237 ml jars

---

2 lb/900 g mulberries, stems removed
1½ c/300 g sugar
3 oz/89 ml freshly squeezed orange juice

1½ oz/45 ml freshly squeezed lemon juice
1 Tbsp/ml grated lemon zest

DIRECTIONS

Add the berries and sugar to a medium saucepan and let macerate overnight at room temperature to draw out the fruit juices. The next day, add a plate to the freezer to use later. Place the sugar and fruit over medium heat and cook until it starts to boil, around 10 minutes. You'll need to stir occasionally when the liquid boils rapidly, gradually increasing the frequency to a constant stir to prevent scorching as the boiling slows and the jam thickens.

Once the jam reaches a thick boil, add the citrus juices and cook until thick again (another few minutes), stirring constantly. Remove from the heat and add in the lemon zest. Stir to incorporate.

Pull your plate out of the freezer, place a bit of jam on it, and wait 30 seconds. Push your spoon through it. If it wrinkles up, it has reached its setting point. If it doesn't, keep cooking and conducting the same test every few minutes until it reaches a jam-like consistency.

Funnel into two 8 oz/237 ml canning jars, filling to just under the glass threading. Cover, move to the refrigerator, and consume within a few weeks or months, or process the jars in a boiling water bath for longer-term storage.

MULBERRY WHISKEY SMASH

Makes 1 cocktail

---

2 oz/60 ml bourbon

1 oz/30 ml freshly squeezed lime juice

6 mint leaves

2 Tbsp Mulberry Jam (see page 131)

Mint sprig, for garnish

DIRECTIONS

Fill a cocktail shaker with ice and add the bourbon, lime juice, and mint leaves and gently muddle to release the mint's oils. Next, add the mulberry jam and shake vigorously for 5 seconds, then double strain into a rocks glass filled with pebble ice. Garnish with a mint sprig.

CHERRIES | *Prunus*

Far too many people have had their introduction to preserved cherries in the form of a neon red orb perched atop their ice cream sundae or floating at the bottom of their Shirley Temple.

What I didn't find out until too late in life is that these "maraschino" cherries are more of a Frankenstein living-dead creation than an actual fruit. The cherries are first soaked in a solution of sulfur dioxide to bleach them, followed by calcium chloride to make them firm once again. They are then soaked in a solution of Red Dye 40, corn syrup, bitter almond extract, and preservatives to create a shelf-stable version of the cherry variety they are meant to imitate: the maraschino. True maraschino cherries get their name from the marasca cherry, a prized heirloom sour cherry native to the central coast of Croatia.

The name *marasca* comes from the Italian word *amarasca*, which is a derivative of the word *amaro*, meaning bitter. Marasca cherries came to northern Italy with Croatian citizens fleeing the war-torn region with their prized possessions (including cherry tree cuttings). One such asylum seeker was the last surviving member of the Luxardo family, who left the family's distillery behind after it was repeatedly bombed in World War II, in order to build a new facility in Italy. There, he began making preserved marasca cherries the way his family had for over a century: by first fermenting the cherries into a wine, then distilling that wine into a clear brandy (cherry brandy is commonly consumed in Germany, Switzerland,

and elsewhere, where it is known as *kirsch* or *kirschwasser*). The brandy was then sweetened into a liqueur to which cherries brined in ocean water were added to preserve them. These are true maraschino cocktail cherries, and no matter where you live, you can make an easy, delicious version with whatever variety is available to you.

Here in the United States, which cultivated variety you find depends largely on which coast you live on. Out west, it is more common to find sweet cherries (*Prunus avium*) like Bing, Tulare, and Rainier, which are most commonly eaten out of hand. On the East Coast, you are more likely to find sour cherries (*P. cerasus*), which are often referred to as "pie cherries" due to the fact that they are most commonly used for cooking and preserves. There are two subspecies of sour cherries, *amarelle* and *morello*. Amarelle cherries, like Montmorency and Early Richmond, are characterized by their highly acidic, bright red fruit. Morellos, like marascas and English morellos, are darker in color and more bitter than amarelles.

When it comes time to pick cherries each spring, I have a few go-to spots I visit as I wait for the two cherry trees in my yard to mature and bear fruit. After harvesting comes the hard part: painstakingly pitting them one by one. Though some people swear by the hole punch pitters, the metal straw is my preferred tool of choice. It takes a while, but good things often do.

CONTINUED

Cherries (like their other *Prunus* relatives, almonds, peaches, plums, nectarines, and apricots) have a delicious "nut" locked inside of their pits, which can be infused in brandy or cognac to make a traditional European liqueur known as *noyaux* (see page 137). If you've never tried a noyaux of any sort, it tastes like what you wish amaretto tasted like and can be substituted in recipes as such. Remember the bitter almond extract that is added to the fake maraschinos? This is meant to mimic the flavor of submerging the cherries intact and having their pits, known as *noyau*, impart their flavor to the brine.

To preserve the cherries, I like to make a brine with Luxardo Maraschino Liqueur, balsamic vinegar, a pinch of salt, and just a splash of stone fruit noyaux. The liqueurs add the important flavor of maraschinos and bitterness to the cherries; the balsamic gives it the deep, dark color and a nice touch of acidity.

These Luxardo cherries can be used to garnish all the classics that call for cocktail cherries (Manhattans, Old Fashioneds, etc.), and the brine is a really delicious addition to cocktails as well. You can pour some in a champagne flute and top with dry sparkling wine or substitute it for Luxardo Maraschino in the classic Last Word Cocktail as I've done in Spring's Last Word (see page 138).

N/A Alternatives: Sour cherries make delicious shrubs, jams, fermented sodas, vinegars, and kombuchas.

CHERRY PIT NOYAUX

This recipe is based on the Liqueur Master Recipe, page 75.

Makes approximately 3 c/720 ml

¼ c/60 ml noyau

honey syrup (see page 25)

2 c/475 ml brandy, cognac, or kirsch

DIRECTIONS

Preheat the oven to 300°F/150°C. Spread the noyau on a baking sheet and toast for 10 minutes. Allow to cool and repeat the roasting process, toasting again for 10 minutes, until all of the noyau are double roasted. Place the roasted noyau and brandy in a 1 qt/1L jar, seal, and let macerate for 4 months, shaking occasionally. After 4 months, strain out the noyau and sweeten the noyaux to taste, using about ½ oz/15 ml per cup/240 ml.

MARASCHINO COCKTAIL CHERRIES

Makes 1 pt/475 ml

---

1 pt/280 g pitted sour amarelle or morello cherries (sweet cherries will also work if you can't find sour)

¾ c/175 ml Luxardo Maraschino liqueur

2½ Tbsp/35 ml balsamic vinegar

¾ oz/22 ml Cherry Pit Noyaux (see above), Stone Fruit Amaretto (see page 170) or plain brandy

Pinch of salt

DIRECTIONS

Add the cherries to a 1 pt/475 ml wide-mouth mason jar. In a saucepan, bring the remaining ingredients to a boil, pour over the cherries, and cover with an airtight lid. The high alcohol content, vinegar, and sugar from the liqueur will render these shelf stable.

SPRING'S LAST WORD

Makes 1 cocktail

¾ oz/22 ml London dry gin

¾ oz/22 ml Green Chartreuse

¾ oz/22 ml cherry brine (from the
Maraschino Cocktail Cherries, page 137)

¾ oz/22 ml freshly squeezed lime juice

Maraschino Cocktail Cherry (see page 137),
for garnish

DIRECTIONS

Fill a cocktail shaker with ice and add the gin, Chartreuse, cherry brine, and lime juice. Shake vigorously and double strain into a chilled Nick and Nora glass. Garnish with a cocktail cherry.

SPRING "RABARBARO" AMARO

Rhubarb and rhubarb root are popular ingredients in many different amari, with the two most popular rabarbaro-style amari brands being Zucca Rabarbaro and Cappelletti Amaro Sfumato Rabarbaro. Both of these use Chinese rhubarb root, which takes on a smoky flavor when dried. Amaro sfumato further amplifies this flavor by actually smoking the roots (*sfumato* is the Italian word for "smoked"). While I love both of these brands, the rich smoky flavor isn't the profile I'm aiming for with spring ingredients. I want to show the delicate, fleeting flavors of the season, with something as light and bright as spring itself. To achieve this, I prefer to use the rhubarb stalks in place of the roots as my main flavoring agent.

For all the amaro recipes in this book, the goal is not to be overly precise, but rather to offer a framework for creating something evocative of the season, no matter where you live. My ingredients and their quantities change from year to year depending on what is available in the garden and in nature at that time. Maybe you had a late frost that wiped out your honeysuckle. Or perhaps the valerian you planted last year finally flowered and you want to include the incredibly fragrant blooms in this year's batch. I encourage embracing the unpredictable elements of the process. For me, each batch of amaro serves as a snapshot of that year in all its variation and uniqueness.

Before I assemble my jars of amaro, I like to break the ingredients down into their respective flavor profiles. Here is an example with the spring ingredients:

Bittering agents: dandelion root, horehound, wormwood

Acidic: rhubarb stalks, lemon balm

Floral: chamomile, honeysuckle, yarrow

Sweet: strawberries, mulberries

Herbaceous: mint, sage, bronze fennel fronds

Spice: spruce tips, green coriander seeds

One piece of advice is to make sure to document rough amounts of each ingredient before it goes in the batch. This way, if you have one flavor that is too strong, you can dial it back next year, or if you feel like you loved this year's recipe so much you never want to deviate from it again, you'll have the specs written down for years to come.

Here is a recipe for my amaro from last spring. Think of it as more of a suggestion than a hard-and-fast recipe. If you don't have an ingredient, skip it. If you want to add other ingredients, by all means do it. Just keep in mind the aforementioned flavor categories and try to include an ingredient or two from each. I highly recommend that you embrace the experimental nature of the process and don't get bogged down with specifics.

SPRING AMARO

This recipe is based on the Amaro Master Recipe on page 80.

Makes approximately 2 qt/1.9 L

---

375 g rhubarb stalks, cut into 3 in/7.5 cm pieces (2 or 3 stalks)

275 g halved strawberries (approximately 2 c/475 ml from roughly 24 medium strawberries)

80 g mulberries (approximately ½ c)

30 g honeysuckle flowers (approximately 1 c)

12 g (approximately ¼ c) of fresh chamomile flowers (can substitute 4 g dry)

15 g roughly chopped spruce tips (approximately ½ c)

10 g bronze fennel fronds (approximately 2 large sprigs)

10 g yarrow flower heads (approximately 12 flowers)

5 g lemon balm (approximately two 6 in/15 cm sprigs)

5 g sage leaves (approximately one 6 in/15 cm sprig)

5 g wormwood (approximately three 6 in/15 cm sprigs)

5 g horehound (approximately three 6 in/15 cm sprigs)

5 g mint (approximately one 6 in/15 cm sprig)

1 Tbsp green coriander seeds (can substitute dry)

1 Tbsp ground, roasted dandelion or chicory root (see page 266)

151-proof vodka, for topping (approximately 5 c/1.2 L)

8 oz/240 ml 3:1 honey syrup (see page 25)

6 oz/177 ml simple syrup (see page 25)

20 oz/591 ml water

DIRECTIONS

In a 2 qt/2 L glass jar, combine the rhubarb, strawberries, mulberries, honeysuckle, chamomile, spruce tips, fennel fronds, yarrow flowers, lemon balm, sage, wormwood, horehound, mint, coriander, and dandelion root and top with the vodka. Tightly secure the lid and let it macerate for 5 weeks.

After 5 weeks, strain out the solids and reserve the liquid (it should yield approximately 4¼ cups/1 L). Add the strained liquid to a 3 qt/3 L oak barrel and let age for an additional month (or longer), or skip this step if you don't have an oak barrel.

Next, add the honey syrup, simple syrup, and water. Stir to incorporate, and adjust the sweetness and dilution to taste. This can be stored indefinitely at room temperature. Its flavors will meld and mellow over time.

ORANGE SHERBET

This recipe is based on the Oleo-Saccharum & Sherbet Master Recipe, page 89.

Makes 1½ c/360 ml

---

4 orange peels   1 c/240 ml water

1 c/200 g sugar

DIRECTIONS

To make the oleo-saccharum, put the orange peels in a food-safe container and top with the sugar. Muddle the peels to release their oils. Cover the container and let sit overnight at room temperature.

The next day, add the water and oleo-saccharum to a medium saucepan and gently heat until all the sugar dissolves. Pass through a fine-mesh strainer into a bowl, being sure to squeeze as much liquid from the peels as possible. Discard the solids after straining and store the sherbet in the refrigerator for up to 1 month.

NO SWILL

Makes 1 cocktail

---

2 oz/60 ml rye whiskey

½ oz/15 ml Spring Amaro (see page 142)

½ oz/15 ml Orange Sherbet (see page 143)

2 dashes of Angostura bitters

Maraschino Cocktail Cherry (see page 137), for garnish

DIRECTIONS

Fill a mixing glass with ice and add the whiskey, amaro, sherbet, and bitters. Stir until well chilled, approximately 15 seconds. Strain into a rocks glass over a large cube and garnish with a skewered cocktail cherry.

CHAPTER 4

SUMMER

Walnuts | Elder | Blueberries | Stone Fruits | Watermelon | Tomatoes

Hot Peppers | Sweet Peppers | Summer "Carciofo" Amaro

When the longest day of the year arrives with the summer solstice, I find my energy mirrors nature in that moment—frenzied and prolific. The foraging trips and garden planning that filled my head all winter are now coming to fruition, and I am fully in the throes of the busiest time of the gardener and forager's year. What happens between the summer solstice and the fall equinox can only be described as wild and intense. The end of June marks the slim timeframe to pick unripe walnuts for nocino, the peak window for elderflowers, and the beginning of berry and stone fruit season. Melons come next, and from the middle of July until September, I find myself immersed in the nightshade garden glut, where harvesting, processing, cooking, and preserving becomes an almost full-time job.

I am not one of those people who claims that summer is their favorite season; I much prefer the cooler days of fall and spring. When September arrives, I'm ready for the cool weather and an end to gardening season, as I've been hot, tired, and overworked for months by this point. Regardless, as soon as the days start to get shorter and the nights get colder, I find myself yearning for those early, hopeful days of summer once again.

With the exception of walnuts and elderflower, all the ingredients highlighted in the following pages can be purchased from your local farmers' market or from the shelves of your grocery store. Or, for the do-it-yourself types, can be grown in your garden. And while there are plenty of longer-term preservation projects included here, I have also tried to strike a balance with shorter turnaround recipes that can be enjoyed quickly as a means to beat the summer heat.

WALNUTS | *Juglans*

My yearly foraging schedule can be described as loose at best. When I venture back outside after the end of winter, it's time to search for ramps, elderflower season starts around the solstice, pawpaws at the fall equinox, and persimmons after the first frost. My one exception to this lax approach is walnuts, which I harvest each year on June 24, when they are still in an unripe state and perfect for making a green walnut liqueur known as *nocino*. This date is not one that I made up; this is the date that walnuts have been harvested to make nocino in Europe for centuries.

The first written account of nocino production comes from the days of the Roman Empire, when Roman soldiers learned of the practice from the Celtic Pict tribe of Eastern Scotland. Each year on June 24, during the Midsummer solstice celebrations, the paganistic Picts would harvest walnuts to infuse with alcohol for a brew that was thought to contain supernatural properties. This June 24 date was not chosen for ritual purposes, however. The Picts knew that, at this early point in the walnut's development, the hard outer husk had yet to develop, making it significantly easier to cut through. More important is the liquid that can be found at the walnut's center during this young stage, which, if left unpicked, would begin to harden into the walnut just a few days later. When timed right, this white liquid will dissolve into the surrounding alcohol and, over the course of the next six months, imbue it with its jet-black color and spicy, earthy, and slightly bitter flavor.

The Romans adopted the practice from the Picts and brought it back to Italy where nocino production became deeply embedded in Italian culture. According to ancient lore, Romans would send an odd number of barefooted virgins into the trees each year on the night between June 23 and June 24 to collect the walnuts. The nuts were then cut in half and submerged in alcohol to macerate until December, when the nocino was consumed during the rituals that accompanied the winter solstice. During the fourth century, after Christianity was adopted as the official religion of the Roman Empire, these practices were changed to coincide with the corresponding Christian holidays of the Feast of Saint John and Christmas, respectively.

The tradition of making nocino eventually spread throughout the Roman Empire and remains intact in much of rural Europe today. In France, black walnuts are used to make the French counterpart to nocino, known as *liqueur de noix*, as well as *vin de noix*, in which the nuts are placed in red wine and result in a product that's more similar to vermouth. In the Italian peninsula, you can still find families making their proprietary nocino (or *ratafia di noci*, as it's known in the Piedmont) on the Feast of Saint John, the same way they have for centuries.

CONTINUED

While most commercial *nocini* available today are made from the European species, *Juglans regia*, known colloquially as the "common," "English," or "Persian" walnut, there are many other species in the *Juglans* genus. Here in the eastern United States, where I live, the native walnut species are the prolific black walnut (*J. nigra*), as well as the more sparsely dispersed butternut or white walnut (*J. cinerea*), whose numbers have been greatly reduced in recent years due to a fungal infection known as butternut canker. Both species were incredibly important to Native American groups east of the Mississippi as food, medicine, dye, and lumber. The Iroquois were even known to make a drink from black and white walnuts by crushing and boiling the meal into a sort of atole-like beverage.

Hypothetically, each of the approximately twenty *Juglans* species could be used to make nocino unique to their native regions. However, until my dream of an international web of nocino producers is realized, I am very content making a few gallons of nocino each year using black and white walnuts that grow within walking distance of my home. I pick my black walnuts on the running trail in the town where I live in suburban New Jersey, attracting weird looks from joggers in the process. Even more odd is my white walnut foraging spot, which is located along the edge of a parking lot in a corporate office park nearby, which tends to attract weird looks from businesspeople leaving for their lunch breaks. Although it's far from a bucolic foraging scene, it's the only place I've ever found them growing around me.

Once I've collected a sufficient haul, I bring them home and immediately get to work on halving them and packing them in 2-quart/2 L mason jars. From there, I cover them with 151-proof vodka, put them on the shelf, and forget about them until just after Thanksgiving, when I strain out the nuts and subsequently dilute, sweeten, and spice the liquid.

After letting it rest for an additional month, it's ready to be shared with restaurant guests, friends, and family just in time for the holidays. Nocino is wonderful on its own as a *digestivo*, but it can really shine in cocktails like the Black Walnut Old Fashioned (see page 153).

Regional Substitutes: Here in North America, black walnuts and, to a lesser extent, butternuts can be found growing throughout almost the entire eastern half of the continent. As you move farther west, you can find the Texas walnut (*J. microcarpa*), the Arizona walnut (*J. major*), the California black walnut (*J. californica*), and the Northern California walnut (*J. hindsii*). Then there are the southern Central and South American species that stretch as far as Argentina, and, in Eurasia, there are several other walnut species that can be found from the British Isles to Japan.

WALNUT NOCINO

This recipe is based on the Liqueur Master Recipe, page 75.

Makes approximately 2¼ qt/2.13 L

_____

2 qt/1.9 L young black walnuts, butternuts, or any other walnut species

151-proof grain spirit, for topping

3½ c/830 ml water

1½ c/360 ml rich demerara syrup (see page 25)

1 oz/30 ml Angostura bitters

DIRECTIONS

On or around the date of June 24, before the shells have hardened and the immature walnuts can easily be cut with a knife, harvest as many black walnuts as you can find (or as many as you want). Cut them in half, place them in a 2 qt/2 L mason jar, cover them with 151-proof vodka, and allow to macerate at room temperature for approximately 5 months.

In late November, strain out the walnuts and reserve the liquid (it should yield about 4 cups/950 ml). To this, add the water, demerara syrup, and bitters. Store at room temperature and allow to sit for an additional month for the volatile compounds to subside, yielding a smooth, spiced flavor that will continue to improve and mellow with time. Will keep indefinitely.

BLACK WALNUT OLD FASHIONED

Makes 1 cocktail

2½ oz/74 ml bourbon

¾ oz/22 ml Walnut Nocino (see page 151)

½ oz rich demerara syrup (see page 25)

Dash of orange bitters

Dash of Angostura bitters

Orange peel, for garnish

Maraschino Cocktail Cherry (see page 137), for garnish

DIRECTIONS

Fill a mixing glass with ice and add the bourbon, nocino, demerara syrup, and bitters. Stir until well-chilled and strain into a rocks glass over a large ice cube. Peel a long strip of orange and express over the drink (to release its oils), then skewer the peel along with the cocktail cherry and add to the drink.

ELDER | *Sambucus*

A few years ago, a long-standing community garden in northeast Philadelphia was going to be demolished to make way for one of the many new residential builds in the city. To save some of the perennials that had been established there, the organizers put out a notice on social media for the community to come rescue the plants from impending destruction. I jumped at the opportunity and brought home a rather measly elderflower bush (among other things) that I wasn't sure would survive relocation. In the years since, this bush has grown into the largest and one of the most beautiful shrubs in our backyard. It even has new shoots from its base that I gift each spring to friends and family, furthering the legacy of this piece of Philadelphia agricultural history.

I have come to value my elder plant more and more each year, and I am far from alone in this sentiment. In Greek mythology, Prometheus was said to have created civilization by delivering fire to humankind in a hollowed elder branch. Both the Brothers Grimm and Hans Christian Andersen wrote about the Scandinavian and English folktale of the Elder Mother, the guardian of the elder shrub whose permission needed to be granted before harvesting the plant's bounty.

There are more than twenty species of elder around the world, present on every continent except Antarctica, and people everywhere have long revered it for its culinary, medicinal, and utilitarian applications. I have seen species of elder growing in the mountains of Bolivia, parks in the center of Tokyo, and along the New Jersey Turnpike. Across most of the continental United States, you can find one elder species or another growing wild along the sides of roads, wood clearings, and as an ornamental landscape fixture. The varieties of elder most commonly used in culinary applications are *Sambucus nigra*, which grows wild across most of North America and northern Europe, *S. canadensis*, which is native to eastern North America, and *S. mexicana*, which can be found in the more arid regions of the southwestern United States and Mexico.

Elderflowers first appear at the end of the spring, when the dinner plate–size white flowers begin to bloom and their aroma fills the air. The smell is sweet, with perfumey floral and vanilla notes (I think of it like nature's equivalent to Johnson & Johnson baby powder). The flowerheads (corymbs) are best harvested in early summer when most of the blooms have opened, revealing the dusty pollen inside. This pollen attracts lots of tiny pollinators, which are best dealt with by placing the flowers in a metal bowl in the sun for a few hours, which will force the insects to evacuate.

If you leave the flowers undisturbed, they will eventually become elderberries. The berries can be cooked down into a jam, preserved as a syrup, or fermented to make elderberry wine or a traditional elderberry beer known in Europe as *ebulon*. Here in North America, Indigenous American groups far and wide

CONTINUED

utilized the berries of various *Sambucus* species fresh, juiced, dried, and preserved, and there is evidence that groups such as the Apache and Cherokee fermented the berries into wine.

My elder bush is so prolific, I can get a bumper harvest of both flowers and berries each year. To capture the essence of the flowers, I preserve them as both a liqueur and as a kombucha, and I mostly use the berries to make wine and more kombucha.

To make the liqueur, submerge the flowers in 151-proof vodka for 3 months, though if you have the patience, leaving them for up to 6 months or a year will really bring out their essence. As Amy Stewart says in her book, *The Drunken Botanist*, "No other spirit tastes quite like a meadow in bloom; if one tries to imagine what honeybees taste when they dive between flower petals, this drink is surely it."

Safety: It is important to keep in mind potential dangers associated with elder before experimenting with it. Due to the presence of cyanogenic glycosides, elderberries are mildly toxic when they are unripe and can induce nausea and vomiting if too many raw ones are consumed. These compounds are also present in the leaves, bark, and stems at much higher levels, so it is never safe to consume any of these parts of the shrub. Cyanogenic glycosides are not an issue once they are cooked, and studies also suggest that fermentation renders them inactive. For the recipes that follow, make sure to remove the white flowers and berries completely from the stems and to use berries that are fully ripe before cooking.

Foraging Advice: It is not uncommon for elderflowers to be mistaken for their dangerous lookalike, poison hemlock. Additionally, the berries can be mistaken for toxic pokeberries and nontoxic devil's walking stick. One main difference is that elderberries grow from large bushes/shrubs, whereas the other plants mentioned all grow from the ground. As always with foraging, it is important to be certain you are harvesting the desired plant and not something that could harm you or anyone else. Consult a guidebook or an experienced forager in your area.

Regional Substitutes: There are over twenty species in the elder genus, *Sambucus*, found in many different environments throughout North and South America, most of Eurasia, northern Africa, and northern Australasia. The flowers and fruits of all these should be safe to use in culinary applications once cooked or fermented, but double-check your local variety prior to consuming.

N/A Alternatives: In addition to the kombucha recipe below, elderflower can be fermented into a delicious nonalcoholic soda and works equally well in syrups, dried herbal tea blends, and vinegars. The berries are also excellent as jams, kombuchas, vinegars, and shrubs, and people swear by elderberry syrup as a cold and flu remedy.

ELDERFLOWER LIQUEUR

This recipe is based on the Liqueur Master Recipe, page 75.

Makes approximately 3½ qt/830 ml

_____

3 c/720 ml packed elderflowers, picked from the stem

6½ c/1.5 L 151-proof vodka

5¾ c/1.4 L water, plus more to taste

1¾ c/415 ml honey syrup (see page 25), plus more to taste

DIRECTIONS

Add the elderflowers and vodka in a 2 qt/2 L mason jar and let it sit for 3 to 6 months or upwards of 1 year. When you're happy with the taste, strain out the flowers, making sure to squeeze as much liquid from them as possible, before adding the water and honey syrup. Add additional honey and water to taste. Will keep indefinitely at room temperature.

ELDERFLOWER KOMBUCHA

Elderflower kombucha may be my favorite flavor of kombucha ever.
It's a wildly floral, tart, sparkling treat that is as nuanced and sophisticated
a nonalcoholic drink as you could ever hope for.

This recipe is based on the Kombucha Master Recipe, page 69.

Makes approximately six 750 ml bottles

---

3 qt/2.8 L water

1 qt/950 ml simple syrup (see page 25),
plus 1 Tbsp per bottle for priming
(see page 43)

4 c/950 ml packed fresh stemmed
elderflower blossoms

2 c/475 ml kombucha from a previous batch
or unpasteurized, store-bought kombucha, or
the liquid that comes with a packaged SCOBY

DIRECTIONS

In a pot, bring the water and 1 qt/950 ml of the simple syrup to a boil. Place the elderflowers
in a heatproof food-safe container, pour the diluted syrup mixture over the elderflowers. Cover
and allow to cool overnight at room temperature.

Once cool, strain the flowers out and squeeze the blossoms to extract as much flavor as
possible. Add the strained liquid to a ceramic fermentation crock, glass jar, or food-safe plastic
container. Culture with a previous batch of kombucha and add the SCOBY to the batch. If you
don't have a SCOBY, one should begin to form after a few days of fermentation, which is also
a good indication of a healthy ferment. Cover with cheesecloth or a tea towel bound with a
rubber band or other non-airtight lid. Let ferment for approximately 1 week (longer for a sourer
brew), tasting frequently until you're happy with the balance of sweetness and acidity.

Prime six 750 ml swing cap bottles with the remaining 1 Tbsp of simple syrup. Remove the
SCOBY, strain out the solids, and transfer the strained kombucha into the bottles.

Allow to sit at room temperature for approximately 1 week, or until the carbonation levels are
to your liking. Once sufficiently carbonated, move to the refrigerator. It will keep for 3 months
or more.

ELDER SPRITZ

Makes 1 cocktail

---

2 oz/60 ml Elderflower Liqueur
(see page 158)

¼ oz/8 ml freshly squeezed lemon juice

Elderflower Kombucha
(see page 159), for topping

Elderflower sprig or lemon wheel, for garnish

DIRECTIONS

Fill a wineglass with ice and add the elderflower liqueur and lemon juice. Top with elderflower kombucha. Garnish with an elderflower sprig (if available) or a lemon wheel.

BLUEBERRIES | *Vaccinium*

For me, the unofficial start to summer is just before the Fourth of July when my family and I pack into the car and drive to the historic village of Whitesbog to pick blueberries. Whitesbog is in the heart of the New Jersey Pine Barrens (known to locals as "the Pinelands" or simply "the Pines"), an area that occupies a huge swath of land along the southeastern part of the state known for its cranberry bogs, sandy soils, cedar swamps, and, of course, pine trees that stretch as far as the eye can see. Much of the landscape you see today in the Pine Barrens was shaped by the original inhabitants of the land, the Lenni Lenape tribe, who used fire to clear unwanted underbrush, in hopes that blueberries and huckleberries, which are most prolific in the immediate years after a fire, would come to dominate the understory of the forest. As a result, fire is still an integral part of the ecosystem, and wild blueberries continue to abound. Today, the Pine Barrens are the self-proclaimed blueberry capital of the world, and Whitesbog is ground zero for blueberry domestication in the United States.

Whitesbog was named after Joseph J. White and the cranberry bogs he built there in the 1800s. White's eldest daughter, Elizabeth White, took an interest in the family business from an early age, and, after receiving a degree from Drexel University in Philadelphia (a relatively rare feat for a woman at the time due to misogynistic societal barriers), decided that she wanted to develop a second crop that could grow in the acidic, sandy soils to complement the fall cranberry harvest. So, with the help of a USDA scientist named Frederick Coville, White set out to domesticate the wild blueberry bushes that grew in the wooded areas between the bogs and throughout the Pines.

To do so, she recruited Pineland locals colloquially known as "Pineys" to bring her the sweetest and largest wild blueberries they could find. They brought specimens of both high- and low-bush blueberries (*Vaccinium corymbosum* and *angustifolium*, respectively), which varied greatly in size, shape, color, and taste. At the end of the season, Elizabeth White and her local helpers returned to the best bushes, dug them up, and moved them back to the experimental "Triangle Field" at Whitesbog.

Just over one hundred wild blueberry bushes were planted on the farm, each named after the person who delivered them to White, and out of those, only a small handful were deemed worthy of propagating for potential domestication. In his Washington, D.C., lab, Coville learned how to take cuttings from these standout bushes and grow genetically identical clones of the originals, and some, like the "Rubel" (named after Rube Leek) are still grown commercially around the world today.

CONTINUED

If you travel to Whitesbog, many of the original bushes planted by White more than one hundred years ago are still growing and producing fruit that are available for the general public to pick for nothing more than a suggested $5 donation. Walking through White's Triangle Field and tasting these long-forgotten varietals—Dixi, Wareham, June, Katherine—is like traveling through the pages of blueberry history and offer flavors that are unavailable in the aisles of grocery stores.

I use the fruit in many ways throughout the season, but it's my annual batch of blueberry wine that gets me most excited. Blueberries exhibit many of the same properties as grapes—sweetness, tannins, acidity, bitterness—and they make a wine that is great still, sparkling, or spiked with alcohol and transformed into a vermouth, as I do on page 166.

Regional Substitutes: Although I think that wild blueberries and the heirlooms at Whitesbog have very distinct tastes, Coville is purported to have once said "all blueberries taste the same, and all taste sour." While we may disagree on the fine points, I think that we would both agree that any blueberry (wild or cultivated), European bilberry, huckleberry, or any of the many closely related species in the *Vaccinium* genus would work in the recipes that follow. Also, thanks to the work of White, Coville, and other scientists who have followed in their footsteps, blueberries are now commercially grown on every continent and can be sourced at peak season when they are at their most flavorful.

Foraging Advice: If foraging for wild blueberries, it is extremely important to be 100% certain that you are harvesting the desired fruit, and not something that could make you sick or worse. Consult a guidebook or experienced forager in your area, or stick to picking/purchasing cultivated berries.

N/A Alternatives: Blueberries are also great candidates for fermented nonalcoholic sodas, kombuchas, jams, vinegars, or shrubs.

BLUEBERRY COUNTRY WINE

This recipe is based on of the Country Wine Master Recipe, page 53.

Makes approximately nine 750 ml bottles

---

3 lb/1.4 kg blueberries

1 gal/3.8 L ml water

2½ qt/2.4 L simple syrup (see page 25), plus 1 Tbsp per bottle for priming if desired (see page 43)

3 oz freshly squeezed lemon juice

½ c/120 ml Ginger Bug, liquid only (optional, as there is plenty of ambient yeast on the blueberries; see page 39)

DIRECTIONS

Following the blender method on page 48, work in batches to blend the blueberries and water and strain through a cheesecloth into a large bowl or jug, ensuring that no solids pass through (solids will prevent gasses from escaping and can cause your wine to explode). Add the simple syrup and lemon juice and stir to incorporate.

Pour the liquid into a carboy or fermentation bucket equipped with an airlock and let it ferment in a cool, dark place until signs of fermentation have all but stopped (2 to 3 months).

Once fermentation is complete, carefully rack the liquid into a new container (see page 51), being careful not to disturb the yeast on the bottom. Pour the racked liquid into sterilized bottles (here's where to add the sugar for bottle conditioning and carbonating if that's the path you choose to go) and let sit for another 3 to 6 months before enjoying. If you can't wait that long, drink your wine young in the style of nouveau-style wines and try to leave some bottles to age to see how the flavors change. If you decide to carbonate, make sure to check periodically to ensure the bottle hasn't overcarbonated. The wine will keep for a year or more and will continue to change and evolve over time.

BLUEBERRY VERMOUTH

With this vermouth I wanted to make something that encapsulates the terroir of Whitesbog and the surrounding forest. The Winter "Alpine" Amaro from page 210 serves as the fortifying agent for the blueberry wine, resulting in a mix of tart blueberry, pine, and juniper berry notes.

The good thing about the amaro used in this recipe is that its ingredients are available all year long. Once you begin fermenting your blueberry wine, get started on an early batch of the amaro, and they will be ready around the same time. I find that a ratio of five parts blueberry wine to one part amaro works best, but this can be altered to suit your tastes. If you don't feel like tackling this project, Cappelletti's Pasubio Vino Amaro would be a great stand-in with its rich notes of blueberry and pine.

This recipe is based on the Aromatized Wine/Vermouth Master Recipe, page 81.

Makes 3 cups/720 ml

2½ c/590 ml Blueberry Country Wine (see page 165)

½ c/120 ml Winter "Alpine" Amaro (see page 210) or a piney store-bought option, such as Braulio Amaro

DIRECTIONS

Mix together the blueberry wine and winter amaro. Stir well to incorporate.

Store in a swing-cap bottle or mason jar in the refrigerator. It will keep for a month or two before flavors start to oxidize and change.

BLUE MANHATTAN

Makes 1 cocktail

---

2 oz/60 ml Laird's Applejack

1 oz/30 ml Blueberry Vermouth
(see page 166)

DIRECTIONS

Add the applejack and vermouth to a mixing glass with ice. Stir until chilled and serve in a coupe glass without garnish.

STONE FRUITS | *Prunus*

At the center of every stone fruit lies an intensely flavorful, hidden morsel that all too often ends up in the compost bin. I'm not talking about the pits themselves, but the kernels found inside that smell and taste like the purest almond essence. In France, they call this kernel *noyau*, and Europeans have been using them for centuries to make bitter almond extract, marzipan, amaretto, and the alcohol *crème de noyaux*. Most commercially available versions of these ingredients have an artificial taste. Once you make your own amaretto from fresh summertime stone fruits, you'll never go back.

If you're wondering how amaretto, a bitter-almond liqueur, can be made from stone fruit pits, the answer is that almonds are members of the *Prunus* genus of plants, along with peaches, plums, nectarines, cherries, and apricots (and all other stone fruits). The fruits of this family are what's known as drupes, which essentially means that they have a stone (or pit) inside the fleshy, edible part of the fruit.

I use peach pits for my amaretto because those are what I consume the most of, but any member of the *Prunus* genus can be used. The quantity called for in this recipe may seem daunting, but the stone fruit pits can be frozen throughout the summer months. Once you've amassed the pits, the next step is to break open the stones (except for cherries, whose pits I use whole). To do this, I wrap each pit in a towel, then lightly hammer it to get to the almond-sized, lighter-colored stone inside the pit. The goal is to just crack the pits open to expose the noyau, not obliterate them.

There is one final step to ensure safety. Members of the *Prunus* genus all contain trace amounts of amygdalin in their fruit and seeds. Amygdalin undergoes a reaction in the body that yields hydrogen cyanide, a chemical that's toxic to humans. While the cyanide is present in such small amounts that it's not thought to be dangerous, there have been instances reported throughout history where, after long-term cellar storage of amaretto, cyanide collects at the top of the bottle and concentrates enough to deliver a lethal dose. Luckily, you can roast the kernels twice to denature the amygdalin and prevent its conversion into cyanide.

The noyau can then be macerated in alcohol to make the amaretto. I like to use a classic grape brandy (or cognac) as my base spirit, but bourbon and applejack are fine choices as well. If you start in July or August, it should be ready to drink by the holidays in December. Add some to your coffee, stir it with Scotch to make a Godfather cocktail, or use it to make the best Amaretto Sour you've ever had.

Regional Substitutes: There are more than 430 different wild and cultivated *Prunus* species that can be found growing across temperate regions of the Northern Hemisphere throughout North America, Europe, Asia, and Africa. Near me, I can find wild specimens of black cherry (*P. serotina*), American wild plum (*P. americana*), and beach plums (*P. maritima*) (to name a few).

STONE FRUIT AMARETTO

This recipe is based on the Liqueur Master Recipe, page 75.

Makes approximately 2 c/475 ml

¼ c/60 ml noyau

2 c/475 ml brandy, cognac, applejack, or bourbon

honey syrup (see page 25)

DIRECTIONS

Preheat the oven to 300°F/150°C. Spread the noyau on a baking sheet and toast for 10 minutes. Allow to cool. Repeat the roasting process, toasting again for 10 minutes, until all of the noyau are double roasted. Place the roasted noyau and brandy in a 1 qt/1 L jar, seal, and let macerate for 4 months, shaking occasionally. After 4 months, strain out the solids and sweeten the amaretto to taste using about ½ oz/15 ml honey syrup per 1 cup /240 ml strained amaretto.

AMARETTO SOUR

Makes 1 cocktail

---

2 oz/60 ml Stone Fruit Amaretto (see above)

1 oz/30 ml freshly squeezed lemon juice

¾ oz/22 ml honey syrup (see page 25)

½ oz/15 ml egg white

Dash of Angostura bitters

Lemon twist, for garnish

Maraschino Cocktail Cherry (see page 137), for garnish

DIRECTIONS

Fill a cocktail shaker with ice and add the amaretto, lemon juice, honey syrup, egg white, and bitters. Shake vigorously and double strain through a fine-mesh strainer into a separate glass, then discard the ice and return the drink to the cocktail shaker. Shake again without ice (this is called dry shaking) for 10 seconds, until the egg white becomes frothy. Strain into a rocks glass and garnish with a lemon twist and cocktail cherry.

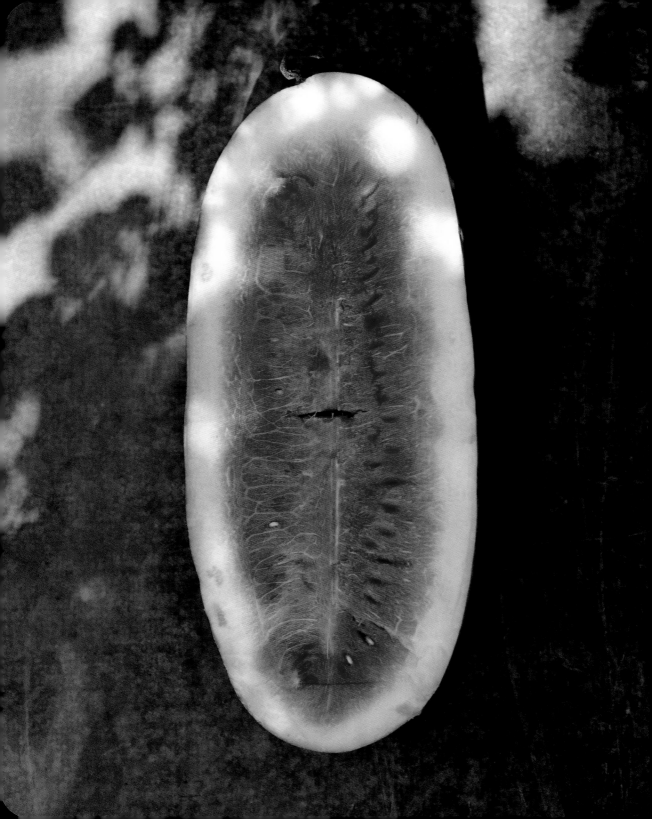

WATERMELON | *Citrullus lanatus*

Next time you bite into a watermelon and juice drips down your chin and shirt, remember that their juiciness is exactly why they were domesticated by humans in the first place. Thousands of years ago, the watermelon's ability to store water provided a safe, reliable drinking source for the inhabitants of the arid Kalahari Desert during the dry season. About 4,000 years ago, the seeds of this coveted crop spread across the African continent and became an important food in the Egyptian empire, even making its way into the tomb of Pharaoh Tutankhamun (a.k.a. King Tut) to symbolically accompany him to the afterlife. From Egypt, watermelon cultivation spread throughout the Mediterranean and became ingrained in the culinary traditions of the Arabs, Turks, Spanish Moors, and nearly every corner of the Roman Empire in the process. They came to the Americas in the 1600s via Spanish merchants and seeds smuggled on ships with West Africans during the slave trade.

Watermelons are members of the gourd family, *Cucurbitaceae*, along with squash, pumpkins, cucumbers, melons, and zucchini. Like all cucurbits, watermelons are promiscuous and will readily cross and hybridize with any botanical relative growing within a one-mile/1.6 km vicinity, creating mutant cucurbit progeny in the process. In the early 1800s, when the first seed companies were beginning to appear in the United States, and plant breeding was becoming more of a scientific discipline, the demand for pure, untainted watermelon seed that could be grown year after year skyrocketed, and the big business of breeding pure, genetically distinct watermelons began. One of the earliest sought-after melons came from a Revolutionary War officer named John Franklin Lawson who saved seeds from a watermelon slice he was given while imprisoned on a British ship in the West Indies. Upon his return to Georgia, Lawson began growing the seeds on his family farm. His son, A.J., continued the legacy and eventually earned the Lawson melon the reputation of being the sweetest, most delicious in the United States.

A. J. Lawson sent his father's seeds to a contemporary breeder, Nathaniel Bradford, who crossed the seeds with the popular "Mountain Sweet" melon to develop his own breed, which became known as the "Bradford" watermelon. Bradford's namesake fruit usurped the Lawson as the most coveted melon of the day, and those growers in possession of Bradford watermelons went to great lengths

CONTINUED

to protect them. Farmers would station armed guards overnight to protect their patches from the so-called watermelon gangs that plagued the fields of the south. Others took a more drastic line of defense, injecting unmarked melons with poison, and, once America had electricity, wiring them to deliver fatal shocks to potential melon thieves. Unfortunately, far too many farmers forgot which melons were meant for would-be invaders, and in a statistic that seems almost too insane to be true, watermelon patches became the second most fatal sector of the agricultural industry after livestock-related deaths in the late 1800s.

The Bradford melon's popularity eventually waned in the early 1900s, replaced by "rhino hide" melons that could be stacked high and shipped cross country. The Bradford melon would have likely gone extinct if not for the efforts of Nathaniel Bradford's descendants who continued growing the seeds for generations. Today, Nat Bradford is carrying the torch his forefather lit eight generations prior, and has succeeded in bringing the variety back into the culinary spotlight with the help of Slow Food USA, USC professor Dr. David S. Shields, the Carolina Gold Rice Foundation, and Chef Sean Brock.

Knowing that people used to risk their lives to get their hands on Bradford watermelon seeds, I always feel very fortunate when I go on the Bradford family website and add the seeds to my online shopping cart. I've grown Bradford melons for years now, and although some seasons have been less than favorable, I have had plenty of successful melon harvests that keep me coming back for more. Considering that a ripe Bradford melon can weigh between 30 and 40 pounds/13.6 to 18 kg, there are many opportunities to use them. Each summer, I make a watermelon–white balsamic shrub and watermelon rind pickles to enjoy all year long. For more immediate consumption, I like to make a salted fermented watermelon, agave, and lime soda. It's delicious on its own as a nonalcoholic drink or spiked with an aperitif or clear spirit of your choosing. The winning combination for me is watermelon soda and tequila, with their complementary agave and salty flavors that go down way too easy after a few hours in the garden.

FERMENTED WATERMELON SODA

This recipe is based on the Ginger Beer Master Recipe, page 43.

Makes approximately six 750 ml bottles

---

9 lb/4 kg watermelon flesh
(Bradford or other)

4 c/950 ml water

2 c/475 ml Agave Syrup (see page 25)

1¼ c/300 ml freshly squeezed lime juice

½ c/120 ml Ginger Bug (see page 39)

2 pinches of salt

DIRECTIONS

Remove the watermelon flesh from the rind by scraping it into a bowl (don't worry about separating the seeds).

Working in batches, add the watermelon and water to a blender and blend on high until liquefied. Use a fine-mesh strainer to remove the solids.

Add the blended watermelon, agave syrup, lime juice, ginger bug, and salt to a food-safe container.

Cover with cheesecloth or a tea towel secured with a rubber band or other non-airtight lid, and allow to sit at room temperature for 24 hours for the primary fermentation.

After 1 day has passed, decant the soda into six 750 ml bottles. Cap tightly and let sit for 24 hours out of direct sunlight. Check after 12 to 16 hours to make sure that too much pressure hasn't built up (watermelon is very active and can sometimes carbonate very rapidly). After fermentation is complete, place the bottles in the refrigerator and consume within a week or two.

TEQUILA-WATERMELON COOLER

Makes 1 cocktail

---

2 oz/60 ml blanco tequila (or any other spirit/aperitivo of your choosing)

Fermented Watermelon Soda (see page 175), for topping

Watermelon wedge, for garnish

DIRECTIONS

Fill a Collins glass with ice, pour in the tequila, and top with watermelon soda. Garnish with the watermelon wedge.

TOMATOES | *Solanum lycopersicum*

Nothing is more emblematic of summer than the first ripe tomato of the year. Waiting for that moment is an act of patience. Tomatoes are among the first seeds sown indoors in late winter, and one of the last to bear fruit, but that first bite into a perfectly sweet, juicy, vine-ripened tomato makes the wait well worth it. Though they come on slowly at first, once the intense heat of late July and early August arrives, they provide a surplus that is unparalleled by any other plant in the garden.

The use of wild tomatoes dates back millennia in their ancestral homeland in the South American Andes where they were long foraged and consumed by humans, but never domesticated. These seeds migrated north through the tropics until they arrived in Mexico, where the Aztecs domesticated them and gave them the Nahuatl name *tomatl*, which roughly translates as "swelling fruit" or "fat thing." Cortez observed the importance of tomatoes in Mexican cooking during the Spanish conquest period and is credited with first bringing tomato seeds to Europe in the early 1500s.

Tomatoes were first met with skepticism in Europe due to their inclusion in the nightshade family, *Solanaceae*, which includes mandrake, henbane, and belladonna, all of which are toxic hallucinogens maligned for their use in witchcraft. For this reason, in their earliest days in Europe, tomatoes were most commonly grown as ornamental plants rather than food. Over time, this perception changed, and it's now hard to imagine Italian food without red sauce, Spain without gazpacho, Israeli salad without fresh tomatoes, or tomato-less shakshuka in North Africa.

Here in North America, the first written evidence of tomato cultivation comes in the early 1700s in the Carolinas, though they didn't catch on for another 150 years because of the same suspicions they received when they arrived on European shores. In the 1850s, after the industrious New Jerseyan Joseph A. Campbell (the founder of Campbell's Soup) demonstrated that tomatoes responded well to canning and storage, Americans became enamored with the fruit, especially those "Jersey tomatoes" from Campbell's home state. Today, there is no symbol more iconic of the American home gardener than the tomato.

The greatest thing to me about tomatoes is their versatility. They are simultaneously sweet and sour, accentuated by a savory umami kick from their naturally high levels of MSG (monosodium glutamate). Once a bit of salt is added, you can taste all these flavors one by one. It is this phenomenon that first gave me the idea to swap the tomato in for olives in a Dirty Martini. The result is the Nightshade Martini (see page 182), a drink that hits every taste receptor—salty, sweet, sour, umami, with a fleeting bitterness and incredible mouthfeel imparted by the Tomato Leaf Oil (see page 181). This is a great cocktail to make a large batch of at the peak of tomato season and keep in your refrigerator or freezer all year long.

FERMENTED TOMATO WATER

This recipe is based on the Dry-Salted Lacto-Fermentation Master Recipe on page 63.

Makes approximately 2½ c/590 ml

2¼ lb/1 kg ripe tomatoes of
any juicy, non-plum variety

2½ Tbsp/20 g kosher salt

DIRECTIONS

Remove the stems, chop the tomatoes into 1-inch/2.5 cm pieces (if using cherry tomatoes, just halve them), and add to a jar or crock. Add the salt and stir to evenly coat the tomatoes. Let sit for 1 hour until the tomatoes begin to "sweat" out their moisture. Pack into a clean, food-safe container or fermentation vessel and press the tomatoes down until they are submerged in their liquid. Add a weight or zip-top bag filled with water on top to keep the tomatoes submerged under the brine. Loosely cover the container with a cheesecloth or tea towel bound with a rubber band or other non-airtight lid, so that gas can escape but insects can't enter.

Let the tomatoes ferment for 5 to 7 days at room temperature, until they smell slightly sour. It's more than likely that there will be a harmless bloom of Kahm yeast that forms at the liquid-air interface. Scrape away as much as you can using a spoon.

Blend the tomatoes until smooth and strain through a fine-mesh strainer lined with a few layers of cheesecloth or tea towels. The resulting liquid should be clear. If there is still some tomato sediment, strain again. It will keep in the refrigerator for 6 months or more.

TOMATO LEAF OIL

For me, the smell and stain of tomato leaves on my hands after a long
day of harvesting in the garden is peak summer. This tomato leaf oil perfectly
encapsulates that tomato leaf essence.

Makes approximately ¾ c/175 ml

¾ c/175 ml coarsely chopped tomato
leaves and stems

¼ c/15 g coarsely chopped parsley leaves
1 c/240 ml olive oil, chilled

DIRECTIONS

Bring a medium pot of water to a rolling boil and have a bowl of ice water nearby. Blanch the
tomato leaves and stems and parsley in the boiling water for 20 seconds, then transfer them to
the bowl of ice water.

Remove the blanched greens from the water and squeeze until there is no residual water left.

Add the oil followed by the greens to a high-speed blender and purée on the highest speed until
the greens are totally liquefied. Strain through a fine-mesh strainer lined with a few layers of
cheesecloth or tea towels, squeezing as much oil from the greens as possible.

It will keep in the refrigerator for 6 months or more.

TOMATO LEAF OIL–WASHED VODKA

Makes approximately 3 c/770 ml

¾ c/175 ml Tomato Leaf Oil (see page 182)

One 750 ml bottle vodka

DIRECTIONS

Add the tomato leaf oil and vodka to a 2 qt/2 L food-safe container and whisk well. Place in the freezer for 3 days until the oil has frozen and risen to the top of the vodka. Remove the frozen oil and discard. Pass through a fine-mesh strainer lined with a few layers of cheesecloth or tea towels to remove any additional oil. Oil-washed vodka will keep in the refrigerator or freezer indefinitely.

NIGHTSHADE MARTINI

Makes 1 cocktail

---

2 oz/60 ml Tomato Leaf Oil–Washed Vodka (see page above)

½ oz/15 ml dry vermouth

½ oz/15 ml Fermented Tomato Water (see page 180)

Cherry tomato, for garnish

DIRECTIONS

Fill a mixing glass with ice and pour in the vodka, dry vermouth, and tomato water. Stir until ice-cold (approximately 30 seconds). Strain into a chilled coupe over a fresh cherry tomato.

HOT PEPPERS | *Capsicum*

Of the estimated fifty thousand varieties of domesticated peppers grown around the planet today, each can be traced back to a single parent species that originated between fifteen and twenty thousand years ago in the eastern foothills of the Bolivian Andes. This prehistoric ancestor evolved into more than thirty species of wild chile, before humans intervened and domesticated five of those species into the fifty thousand chile varieties we have today.

When I first traveled to Peru in my early twenties as a self-proclaimed "chile head," I tried a myriad of *ajíes* (the most commonly used word for peppers in South America) from mildly spiced *ají panca*, to the medium heat *ají limón* and *ají amarillo*, all the way to the excruciatingly hot *rocoto* and *charapita* peppers. When I traveled south into Chile, I expected to find an equally thriving hot pepper culture, but the country's name turned out to be a misnomer. During my time in the north and central parts of Chile, I found the cuisine almost entirely devoid of spice, much to my dismay. It wasn't until I went farther south to Temuco, the capital of Chile's Araucanía region, that I finally encountered a source of Chilean heat in a dried pepper seasoning called *merkén*, made with the pre-Columbian pepper varietal known as *ají cacho de cabra* (goat's horn pepper).

Araucanía is home to the majority of the Mapuche, Chile's predominant Indigenous population whose ancestors have lived there for thousands of years. The Mapuche, who make up about 10% of the Chilean population, have managed to maintain a very strong cultural identity despite longstanding conflicts with outsiders. They were one of the few Andean societies to never be conquered by the Incan Empire; they resisted Spanish forces for three and a half centuries until ultimately surrendering in 1882; and they continue to have ongoing disputes today with the Chilean government over land rights and cultural recognition.

Eager to learn about how the Mapuche exist in modern-day Chile, I traveled to Temuco and stayed with a tribal elder named Olvado in a traditional straw-thatched longhouse, called a *ruka*. The ruka had a central firepit with dried cacho de cabra peppers hung from the rafters above it, which served to dehydrate them as well as impart a smoky flavor similar to paprika. Olvado's wife, Meriam, showed me how to prepare merkén by grinding the dried peppers, salt, and coriander seeds in a mortar and pestle. That night for dinner, we ate the traditional Mapuche dish of *charquicán* seasoned heavily with merkén, while sipping *chicha de manzana*, a wild-fermented apple cider (similar to the one on page 220) that the region is known for. After dinner, we sat around the fire pit and passed around a gourd of yerba mate as Olvado and his family told me about their culture's worldview, foodways, and day to day life until it was time for bed.

CONTINUED

I returned to Temuco again the following year to study with a Mapuche shaman to document and collect their medicinal plants. A few months after that, I began working with a Mapuche population in Santiago to see firsthand how they maintained an intact cultural identity in a bustling metropolis. On my fourth and final trip, I worked with this same population in Santiago to study their healthcare decisions, including whether to visit a Western medical practice or a tribal shaman when they fell ill.

To make ends meet during this last stint with the Mapuche, I picked up my first-ever bartending gig at a friend's restaurant, La Casa de la Luna Azul. The first two drinks I learned how to make there were the Pisco Sour and Michelada. Micheladas originated in Mexico before spreading throughout Latin America, and while there are probably as many Michelada variations as there are Michelada drinkers, our mix consisted of tabasco sauce, Worcestershire, salt, pepper, lemon, lime, and tomato juice. One day, the bar owner, Felipe, suggested we put smoky merkén on the rim. I now include it on my own cocktail menu with homemade merkén and a fermented hot sauce made with long hot peppers from my home garden.

N/A Alternative: The Michelada recipe can easily be made with a nonalcoholic beer. I enjoy these quite frequently thanks to the abundance of delicious, craft N/A beers on the market today.

MERKÉN

Makes approximately ½ c/120 ml

1¾ tsp whole coriander seeds

½ c/30 g dehydrated, fermented red chile flake (see opposite) or another dehydrated red chile flake (such as guajillo)

2 tsp smoked Spanish paprika

1 Tbsp plus ¼ tsp kosher salt

DIRECTIONS

In a skillet over medium heat, toast the coriander seeds until fragrant, 2 to 3 minutes.

Add the chile flakes to a mortar and pestle or spice grinder along with the paprika, salt, and toasted coriander seeds and grind into a coarse powder.

Store in an airtight container. It will keep indefinitely, though flavors may change with time.

FERMENTED LONG HOT SAUCE

Fermentation reduces the spice levels of peppers, so choose your pepper variety accordingly depending on your heat preference. Pro tip: Save your solids and dehydrate them to use in the Merkén recipe (opposite).

This recipe is based on the Lacto-Fermentation Master Recipe on page 63.

Makes approximately 3 c/710 ml of hot sauce and 1 c/60 g of dehydrated chile flakes

---

2¼ lb/1 kg long hot peppers or another variety of your choosing

3¾/30 g Tbsp kosher salt

¼ cup/60 ml water

6 Tbsp/90 ml Cider Vinegar (see page XX)

DIRECTIONS

Remove the stems (but not the seeds) from the peppers and chop into 1-in segments. Add to a fermentation crock or jar with 20 g of the salt and mix to coat the peppers evenly.

After 24 hours, muddle the peppers until they release enough of their liquid that they are fully submerged once a weight is added on top. Allow to ferment for 14 days at room temperature. If any Kahm yeast (see page 62) forms at the liquid-air interface, don't worry, just scrape it off and discard.

After the 2 weeks have passed, blend the peppers until smooth using an immersion blender or by transferring them to a blender. Pass through a fine-mesh strainer so that the largest solids and seeds are removed (some solids are okay, as they will help give the sauce body).

Add the remaining 10 g of salt, the water, and apple cider vinegar.

Store in a sealed container in the refrigerator and eat within 1 year. Put on top of anything and everything.

MICHELADA MIX

Makes approximately 2¼ c/530 ml, enough for approximately 9 Micheladas

---

¾ c/175 ml canned tomato juice
(I prefer Sacramento brand)

½ c/120 ml Worcestershire sauce
or Maggi Seasoning

5 Tbsp/75 ml freshly squeezed lemon juice

5 Tbsp/75 ml freshly squeezed lime juice

6 Tbsp/90 ml Fermented Long Hot Sauce
(see page 187) or your favorite
store-bought hot sauce

Big pinch of kosher salt

1 tsp freshly ground black pepper

DIRECTIONS

Combine all the ingredients in a 1 pt/475 ml jar and mix well. Store in the refrigerator for up to 3 months.

MICHELADA

A lot of people like their Micheladas over ice. I, however, am not one of those people. Feel free to add ice if you'd like.

Makes 1 cocktail

Lemon slice

Merkén (see page 186), for the rim

¼ c/55 g Michelada Mix (see above)
or more to taste

One 12 oz/355 ml can or bottle of a light,
crisp lager, chilled

DIRECTIONS

Wet the rim of a pilsner glass with a slice of lemon and dip in the merkén.

Add the michelada mix and top with an ice-cold lager. It will be quite bubbly, so be careful not to let it wash the rim away.

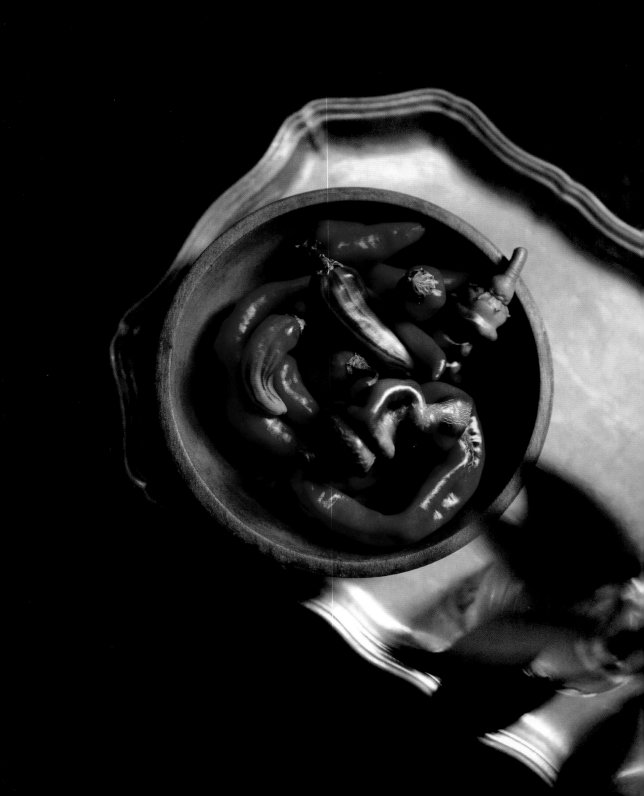

SWEET PEPPERS | *Capsicum annum*

For thousands of years, four of the world's five domesticated pepper species didn't venture far from their homeland in the Bolivian and Peruvian piedmont. Something that has stumped archaeobotanists, however, is how the fifth species of pepper, *Capsicum annum*, was domesticated in Puebla, Mexico, nearly four thousand miles to the north, almost five thousand years later with no evidence of how it arrived there.

The oldest living wild ancestor of the *C. annum* peppers is the incredibly spicy wild variety known as *chiltepín* (from the Nahuatl words *chīlli* meaning "pepper" and *tecpin* meaning "flea," referring to the small size of the fruit), which is native to southern North America and northern South America. The most commonly agreed-upon domestication theory is that the people in and around Puebla began discarding the seeds of these wild chiltepines around their settlements, weeding and tending to these dedicated patches, and saving seeds from the offspring with the most desirable traits—larger fruit, adaptiveness to specific climates, disease resistance—in a process known as artificial selection. Over time, these peppers became dependent on human intervention for their reproduction and dissemination, a telltale sign of plant domestication.

These earliest pepper seeds were saved and traded, and eventually spread to all reaches of the Aztec and Mayan Empires. As they moved across Central America, they continued to be selected for specific traits and suitability for different climates, creating dozens of pepper varieties in the process. One such modification was the expression of a recessive gene that prevents the synthesis of capsaicin, the chemical responsible for heat. This gave rise to the vast majority of sweet peppers in the world today.

Of all the *C. annum* varieties, poblano peppers (which hail from the epicenter of domestication in Puebla, Mexico) are my favorite, as they are equally flavorful in their unripe, green state as they are when they have ripened to a crimson red. Sometimes they have no detectable heat at all, and other times can be as spicy as a jalapeño. We grow poblanos each year in our restaurant garden, along with a potent Mexican herb called *papalo*, which has a complex flavor profile with hints of cilantro, nasturtium, arugula, and mint.

I wanted to combine these two ingredients in a Mexican-inspired cocktail and worked closely with our Puebloan sous chef, Poncho Hernández, to do so. The result was a drink we dubbed La Poblanita. When people ask me what my favorite cocktail is, I can say without hesitation it's La Poblanita. There are a lot of strong flavors vying for your attention in this drink—vegetal blanco tequila, smoky mezcal, spicy poblano syrup, herbaceous papalo, lime, salt—that result in a final product that is greater than the sum of its parts. It's a perfect example of how a cocktail can perfectly embody a sense of place.

PEPPER SYRUP

If you are making this while the peppers are green, throwing a half bunch of parsley in will help keep it vibrant green for a few days. The red pepper syrup will remain good for about 2 weeks. The spice level of the poblanos can vary greatly. If you want to make the recipe a bit spicier, add a green jalapeño or red serrano. Personally, I think it makes the drink.

This recipe is based on the Flavored Simple Syrup recipe, page 85.

Makes approximately 3½ c/830 ml

---

3 c/447 g roughly chopped stemmed poblano peppers (from about six peppers)

3 c/720 ml simple syrup (see page 25)

½ bunch parsley (if using green peppers; omit if using red)

5 papalo leaves (omit if you can't locate)

1 jalapeño or serrano pepper, stemmed (optional)

DIRECTIONS

Add all the ingredients to a blender and blend on high for 10 seconds. Strain through a fine-mesh strainer. It will keep in the refrigerator for around 1 week, though the color will fade with time.

LA POBLANITA

Makes 1 cocktail

1½ oz/45 ml blanco tequila

½ oz/15 ml mezcal

1 oz/30 ml freshly squeezed lime juice

1¼ oz/37 ml Pepper Syrup (see above)

Pinch of kosher salt

Papalo leaf, for garnish (optional)

DIRECTIONS

To a cocktail shaker, add the tequila, mezcal, lime juice, pepper syrup, and salt and shake vigorously for 10 seconds. Double strain over a large cube in a rocks glass. Garnish with a papalo leaf, if desired.

SUMMER "CARCIOFO" AMARO CYNARA

Artichokes and cardoons are two close relatives in the thistle genus, *Cynara*. Scientifically, the two are characterized as the same species, *C. cardunculus*, but while artichokes have been selected for their oversized flowerheads, cardoons have been bred for their long leaf stalks. I grow both in my home garden, and they are gorgeous landscape fixtures that are two of the first plants to emerge in the spring and two of the last survivors in the cold days of winter. Both are armed with sharp spines meant to deter would-be grazers and can grow up to 4 feet/1.2 m tall, producing beautiful purple flowers at the height of summer.

Artichokes, along with their *Cynara* cousins, are featured in a category of Italian amaro called *carciofo*, the Italian word for artichoke. While the two most popular brands on the market are Cynar, made with Italian artichokes, and Cardamaro, made with cardoons, there are quite a few others available.

My goal with this summer amaro is to create something refreshing and light that can be enjoyed on its own or used as an aperitivo in any classic recipe, such as a simple spritz or a twist on Sam Ross's Paper Plane (see page 199).

There are far more ingredients available in summer than I can list here, but here is a breakdown of some of my favorite summer amaro additions and their flavor profiles. As always with the amaro recipes included in this book, it's meant to be a rough outline, not a hard recipe.

Bittering agents: cardoon, artichoke, horehound, hops

Acidic: lemongrass, staghorn sumac, rhubarb, lemon balm

Herbaceous: tomato leaf

Floral: basil flower, yarrow, bronze fennel flowers

Spice: fig leaf

Sweet: peaches, corn cob

Depth of flavor: toasted sunflower seeds and peach noyau (see page 169)

SUMMER "CARCIOFO" AMARO

This recipe is based on the Amaro Master Recipe, page 80.

Makes approximately 1½ qt/1.4 L

---

250 g rhubarb stalks, halved (about 1 or 2 stalks)

100 g lemongrass bulbs, crushed (approximately 5 bulbs)

2 medium peaches, halved and pitted

1 corn cob, kernels removed

60 g artichoke and/or cardoon leaves (approximately 2 large leaves)

50 g sumac berries (approximately 1 c/240 ml), or 1 Tbsp ground store-bought sumac powder

20 g tomato leaves and stems (approximately two 1 ft/30 cm sprigs)

10 g basil flowers on stem (approximately two 8 in/20 cm sprigs)

10 g fresh hops (approximately 70 hops), or 1 g pelleted dry hops

10 g medium fig leaves (approximately 3 medium leaves)

10 g yarrow flowerheads (approximately 12 flowers)

10 g bronze fennel flowerheads (approximately 10 flower heads)

5 g wormwood (approximately three 6 in/15 cm sprigs)

5 g horehound (approximately three 6 in/15 cm sprigs)

5 g lemon balm (approximately two 6 in/15 cm sprigs)

2 Tbsp toasted sunflower seeds

2 Tbsp/8 g double roasted peach noyau (important: see page 170 for noyau roasting instructions)

151-proof vodka, for topping (approximately 5 c/1.2 L)

2½ c/590 ml white wine

1½ c/360 ml simple syrup (see page 25)

DIRECTIONS

To a 2 qt/2 L glass jar, add the rhubarb, lemongrass, peaches, corn cob, artichoke leaves, sumac, tomato leaves, basil flowers, hops, fig leaves, yarrow flowers, fennel flowers, wormwood, horehound, lemon balm, sunflower seeds, and peach noyau and top with the vodka. Tightly secure the lid and let it macerate for 5 weeks.

After 5 weeks, strain out the solids and reserve the liquid (it should yield about 2¼ c/530 ml). Add the strained liquid to a 3 qt/3 L oak barrel and let age for an additional month (or longer), or skip this step if you don't have an oak barrel.

Add the white wine and simple syrup. If the alcohol level feels too high, add more wine or water to mellow it out. It can be stored at room temperature indefinitely. Its flavors will meld and mellow over time.

PAPER PLANE

Makes 1 drink

¾ oz/22 ml bourbon

¾ oz/22 ml Aperol

¾ oz/22 ml Summer "Carciofo" Amaro
(see page 196)

¾ oz/22 ml freshly squeezed lemon juice

Orange peel, for garnish

DIRECTIONS

Fill a cocktail shaker with ice and add the bourbon, Aperol, amaro, and lemon juice.
Shake vigorously until chilled and double strain into a chilled coupe glass. Garnish with
an orange twist.

CHAPTER 5

FALL

Pawpaws | Figs | Apples | Celery | Hibiscus | Chestnuts
Cranberries | Persimmons | Fall "Génépi" Amaro

Come November, the pantry shelves are full of that year's pickles, jams, sauces, and liqueurs, and opening one of these jars transports me back in time to the day that ingredient was collected. There are, however, a few things left to be added to the pantry before my work is done.

While the end of September still feels like summer, the first hints of fall are beginning to creep in. The shorter days bring with them the arrival of the scarlet Harvest Moon and the most bountiful time of the year. The accumulation of energy from the long summer days produces sweet fruits that reach their peak in the early days of autumn. Figs, pawpaws, and apples make their appearance, as well as dense, starchy crops like corn, pumpkins, grains, and nuts that can be harvested and eaten fresh, or stored for the leaner days of winter.

It's always surprising to me how quickly the garden wanes, but thankfully I still have tart, crimson hibiscus and fresh, bright-green celery that offer a nice pick-me-up during the gray days of mid-autumn. Come the first frost, everything dies off quickly, save for the hardiest ingredients like persimmons, cranberries, root veggies, and greens. Where gardening and foraging in the spring and summer comes with a sense of urgency, harvesting ingredients in the autumn feels like a leisurely pursuit before retiring for the year.

As you'll see with the following recipes, the flavors of autumn become darker, hardier, and rich with spice notes. And because this is the season for gathering with family and friends, I've included two large-format punch recipes that can be served to a crowd or squirreled away and stored for your winter hibernation. Every ingredient in this chapter can be grown in your garden or found at a quality farmer's market, and about half of the ingredients can be foraged from the wild if you know where to look. Once everything is harvested and the preserves are up on the shelves, there's nothing to do but sit back and settle into winter's long rest as you enjoy the fruits of your labor.

In what feels like a lifetime ago, I was a twenty-year-old college student conducting research in the middle of the Peruvian Amazon. Walking through the forest with the plant experts from each village was like walking through a drugstore with a pharmacist. In what, to my untrained eye, seemed like a sea of green, they discerned flora they would process for therapeutic purposes for illnesses as varied as the common cold to HIV.

In addition to collecting from nature, each family also tended a plot behind their house where they grew plants for food and medicine. A common staple in many gardens was the *guanabana* tree ("soursop" in English). Suimara, a village matriarch, told me she used the leaves to make a tea for a family member with hepatitis, and that the tea could also be drunk to help cleanse the kidneys. Suimara took a bamboo pole and knocked down a guanabana fruit for me to try. The fruit looked alien. It was almost 12 inches/30 cm long and covered in green spikes, but when she cut it open for us to eat, it was incredible. We used our hands to scoop out the custardy white flesh and then sat quietly, spitting the large black seeds into the grass. The flavor was like a mix of banana and mango with a tropical taste that I thought could be found only in a place as exotic to me as the Amazon.

My misconception was turned upside down five years later when I tried pawpaw, a fruit that grows wild here in New Jersey. As I took my first bites, the creamy yellow flesh, large black seeds, and tropical flavor immediately took me back to the guanabana in Peru. As it turns out, guanabana and pawpaw are cousins in the Annonaceae family of flowering trees, along with sweetsop and cherimoya. Pawpaws branched off from their tropical cousins around 56 million years ago in the southern United States, near what is today the Mexican border. With the help of now-extinct megafauna, such as giant sloths and woolly mammoths and, later, ancient Native American populations, the fruit made its way east of the Mississippi where it can now be found growing from northern Florida to southern Ontario.

Growing between 3 and 6 inches/7.5 and 15 cm long, pawpaws, which are technically berries, are North America's largest native fruit (and perhaps its most delicious). Pawpaws usually grow to around 25 feet/8 meters in height and establish patches by sending up new trees via underground runners. Although these runners are genetically identical, pawpaws still require another variety in order to pollinate and set fruit. Since pawpaws are magnoliids (related to magnolias), which evolved before bees and eudicots (true flowering plants), they rely on other, less common pollinators such as flies and beetles for fertilization. Their window of availability is typically late August to early October.

CONTINUED

Historically, pawpaws have gone by many names, including Indian banana, Quaker delight, hillbilly mango, custard apple, and, most recently, hipster banana, alluding to their importance in many different cultural groups. They were an incredibly important food source for Native Americans who ate them fresh and dried them to be later reconstituted in stews and sauces. Indigenous Americans shared this information with European colonists and, later, enslaved Africans who valued the abundant fruits as a way to bulk up the rations they were given by plantation owners. Pawpaws were said to have saved Lewis and Clark during a particularly lean stretch of their journey, and they were a critical food for soldiers on both sides of the Civil War.

So, how could a fruit with such a rich history and delectable flavor have faded so far from the public eye? One part of the answer is that most Americans no longer forage for their food. The other part lies in the short shelf life (2 or 3 days at room temperature, up to 1 week in the refrigerator), which makes them pretty much impossible to stock in grocery stores.

Lucky for us, people like Neal Peterson (dubbed the "Pawpaw Johnny Appleseed") have been working to help reintroduce them into the American diet by breeding larger, more shelf-stable varietals. Until then, there are three main options to get your hands on pawpaws: foraging them, growing them yourself, or finding a farmer in your region who grows them.

When harvesting pawpaws, timing is key. The goal is to time a trip to the pawpaw patch when the majority of the fruit has ripened on the tree. You can tell which ones are ripe and ready to eat by shaking the tree's trunk. Those that easily detach and fall to the ground are the ones you want.

As for how to enjoy them, there's nothing better than ripping them open under the trees from which they fell, squeezing out the pulp, and spitting the seeds out as you go. They are also excellent in desserts including pies, panna cotta, and ice cream, and I have tried some excellent pawpaw beers over the years. When I encountered pawpaw for the first time, I knew that I wanted to use it in a Pisco Sour, the national drink of Peru, as a tribute to Suimara and the family of fruit she introduced me to in her backyard garden years ago.

The drink, which I call the Pawpaw Pisco Sour (see page 207), has become a favorite of both our staff and guests. Once people have had their first taste, I see their eyes light up as they try to wrap their heads around how an ingredient that tastes so tropical could possibly grow here, and how they could have gone their whole lives without ever hearing about it.

Processing Tip: The easiest way to separate pawpaw pulp from the seeds is by using a food mill.

Regional Substitutes: Pawpaws grow in North American temperate forests east of the Plains from Florida up through southern Ontario. If you live in regions where pawpaws are unavailable, their distant cousins soursop, cherimoya, or one of the other edible species in the Annonaceae family would be suitable, yet distinct, substitutes.

N/A Alternative: Serve the Pawpaw Shrub (see page 205) topped with sparkling water and enjoy the tropical taste of pawpaws year-round.

PAWPAW SHRUB

This recipe is based on the Shrub Master Recipe, page 59.

Makes approximately 3 c/720 ml

---

1 c/200 g sugar   1 c/240 ml pawpaw pulp, mashed

1 c/240 ml Cider Vinegar (see page 221)

DIRECTIONS

In a small pan, mix together the sugar and apple cider vinegar and heat until the sugar dissolves. Let cool, add the pawpaw pulp, and blend until smooth. Cover and refrigerate for 1 week before using. The shrub will keep in an airtight container in the refrigerator for up to 1 year.

PAWPAW PISCO SOUR

Makes 1 cocktail

---

2 oz/60 ml Peruvian pisco (Chilean works fine as well)

1¼ oz/37 ml Pawpaw Shrub (see page 205)

½ oz/15 ml honey syrup (see page 25)

½ oz/15 ml freshly squeezed lemon juice

½ oz/15 ml or 1 small egg white

3 drops Amargo Chuncho or Angostura bitters, for garnish

DIRECTIONS

Fill a cocktail shaker with ice and add the pisco, shrub, honey syrup, lemon juice, and egg white. Shake well and double strain through a fine-mesh strainer into a separate glass, then discard the ice and return the drink to a cocktail shaker. Shake again without ice (this is called dry shaking) for 10 seconds, until the egg white becomes frothy. Strain into a coupe glass and garnish with the bitters.

FIGS | *Ficus carica*

Five years ago, when I was first exploring the neighborhood we had recently moved to, I noticed a massive fig tree laden with fruit overhanging the curb at the end of our street. The tree was growing alongside a six-lane highway, and the building on the property appeared to be a former residence that was converted into an office for a construction company. After a week of driving by to check on the tree, and never seeing anyone pick the ripe figs, I decided to knock on the door to ask if they minded if I harvested the fruit, but no one answered. After mulling it over a bit, I thought that the tree must have been a relic from a previous owner, and I ultimately decided that it would be harmless to pick a few for home consumption.

I returned the next day with Katie, and within a few minutes our hands (and bellies) were full of perfectly ripe figs. Suddenly, a car screeched up and out jumped a visibly angry elderly man in a tracksuit with another younger and larger man who I assumed to be his son. The older gentleman ran towards me and shouted through a thick Italian accent, "Whaddya doin' with my figs!?" I stammered something—how, because the figs were outside of a business, I didn't think anyone would pick them and I didn't want them to go to waste. He replied, with a straight face, "Buddy, the figs don't go to waste." His son echoed his statement, "They don't go to waste."

My heart was beating fast. The old man stood quietly deciding what to do with us. He looked at my loot, looked at Katie's, then turned back to me and said, "Give me your figs." Then, he looked at Katie and with a level of charm that only an old Italian man could have, patted her on the arm, smiled, and said, "You can keep your figs." Bruno was his name, and he played me right there in front of my wife.

Bruno's attachment to his fig tree isn't uncommon in this area. While it was Spanish missionaries who originally brought "mission" figs to California in the 1500s, most figs arrived on American shores with Italian immigrants in the late-nineteenth and early-twentieth centuries. If I drive fifteen minutes to Philadelphia's Bella Vista neighborhood, originally settled by Italian immigrants in the 1800s, it's not uncommon to see multiple fig trees growing on a single city block. Originally native to the Mediterranean, they are easily picked out in the urban Philadelphian landscape by their sprawling green foliage in the summer. In the winter, they are equally recognizable when they are wrapped with burlap to insulate them, or with their branches bent in half and buried in the ground to accomplish the same task.

The following spring, I thought it would be a good idea to go out and get my own fig tree to avoid another run-in with Bruno, although I would still occasionally drive by to spy on his behemoth tree. A few years later, I noticed that the construction company had closed, and the building was shuttered with a vacancy sign in the window. You can be sure that come fig season, I was back at the tree harvesting figs, relishing in having the last laugh with old Bruno.

CONTINUED

Fig harvest begins each summer with fruit from old growth branches known as *breba*, but peaks in the beginning of fall when the "true figs" arrive. Between the "Brown Turkey" fig tree in my yard and Bruno's tree, I came to a point where I had more figs than I knew what to do with. That's when I turned to the southern Italian playbook for inspiration.

In addition to eating them fresh, dehydrating them, and of course making fig jam, there is another Italian method of fig preservation called *miele di fichi*, which translates to "fig honey." Miele di fichi is made by boiling figs, either ripe or dehydrated, in water and reducing them until they have the consistency and sweetness of honey. In addition to miele di fichi, I discovered that Italians also use the leaves to wrap fish and cheeses prior to baking to impart their sweet flavor of cinnamon, vanilla, and coconut. Using both the leaves and fruit this way truly exemplifies the *cucina povera*, literally "poor kitchen," approach of southern Italian cooking. I realized that when Bruno told me that his figs "don't go to waste," he was honoring a tradition of generations before him. I now make a delicious figgy Whiskey Sour with fig leaf–infused bourbon, miele di fichi, and fresh lemon. Each time I make myself the drink, I smile and think of Bruno and the brief, but unforgettable interaction we had over his beloved fig tree. *Salute*, Bruno.

Harvesting Advice: Wear long sleeves when picking figs as they, like many members of the Moraceae family, contain a milky sap that can cause skin irritation.

FIG LEAF BOURBON

Fig leaves impart the bourbon with a rich coconut flavor that is equally at home in an Old Fashioned, Manhattan, or Whiskey Sour.

This recipe is based on Infusions and Tinctures, page 72

Makes approximately 3 c /720 ml

One 750 ml bottle bourbon

2 oz/50 g fresh fig leaves
(about 15 medium leaves)

DIRECTIONS

In a food-safe container, combine the bourbon and fig leaves and allow to infuse overnight. Strain the fig leaves out, squeezing as much liquid from them as possible, and decant the bourbon back into the bottle. It will keep indefinitely at room temperature.

MIELE DI FICHI

While the recipe below can be made with fresh figs, it would take around 20 lb/9kg! I prefer to dehydrate figs by setting them out on a screen in the sun for about a week.

Makes approximately 2 cups/475 ml

---

2 lb/900 g dried figs, halved   1 gal/3.8 L water

DIRECTIONS

Place the figs in a large pot, cover with the water, and bring to a boil. Simmer until the liquid has reduced by half and the figs have softened, about 1 hour. Strain the figs through a fine-mesh strainer lined with cheesecloth. Once cool, squeeze the liquid out of the figs. Discard the solids.

Transfer the liquid to a medium saucepan and bring to a boil. Simmer for 30 minutes, until it reaches a honey-like consistency. It will keep in an airtight container in the refrigerator for 2 months, or you can process it in a boiling water bath and store at room temperature for 1 year.

SALUTE, BRUNO

Makes 1 cocktail

---

2 oz/60 ml Fig Leaf Bourbon (see page 211)   Dash of Angostura bitters

¾ oz/22 ml Miele di Fichi (see above)   Fig leaf, for garnish

¾ oz/22 ml freshly squeezed lemon juice

DIRECTIONS

Fill a cocktail shaker with ice and add the bourbon, miele di fichi, lemon juice, and bitters. Shake vigorously until chilled and double strain into a rocks glass over a large cube. Garnish with a fig leaf.

N/A Alternative: Brew a fig leaf tea to replace the bourbon. Let cool and mix 2 oz of the tea, 1 oz miele di fichi, and 1 oz lemon juice in a shaker. Shake and serve over ice and garnish with a fig leaf. Also, try miele di fichi over vanilla ice cream with a bit of sea salt.

APPLES | *Malus*

In the early days of the American colonies, Spanish, English, French, and Dutch settlers brought alcohol from their respective countries to tide them over for the first few months. But as reserves dwindled, it became apparent that producing alcohol from familiar grains and Old-World grapes in the colder climates of New England wasn't so easy to do. Instead, they turned to a resource that was both familiar from home and prolific on the east coast of North America: crabapples.

The first documentation of European cider making comes from 55 BCE when Romans invaded England and encountered the Celtic Britons producing and consuming it. We can't be sure exactly which variety of apple they were using, but it was probably a mix of wild crabapples and cloned cultivars. The word *crabapple* is used to refer to both apples grown from seed, as well as the other thirty-five to fifty nondomesticated *Malus* species native to the Northern Hemisphere. Cloning apples is a process that predated the Roman invasion of Great Britain, and results from the process of grafting shoots from desirable trees onto the rootstock of another to produce fruit that is identical to the parent tree. Grafting is especially important with apples, as offspring grown from seed neither look nor taste anything like their parents. This process is responsible for perpetuating and preserving each of the estimated 7,500 varieties of domesticated apple consumed around the world today.

When the first Europeans came to eastern North America, they began brewing cider with indigenous American crabapples, such as sweet crabapple (*M. coronaria*) and southern crabapple (*M. angustifolia*), which were prized by Indigenous populations including the Cherokee, Iroquois, and Ojibwa. Later, they began to use apples from genetically unique fruit started from seed, as well as grafted varietals brought from Europe. By the 1670s, hard cider was the most widely consumed beverage in the United States. In the 1680s, a Scottish distiller named William Laird immigrated to America and settled in the heart of New Jersey cider country and decided to apply his distillation skills to make "cyder spirits." While this practice was already established with English cider brandy and French *lambig* and *calvados*, Laird went on to produce the first spirit born on American shores, which we now know as "applejack." His great-grandson, Robert Laird, eventually incorporated Laird & Company as the United States' first commercial distillery, receiving license US No. 1 from the US Department of the Treasury. The company is still run by the Laird family today.

Apples can vary greatly in size, color, texture, sweetness, acidity, and tannins. Each of these variables plays a role in determining the most suitable ways to use them. Some are best eaten fresh out of hand, others are meant for storing, and still others are best when dried, cooked, or turned into sauce. Then there are the cider apples, which are usually far too tart and tannic to eat on their own, but it's these very characteristics that make them shine in the glass. When apple season arrives each fall, I travel to quite a few different spots in my region to collect fruit of varying shapes, sizes, and flavors. There are the gnarly old trees I visit in the Pocono mountains in Pennsylvania, the South Jersey farmer who sells "deer apples" for an absurdly low price ($80 per cubic yard!), the cemetery with two golden apple trees tucked behind the church, the quarter-size crabapples that grow in the parking lot behind the restaurant, and the apartment building where tenants give me sidelong looks as I wield my extendable fruit picking pole out front.

While brainstorming the best way to use all these apples a few years back, I decided I wanted to make a Lairds cocktail that early Americans may have enjoyed during the colonial era. For my inspiration, I didn't have to look much farther than about an hour west of the Laird's distillery along the banks of Philadelphia's Schuylkill River, to the home of the Philadelphia Fish House Punch. The punch was invented by the Schuylkill Fishing Company of Pennsylvania (also known as the State of Schuylkill), which was founded in 1732 by an unruly group of colonial Americans who dubbed the assemblage a sovereign state. Today, nearly three hundred years later, the group still meets, making them one of the oldest social clubs in the world.

On the State of Schuylkill's "fishing days," punch preparation would begin early in the morning, starting by peeling lemons for the oleo-saccharum (see page 89) in a bowl so large that it was said to have doubled as a baptismal font. The rest of the ingredients were then added—lemon, rum, cognac, old-fashioned peach brandy (a spirit that never really bounced back after Prohibition), and extender (such as tea or water)—before serving it over a large block of ice with lemon slices and freshly grated nutmeg. The resulting concoction is delicious, but deceptively innocent. An 1896 article from the *Philadelphia Times* states that the mild taste of the punch is as "false as dicers' oaths. . .He who sips for the first time imagines that he has been made immortal. . .and only realizes when he is under the table, that he still belongs to the earth."

Using this recipe as a rough template, I made an apple-laden punch by swapping in applejack for peach brandy and cognac and using unfiltered apple cider as the extender. The resulting punch became our number one seller at the Farm and Fisherman, and earned a forever home on our menu as "The Farm and Fish House Punch." And while we don't include the wild-fermented cider in our version at the restaurant, I'm including it here as an optional sparkling addition, or to be enjoyed on its own.

THE FARM AND FISH HOUSE PUNCH

Makes approximately 7 c/1.6 L, enough for 16 servings

8 medium lemons, plus more if needed for 1½/360 ml cups juice

½ lb/225 g demerara sugar (approximately 1 c/240 ml)

½ cinnamon stick

1 star anise

2 cloves

10 coriander seeds

2½ c/590 ml unfiltered and unsweetened apple cider

1¼ c/300 ml Laird's Applejack

1¼ c/300 ml funky, ester-rich Jamaican rum (like Smith & Cross or Plantation Xaymaca)

Wild Fermented Cider (see page 220), for serving (optional)

Grated nutmeg, for garnish

DIRECTIONS

To make the oleo-saccharum, peel 8 lemons, being careful to stop short of peeling the white pith. Set the peeled lemons aside to juice later. Place the peels in a medium bowl along with demerara sugar. Grind the cinnamon, star anise, clove, and coriander in a spice grinder or mortar and pestle and add to the bowl along with the lemon peels and sugar. Mix well and muddle to release the oils from the peels. Cover the bowl with a towel or plate and let sit at room temperature overnight. In the meantime, juice the peeled lemons (though you may need a few more to reach 1½ cups/360 ml of juice), and refrigerate the juice in an airtight container.

The next day, use a silicone spatula to scrape the oleo-saccharum into a medium saucepan along with the lemon juice and gently heat until all the sugar dissolves. Pass through a fine-mesh strainer into a large bowl (this strained liquid is called a "sherbet"), being sure to squeeze as much liquid from the peels as possible (it should yield about 2¼ cups/530 ml). Discard the solids after straining. Next, add the apple cider, Laird's, and rum to the sherbet and stir well to combine. Congratulations, you've successfully made your punch! Transfer to airtight bottles or containers and refrigerate. It will keep in the refrigerator for at least a few months, but there's no chance it won't get consumed before then.

To serve the punch to a crowd, pour into a punch bowl over a large block of ice and add one 750 ml bottle Wild Fermented Cider (page 220, optional). Garnish with grated nutmeg and lemon slices.

For an individual serving, pour 3½ oz/104 ml in a rocks glass with a large ice cube and top with 1 oz/30 ml Wild Fermented Crabapple Cider. Garnish with freshly grated nutmeg.

WILD FERMENTED CIDER

The following recipe can be made with unsweetened cider purchased from a local farm or supermarket. Alternatively, you can juice any apple variety of your choosing.

This recipe is based on the Beer Master Recipe, page 49.

Makes approximately five 750 ml bottles

---

1 gal/3.8 L unsweetened fresh-pressed or store-bought unfiltered raw apple cider

½ c/120 ml Ginger Bug, liquid only (optional, as there is plenty of ambient yeast if using fresh apples, see page 39)

1 Tbsp honey syrup, for priming (see page 43)

DIRECTIONS

Pour the cider into your fermentation vessel. This can be a rudimentary setup like a food-grade container covered with cheesecloth or a tea towel secured with a rubber band or other non-airtight lid, or you can use a carboy or fermentation bucket outfitted with an airlock. Let the cider ferment for approximately 4 weeks, until bubbles subside almost entirely.

Rack off the sediment and bottle in 750 ml bottles primed with 1 Tbsp honey syrup. Allow to carbonate in a cool, dark place, checking occasionally to make sure it hasn't overcarbonated. Once sufficiently bubbly, move to the refrigerator where it will keep for 1 year or more.

N/A Alternatives: This hard cider can be stopped short during its fermentation to make a great soda, or it can be used to make a delicious shrub. This can be done by allowing it to go through a complete fermentation to become cider vinegar (see page 221) that's subsequently sweetened, or you can mix equal parts unfermented apple cider, white balsamic vinegar, and sugar for more immediate results.

CIDER VINEGAR

This recipe is based on the Vinegar Master Recipe on page 57.

Makes approximately 5 qt/4.7 L

---

1 gal/3.8 L unsweetened fresh-pressed apple cider or store-bought unfiltered raw cider

1 qt/950 ml vinegar starter culture from a previous batch of homemade vinegar or unpasteurized store-bought vinegar

Vinegar mother SCOBY (optional, but preferable. If you don't have a vinegar mother, one should form on its own)

DIRECTIONS

Pour the cider into a large jar or fermentation crock along with a vinegar SCOBY (if you don't have a SCOBY, fret not, one should form after a few weeks). Cover with a tea towel or cheesecloth bound with a rubber band or other non-airtight lid. As the weeks pass, you can observe as the brew goes from wort, to sparkling soda, to an alcoholic cider, and finally cider vinegar. Stirring it will help expedite this process.

Hangovers have plagued humans since we first started consuming alcohol millennia ago. Through the years, they have given rise to countless folk remedies involving food, medicine, and of course, more drink. Sometime in my early twenties, I settled on my winning combination: Two Tylenol, a pastrami sandwich on rye, a pickle, and the most crucial piece of the puzzle, an ice-cold can of Doc Brown's "Cel-Ray" celery soda. These days, I can't bounce back from hangovers nearly as quickly, but my love of celery soda lives on, and its restorative properties are something I often mention to bar guests who may have had one-too-many the night before.

You can imagine my vindication when I discovered that celery has been touted as a hangover cure since the days of the ancient Greeks and Romans, although their celery looked much different than ours does today. They were familiar with the wild relative of celery, known as "smallage," that grows in salt marshes throughout the Mediterranean. It was enshrined in the mythology of both cultures and had a reputation as a magical ambrosia of the gods. To rid themselves of a hangover, they would adorn their heads with crowns made from the stalks and leaves, or simply hang a celery stick around their necks to accomplish the same task. It was also valued for various other medicinal applications, including its ability to aid with stomach ailments and act as an aphrodisiac.

Celery's medical use and popularity continued throughout the Middle Ages and spread throughout the rest of Europe. Surprisingly, it wasn't until the 1800s that it began to be cultivated for culinary applications in eastern England, giving rise to the classic "stalk" celery we know today. In those earliest days of cultivation, celery proved difficult to grow, which made it very expensive. The high price of the vegetable made it even more desirable to the well-to-do of the Victorian era, and it came to be seen as a symbol of wealth and a food of the elite, even spurring an entire industry of specially crafted crystal celery vases for displaying celery heads that adorned the tables of the Victorian elite.

In part due to its haute reputation and its longstanding medical associations, celery and celery seed came to be viewed as Victorian superfoods, capable of treating all kinds of ailments. In 1868, "Doctor Brown" (who may have been a fictional marketing scheme rather than a real person) cashed in on celery's curative reputation and began marketing a "celery tonic" that was said to contain all the purported health benefits of celery. The drink

CONTINUED

was sold exclusively to Jewish delicatessens throughout the five boroughs of New York Cit, and became so popular in the Jewish community that it earned the name "Jewish champagne." Its popularity waned over the years, but it is still commonplace to find Doc Brown's Cel-Ray, as well as the brand's other soda flavors, in Jewish delis today.

Unlike Doc Brown's, whose long list of ingredients contains only celery seed extract and no fresh celery, I set out to make a fermented celery tonic from celery grown in my garden, which I try to plant in time for a perfect fall harvest. The recipe below outlines how to make the soda using cultivated stalk celery, although my home-brewed batch often includes shoots of the other two varieties of cultivated celery (leaf celery and celeriac), which offer a more herbaceous, pungent flavor. As for its efficacy as a hangover cure, it probably isn't; however, it does contain

probiotics from fermentation, vitamins, minerals, water, and stress-reducing chemicals called *phthalides*, so it's at least a fresh, healthy start to the day. Plus, it tastes really good. Enjoy the celery tonic on its own, or try spiking it with mezcal as I've done below in the Cel Rey cocktail for a bit of hair of the dog.

N/A Alternative: Celery tonic is an incredible nonalcoholic drink on its own, as well as converted into a shrub. This can be accomplished by brewing nonalcoholic celery tonic and allowing it to go through a complete fermentation to become a tangy, savory vinegar (see page 57) that can later be sweetened, or you can mix equal parts celery juice, white balsamic vinegar, and sugar for more immediate results.

CELERY TONIC

This recipe is based on the Ginger Beer Master Recipe on page 43.

Makes approximately seven 750 ml bottles

---

3 lb/1.3 kg celery, chopped into
1 in/2.5 cm pieces (from approximately
two heads with the base removed)

3 qt/2.8 L water

5 c/1.2 L simple syrup (see page 25)

1 c/240 ml freshly squeezed lime juice

½ cup/120 ml Ginger Bug (see page 39)

DIRECTIONS

Use a juicer or the blender method (see page 48) to extract the juice from the celery. Strain through a fine-mesh strainer lined with a cheesecloth or tea towel to remove the solids, squeezing as much liquid from the solids as possible. Discard the solids.

Add celery juice, remaining water (if blender method was used), simple syrup, lime juice, and ginger bug to a food-safe container, and cover with a tea towel or cheesecloth bound with a rubber band or other non-airtight lid. After 1 day has passed, strain out the solids and decant the soda into seven 750 ml bottles. Cap tightly and let sit at room temperature, checking every 12 hours to make sure that it hasn't overcarbonated (celery tonic is usually pretty active). Once sufficiently carbonated, place the bottle in the refrigerator and consume within 3 to 4 weeks.

CEL REY

Makes 1 cocktail

---

2 oz/60 ml mezcal

¼ oz/37 ml freshly squeezed lime juice

Celery Tonic (see page 225), for topping

Celery leaf, for garnish

DIRECTIONS

Fill a Collins glass with ice and add the mezcal and lime juice. Top with celery tonic and garnish with a celery leaf.

HIBISCUS | *Hibiscus sabdariffa*

Roselle, sorrel, sour-sour, *karkade*, *flor de jamaica*, or, as it is most commonly known here in the United States, hibiscus—the plant with a seemingly endless list of names and just as many culinary uses. Early each March, I start the seeds in my basement, where I will tend to them carefully for months. Come May, it's time to move them outside where they will grow to become one of the flashiest plants in the garden with their red-striped leaves and stems and pinkish-white flowers that are supported by deep scarlet calyxes underneath. Come October, when the plants are done blooming, the calyxes can then be used fresh or dried to lend their bright red color and sharp acidity to food or drink, making the previous 7 months' work well worth it.

The genus *Hibiscus* comprises more than two hundred species in the mallow family, Malvaceae. Many of these are familiar varietals, such as the scarlet, dinner plate–size blooms of Chinese hibiscus (*H. rosa-sinensis*), and the hardy rose of Sharon (*H. syriacus*), both of which you can find growing in gardens around the world. Most are edible and possess some acidity like hibiscus, but none possess its intense pigments that make it a great natural food coloring.

The earliest evidence for hibiscus use comes from around six thousand years ago in Sudan. From there, roselle, as it was known, it spread throughout the rest of Africa and into Asia, where it was a prized food, medicine, and beverage. Its arrival in the Americas came via the African diaspora and the Atlantic slave trade when West Africans brought roselle seeds with them to the Caribbean, and, later, the Americas. Like many foods of the African

diaspora, roselle is celebrated as a cultural and culinary connection to Africa.

One example of this is the modern-day Caribbean Christmas tradition of drinking "sorrel"—a sweetened hibiscus beverage that is spiced with ginger, clove, and cinnamon, and optionally spiked with wine or rum. There is a related tradition of "red drink," a celebratory beverage for Black people in the United States, especially during Juneteenth, a holiday marking the date when the last enslaved people in Texas were finally notified of their freedom two years after emancipation was legalized in the United States. While the modern-day red drink is most often made with powdered mixes, it is widely believed that it was originally made with roselle grown by enslaved people on Southern plantations.

Hibiscus has since permeated into international culinary traditions far and wide. My first introduction came from the Mexican tradition of making agua fresca with *flor de jamaica*, meaning "Jamaica flower," the name most commonly associated with the plant in Latin America, alluding to its importance in

CONTINUED

the Caribbean country. My goal with the cocktail below was to make a drink featuring traditional Caribbean ingredients. To do so, I brewed hibiscus tea and then turned it into a spiced syrup, then mixed with three types of rum, fresh lime juice, and Pierre Ferrand's Dry Curaçao, a triple sec made with bitter oranges from the Caribbean island nation of Curaçao. With its spiced profile and deep ruby color, this cocktail is equally as delicious on a chilly fall day as it is on the beach in the summer.

Safety: Don't consume hibiscus while pregnant.

N/A Alternatives: One of my favorite uses for hibiscus is to brew it into a soda. To do so, follow the Ginger Beer Master Recipe on page 43 and replace the simple syrup with Spiced Hibiscus Syrup and use lime juice instead of lemon. This syrup can also be used to make a delicious kombucha by swapping it in for simple syrup in the Kombucha Master Recipe (see page 69).

SPICED HIBISCUS SYRUP

This recipe is based on the Flavored Simple Syrup recipe, page 85.

Makes approximately 2½ c/590 ml

---

2 c/475 ml water

1 c/240 ml fresh or dried hibiscus

One 2-in/5 cm knob of ginger, grated

1 cinnamon stick

3 cloves

1½ c/300 g sugar

DIRECTIONS

Add the water, hibiscus, ginger, cinnamon, and cloves to a medium saucepan. Bring to a boil, then simmer for 8 minutes. Take off the heat, pour into a heatproof food-safe container, and let it infuse in the refrigerator for 24 hours.

Strain out the solids, being sure to squeeze as much liquid out of the absorbent hibiscus calyxes as possible (should yield about 1½ c/360 ml). Return to a saucepan with the sugar and heat on low until the sugar dissolves. Store in the refrigerator and use within 1 month.

FLOR DE JAMAICA

This recipe tests the adage from Donn Beach, a.k.a. "Don the Beachcomber,"
the founding father of tiki, that "what one rum can do, three can do better."
Be your own judge on this one, but I think the man was right. If you don't have all
three rums, making it with 2 oz/60 ml of just one will still be delicious.

Makes 1 cocktail

¾ oz/22 ml white rum

¾ oz/22 ml aged rum

½ oz/15 ml funky Jamaican rum
(like Smith & Cross or Plantation Xaymaca)

¾ oz/22 ml freshly squeezed lime juice

¾ oz/22 ml Spiced Hibiscus Syrup
(see page 231)

½ oz/15 ml Pierre Ferrand Dry Curaçao
(or another Triple Sec)

Hibiscus flower or dehydrated lime wheel,
for garnish

DIRECTIONS

Fill a cocktail shaker with ice and add the rums, lime juice, Spiced Hibiscus Syrup, and curaçao.
Shake vigorously, double strain into a chilled Nick and Nora glass, and garnish with a hibiscus
flower or dehydrated lime wheel.

In 1904, the chief forester of the New York Zoological Park (now known as the Bronx Zoo) noticed that the park's American chestnut trees (*C. dentata*) were exhibiting a slight yellow discoloration around the trunk. The next year, a mycologist from the New York Botanical Garden isolated and described the cause of this discoloration: a fungus imported on ornamental Asian chestnut trees that came to be known as "chestnut blight." Over the next few years, an unparalleled die-off happened despite the country's best efforts at thwarting it. By 1940, nearly every mature chestnut tree in America had been wiped out by the disease. Estimates place the number of trees lost at around 4 billion.

It would be hard to overstate just how great of a loss this was. For thousands of years, the chestnut had been one of the most important trees in the eastern United States for both people and animals. It is said that one out of every four trees in American forests was a chestnut. Referred to as "the redwoods of the East," these titans formed a 100-foot/30.5 m tall forest canopy that stretched from Maine to Mississippi. Mature trees could produce roughly six thousand nuts that would blanket the forest floor up to 4 inches/10 cm deep each fall. Indigenous American groups such as the Cherokee, Iroquois, and Algonquians consumed the nuts whole, ground them into flour to make chestnut bread, soup, and beverages, and also used various parts of the tree for medicine. Evidence even suggests that these groups and their ancestors actively managed their forest ecosystems to encourage the growth of this vital resource. Later, chestnuts became a staple food for European immigrants, especially in rural Appalachia where they fed livestock with them, used the wood to construct homes, barns, and churches, and exported them to cities up and down the East Coast. It's no exaggeration to say that when the chestnut disappeared, so too did the lifeblood of an entire region.

All is not lost, however. Thanks to the decades-long work of the American Chestnut Foundation, researchers are coming closer to breeding a blight-resistant American chestnut tree. There are also efforts to modify the chestnut genome by splicing it with a segment of wheat DNA that would neutralize the damaging chemical produced by the blight fungus, although introducing a GMO tree on this scale is much more controversial. Finally, there is also the possibility that a blight-resistant American chestnut could be living right under our noses just waiting for its chance to save the species. In any case, the return of the American chestnut is not a matter of if, but when.

CONTINUED

Until that time, it is still possible to harvest chestnuts stateside as blight-resistant Chinese (*C. mollissima*), Japanese (*C. crenata*), and European (*C. sativa*) species all grow well here. There is also the closely related native chinquapin (*C. pumila*), whose name comes from the Powhatan language, which can be found growing in some isolated pockets of the country. Lucky for me, my grandfather has a massive Chinese chestnut tree in his backyard that we make a day of harvesting each fall. One thing I learned the hard way is that it's really important to wear gloves and thick-soled shoes, as the shell, or "burr," in which the nut is contained is covered with incredibly sharp spines. I wore thin-soled shoes our first year and stepped on a shell that pierced through my shoe and into the bottom of my foot. Another piece of foraging advice when harvesting chestnuts is that they are ripe and ready to eat once they fall out of the tree.

Once you pry the burrs open and remove the nuts from the inside, then comes the fun part of roasting them on a gas or wood fire (roasting them in the oven works well, too). After carefully scoring each one with an "X," place them in a cast iron pan on the fire until the shells split open at the incision point, which keeps them from exploding and also helps with shell removal. As they roast, their starches and sugars begin to caramelize and fill the air with a mouthwatering aroma. It's said that you can smell chestnuts roasting across entire cities in France, Italy, Turkey, and Japan during the height of the fall chestnut harvest. Hopefully that is something we can experience with the American chestnut someday in the not-so-distant future.

Foraging Advice: When foraging for chestnuts, be sure not to confuse them with horse chestnuts (*Aesculus hippocastanum*), which are poisonous. The main differentiating characteristic is that edible chestnuts come to a pointed end, or tassel, whereas horse chestnuts are rounded and smooth. Also, horse chestnuts have a more fleshy, bumpy burr, unlike the sharp spiny burr of the edible chestnut.

Regional Substitutes: Chinquapins, or "dwarf chestnuts," are the closest substitute to the American chestnut, although their numbers are a fraction of what they once were since they, like the European chestnut, only display partial resistance. More common are the ornamental Chinese and Japanese chestnuts.

N/A Alternative: Try mixing 2 oz/60 ml of the Chestnut Orgeat (see page 237) with 1 oz/30 ml freshly squeezed lemon or lime juice, and topping with club soda for a delicious alcohol-free alternative.

CHESTNUT ORGEAT

Makes approximately 3½ c/830 ml

---

1 lb/450 g chestnuts (about 34)

4 c/950 ml boiling water

2½ c/500 g sugar

½ tsp orange blossom water

1 oz/30 ml rye whiskey

DIRECTIONS

To roast chestnuts, cut an "X" through the shell of the rounded side, making sure to completely pierce the outer shell and inner skin. Roast over a fire (or for 20 to 30 minutes in an oven at 400°F/200°C) until the shells begin to caramelize and split at the incision point. Use your fingers to peel away the outer shell and papery skin. Sometimes the skin doesn't come off easily, in which case you may have to chisel away at it with a paring knife. If a little is left behind, don't sweat it. After peeling, place the chestnuts on a roasting pan and toast in a 350°F/175°C oven for 10 minutes more.

Next, use a knife or a food processor to coarsely chop the chestnuts. Top with the boiling water, cover, and let sit at room temperature for 3 hours. Strain the liquid through a fine-mesh strainer lined with a tea towel or cheesecloth, being sure to squeeze as much liquid from the nuts as possible (should yield about 2½ c/590 ml) and discard the solids. This strained liquid is now chestnut milk.

Add the chestnut milk to a small saucepan along with the sugar and heat, stirring frequently, until the sugar completely dissolves. Move to the refrigerator to cool. Once chilled, add orange blossom water and rye and store in a swing-cap bottle in the refrigerator for up to 1 month.

STAYCATION

Makes 1 cocktail

---

2 oz/60 ml rye whiskey

1 oz/30 ml Chestnut Orgeat (see page 237)

¾ oz/22 ml freshly squeezed lemon juice

8 dashes of Peychaud's bitters

Mint sprig, for garnish

Grated nutmeg, for garnish

DIRECTIONS

Fill a cocktail shaker with ice and add the whiskey, orgeat, and lemon juice. Shake vigorously for 5 seconds. Strain over pebble ice (pro tip: You can buy 1 lb/450 g bags of pebble ice at a Sonic Drive-In). Dash the bitters around the top of the ice and garnish with a mint sprig and freshly grated nutmeg.

CRANBERRIES | *Vaccinium macrocarpon*

My cranberry harvesting ritual begins in the same place in the New Jersey Pine Barrens where I harvest wild blueberries in July. As I drive down Route 206, I am surrounded by cedar swamps on one side and dense pine forest on the other. My eyes are peeled for a narrow break in the guardrail on the side of the road, though I somehow manage to miss it every time. After I make the U-turn, I take a right down the dirt road, where I continue for a mile or so to the side of an abandoned bog. It's not uncommon to find these in the Pines as the number of cranberry farmers in the state continues to wane. While New Jersey led the nation in cranberry production in the early 1900s, we are now ranked fourth after Wisconsin, Massachusetts, and Oregon.

As I'm picking the berries off the ground, I pause to look around and take stock of how much the landscape has changed since I was there in the summer. The green underbrush has now browned, the wild blueberry bushes have crispy, dehydrated berries hanging from their branches, and the swarms of bugs have (luckily) faded away for the year. I smile thinking of the time my wife, Katie, and I drove here separately and got not one, but both of our cars stuck and had to be towed out by a friend. This spot, though relatively unremarkable, is special to us.

Cranberries have been growing in this area since time immemorial. They were an incredibly important resource to Indigenous American groups as food, dye, and medicine. They were especially crucial for their survival in the winter months when they were used in a mixture with deer meat and fat tallow called *pemmican* by the Cree or *wasná* by the Lakota. These mixtures were preserved thanks to cranberries' naturally high levels of benzoic acid, a food preservative still widely used today. Of the many staples of the modern Thanksgiving table, cranberries are likely the sole surviving dish served at the first Thanksgiving by the Wampanoag tribe, likely in the form of cranberry sauce sweetened with maple syrup or honey.

Cranberries are members of the family *Vaccinium* along with blueberries and huckleberries and can be found growing across the higher latitudes of the entire northern hemisphere. Here in North America, the evergreen vines grow wild in acidic, boggy areas from Newfoundland down to the Carolinas, and as far west as the Mississippi River. On the West Coast, they can be found growing from northern California through Alaska. While cranberry beds were first cultivated in wetlands, the most common method today are manufactured beds surrounded by dikes used for irrigation. Contrary to popular belief, cranberries do not actually grow underwater, but rather they are flooded by commercial farmers to facilitate harvest. Cranberry harvest begins each year in September and will last well into the cold days of November thanks to their thick skin and low sugar content.

CONTINUED

After I take my share from the abandoned bog, I make my way home plotting how I am going to use this year's haul. Truth be told, until I started foraging them, the only time I ever ate cranberries was from a can at Thanksgiving dinners of my childhood. I always hated the stuff, but now that I've discovered the versatility of the fresh fruit, they have become one of my favorite ingredients. Cranberries have a mild sweetness that is counterbalanced with a bright acidity and complex tannic structure.

In the past, I've used them to make bitters, syrups, vermouth, pickles, and a fizzy cranberry and pine soda. With this haul, however, I'm going to make cranberry jam. The jam is a perfect addition to a gin cocktail, as well as a great replacement for the canned cranberry sauce imposter.

Regional Substitutes: Wild cranberries grow across the higher latitudes of the northern hemisphere where they belong to one of several species in the family *Vaccinium* including *V. oxycoccos*, *V. microcarpon*, and *V. vitis-idaea*, better known as the lingonberry. All three of these grow in different parts of North America, in addition to the native American cranberry (*V. macrocarpon*). All have a similar taste and can be used interchangeably in recipes.

N/A Alternatives: In addition to cranberry jam mocktails, the fruit can be used to ferment delicious sodas, kombuchas, and vinegars, and cranberry shrub and club soda is one of my all-time favorite N/A beverages.

CRANBERRY JAM

This recipe is based on the Any Fruit Jam Master Recipe, page 87.

Makes approximately 2 c/475 ml

---

3 c/300 g fresh cranberries
1¼ c/250 g sugar

½ c/120 ml freshly squeezed orange juice

DIRECTIONS

Place a plate in the freezer to use later. In a pot over medium heat, add the cranberries, sugar, and orange juice and stir for 10 to 12 minutes, until the cranberries begin to pop. Transfer to a blender and purée until smooth. Return the purée to the stove and cook over medium-low heat for another 15 to 20 minutes.

Pull your plate out of the freezer, place a bit of jam on it, and wait 30 seconds. Push your spoon through it. If it wrinkles up, it has reached its setting point. If it hasn't, keep cooking and conducting the same test every few minutes until it reaches a jam-like consistency.

Funnel into a clean 1 pt mason jar, filling to just under the glass threading. Process the jam in a boiling water bath for longterm storage or move to the refrigerator and consume within a few months.

PINE BARRENS COCKTAIL

Makes 1 cocktail

1½ oz/45 ml London dry gin

½ oz/15 ml Winter "Alpine" Amaro (see page 310) or a store-bought piney "alpine" amaro brand, such as Braulio or Amaro Pasubio

¾ oz/22 ml freshly squeezed lime juice

2 Tbsp cranberry jam

Evergreen sprig, for garnish

DIRECTIONS

To a cocktail shaker, add the gin, amaro, lime juice, and jam. Shake and strain over fresh ice in a rocks glass. Garnish with an evergreen sprig.

PERSIMMONS | *Diospyros*

On a late-November day a few years back, I went for a hike with my son in the woods near my house. While staring up at the leaf-bare trees, I saw dozens of dark little spheres silhouetted against the gray autumn sky. As I shifted my attention to the forest floor, I noticed some fallen fruit—wild American persimmon (*Diospyros virginiana*)—an ingredient I had been on a years-long search for.

I excitedly ate one, then another, and another, and then it hit me: a mouth-puckering astringency like I had never experienced before. It felt as though I had eaten a piece of chalk. While I drank some water and waited for my tongue to return to normal, I pulled out my phone and did some internet sleuthing and found that American persimmons should only be eaten when they are so ripe that they look almost rotten thanks to a process known as *bletting*. I picked up the most overripe fruit I could find, and had an entirely different experience. It was incredibly sweet, caramelly, and loaded with spice notes, much like a date. To this day, these persimmons are the sweetest wild ingredient I have ever tasted.

Persimmons and their relatives are native to many parts of the Americas, Europe, Asia, Africa, and Australia. Here in North America, you can find American persimmons (*D. virginiana*) growing wild east of the Great Plains from Florida to Connecticut where they go by many names including possum apples, 'simmons, and sugar plums. Persimmons were highly prized by Native American groups throughout this region, especially as a dried food to help sustain them through the winter

(the word *persimmon* is the Anglicized version of the Algonquin word *pessamin*, which means "dry fruit"). Drying persimmons converts the astringent tannins into sugar in the same way that bletting them does. There is also evidence that brewing persimmon beer was a common practice of the Cherokee, Catawba, Rappahannock, and Nanticoke tribes both before and after contact with Europeans.

Much more widely known than the American persimmon are the two domesticated varieties of Oriental persimmon, *D. kaki*, which were first cultivated more than two thousand years ago in China, and, later, Japan and Korea. These include the nonastringent *Fuyu* persimmons, which can be eaten, skin and all, while they are still firm, as well as the astringent heart-shaped *Hachiya*. Like American persimmons, Hachiyas should be left to ripen until they are completely soft, at which time the flesh can either be scooped or squeezed out. East Asians independently arrived at the same solution as Native Americans by realizing they could make Hachiyas more palatable by drying them. The most well-known example of East Asian dried persimmon is Japanese *hoshigaki*, which you can find hanging in windows across the country each fall. Over the

CONTINUED

course of 1 to 2 months, they are given a daily massage to coax the sugars out of the fruit, coating them with a "bloom" of crystalized sugar in the process.

Four years ago, I planted a variety of Ukrainian-bred persimmon called "Nikita's Gift" in my home garden, which was marketed as a hybrid of American and Asian persimmons. Despite being shaped like non-astringent Fuyu persimmons, I was surprised when I tasted the fruit for the first-time last year and found that they still had quite a bit of astringency to them. Which got me thinking that the best way to combat it (besides letting them ripen to mush) would be to use them in a clarified milk punch.

The technique of clarifying punch with milk dates back to the 1700s. When the dairy interacts with the citrus in the punch, it forms a curd, and when passed through a filter, the curd forms a raft of proteins that remove tannins, particles, and color from the original punch. For me, milk punch is the ultimate party trick cocktail—an unassuming, crystal-clear drink that looks like a glass of water, but reveals layer after layer of richness and complexity with each sip.

Foraging Advice: Persimmons are in season from late-October until December. Make sure to wait until the fruit is totally ripe before consuming.

Regional Substitutes: The number of wild persimmon and closely related ebony species growing around the world is so vast, it's a wonder to me that only the widely cultivated Asian species, *D. kaki* gets any attention. Here in North America, you can find *D. virginia* growing in the eastern half of the United States, and the black fruit of *D. texana* growing in Texas, southern Oklahoma, and northern Mexico. Farther south, you can find the black sapote (*D. nigra*), also known as the chocolate pudding fruit, growing throughout Central and northern South America. Africa is home to the jackalberry (*D. mespiliformis*), which has been used to brew beer for centuries. In Europe, the date-plum, or Caucasian persimmon (*D. lotus*) has been held in high esteem since biblical times, and farther east in Asia you'll find the largest variation in the *Diospyrus* family. In Australia, *D. australis* is the most commonly consumed fruit, though there are many other species throughout the continent revered for both the food and as lumber.

CLARIFIED PERSIMMON PUNCH

In Korea, persimmons are brewed into a cinnamon- and ginger-spiced punch known as *sujeonggwa*. Rather than setting out to replicate the Korean punch, I decided to follow the formula for the Farm and Fish House Punch (see page 219), while incorporating ingredients from east Asia. You might have to do some digging to get your hands on some of the ingredients listed below, but it will be worth it. If that seems daunting, I have included some easier-to-find substitutes, as well.

Makes approximately 11 c/2.6 L, enough for 25 servings

---

1 Buddha's hand (a.k.a. fingered citron) (or substitute the peels of 16 lemons)

1 lb/450 Okinawa black kokuto sugar (or substitute another raw sugar, such as piloncillo, unrefined muscovado, jaggery, or demerara)

1 tsp ground ginger

1 cinnamon stick

1 star anise

3 cloves

20 coriander seeds

¾ lb/340 g ripe persimmon pulp, Asian, American, or other

3 c/720 ml freshly squeezed lemon juice

2 c/475 ml Barley Tisane (see page 281) (or substitute any brewed black tea)

2¼ c/530 ml Japanese whiskey (I prefer Akashi "White Oak" single malt)

2¼ c/530 ml aged rum, Caribbean (or Japanese if you can find it)

1 c/240 ml Japanese shochu (I prefer Honkaku Kana Shochu, distilled from kokuto sugar and rice and bottled at 30% ABV) (or substitute with any shochu)

3 c cold whole milk

Grated nutmeg, for garnish

Dried persimmon, for garnish

DIRECTIONS

Begin by making an oleo-saccharum: Add the Buddha's hand (or lemon peels), sugar, and ground ginger to a medium bowl. Grind the cinnamon, star anise, cloves, and coriander seeds in a spice grinder or mortar and pestle, and add to the bowl. Mix well and muddle to release the oils from the citrus. Cover and let sit at room temperature overnight.

CONTINUED

The next day, use a silicone spatula to scrape the oleo-saccharum into a medium saucepan along with the persimmon pulp and lemon juice, and gently heat until all the sugar dissolves. Pass through a fine-mesh strainer into a large bowl (this strained liquid is called a "sherbet"), being sure to squeeze as much liquid from the strained solids as possible. It should yield approximately 5 c/1.2 L. Discard the solids after straining.

Make the barley tisane following the directions on page 281, then add the Japanese whisky, rum, and shochu to the sherbet and stir well to combine. You have successfully made your punch. Let come to room temperature, then try some at this stage and take note of its color and flavor. These will both change drastically after the punch is clarified.

Pour the cold milk into a 6 qt/6 L container. Slowly pour your room-temperature punch over the surface of the milk (not the other way around!), being sure to pour over any areas that have yet to curdle. After your punch is added, gently stir as the milk continues to break. Let sit for 30 minutes for the mixture to finish curdling.

Line a fine-mesh strainer with multiple layers of tea towels or cheesecloth. After the 30 minutes are up, strain the punch through the tea towels. Wait another 30 minutes, then take the first pass of the strained liquid and restrain it through the curd. After all the liquid has been strained, add the clarified punch to airtight bottles or containers and refrigerate. It will keep indefinitely.

For communal serving, place a large block of ice in a punch bowl and pour the punch over it. Garnish with freshly grated nutmeg and dehydrated persimmons.

For individual serving, pour 3½ oz/104 ml over a large ice cube in a rocks glass and garnish with freshly grated nutmeg and a dehydrated persimmon.

FALL "GÉNÉPI" AMARO | *Artemisia*

The three hundred or so species included in the wormwood genus, *Artemisia*, comprise one of the most important groups of botanical relatives in the history of alcohol production. This group provides the essential ingredients to make vermouth (coming from the German word for wormwood, *vermut*), absinthe (from the Latin name for "grand wormwood," *A. absinthium*), a whole class of amaro known as *génépi* (from the species *A. genipi*), and a wormwood-based beer known as *purl*. Wormwood's chemical footprints have even been found in some of the earliest fermented beverages of ancient Egypt.

Wormwood also has one of the most tumultuous histories of any botanical ingredient in the history of alcohol. Absinthe, a product containing wormwood, fennel, and green anise, was first marketed by Dr. Pierre Ordinaire in the late 1700s as an antiparasitic used to treat French soldiers who contracted malaria while stationed in Northern Africa. By the early 1800s, it began to catch on in France as a recreational spirit. By the mid 1800s, its consumption skyrocketed due to the crumbling European wine industry caused by the phylloxera epidemic. It was especially popular among intellectuals during the Belle Époque, including Van Gogh, Picasso, Henri de Toulouse-Lautrec, and Ernest Hemingway.

Anti-absinthe furor, led by social conservatives and prohibitionists, swept the world over with claims that absinthe made people hallucinate and devolve into "absinthe madness" due to one of wormwood's main active chemicals, thujone. As it turns out, the madness associated with absinthe wasn't caused by thujone at all, but rather the addition of adulterants by absinthe bootleggers, including copper salts used for green coloring and antimony trichloride used to mimic the clouding, or "louching," effect of authentic absinthe. It's also possible that the "madness" was just the result of absinthe making people really drunk, as it's bottled at 70 to 80% ABV (nearly twice the level of other conventional spirits).

Still, thujone remained blacklisted for decades despite its presence in many ingredients we view as safe, including sage, mint, and oregano. This was largely predicated on experiments where incredibly high levels of the chemical were given to rats over a long period of time, resulting in convulsions, muscle breakdown, and kidney failure. (If this sounds familiar, it's almost the same thing that happened with sassafras when it was discovered that the drug MDMA could be synthesized from safrole.) As a result of these tests, as well as lobbying funded by the rebounding wine industry's anti-absinthe campaign, production and consumption of the spirit was banned in the early 1900s, despite it being next to impossible for a human to consume the levels of thujone given to rats solely from drinking absinthe.

A few decades later, governmental bodies finally recognized that the dangers of drinking absinthe were no greater than the risks associated with consuming any other type of alcohol, and the ban was lifted, though there are still thujone safety levels in place. (Here in the United States, alcoholic products are considered safe under 10 ppm and are labeled as "thujone-free" at this very low level; in Europe the legal level is 35 ppm for alcohol.) Armed with this information, I use only a small bit of wormwood when making my fall "génépi" amaro, but luckily a little goes a long way, as another of wormwood's primary chemicals, *absinthin*, is one of the most bitter compounds ever discovered. My goal here is to create something that tastes like fall, with bold spice and a lingering bitterness. This amaro can sipped neat as a digestivo, served warm with a bit of apple cider, or swapped into my favorite fall cocktail, the Boulevardier. Here is a breakdown of the ingredients.

Bittering agents: wormwood, horehound

Acidic: orange peels (I use trifoliate "hardy" orange), cranberry, lemongrass, staghorn sumac

Spice: fig leaves, juniper

Herbaceous: sage, rosemary, thyme

Sweetness: apples (or crabapples)

Depth: toasted pepitas

Safety: Wormwood should not be consumed if you're pregnant, breastfeeding, taking medication, or experience epilepsy or kidney problems. The common consensus is, however, that occasionally consuming wormwood in small concentrations, like in the recipe that follows, poses little to no health risks as the amount of thujone is negligible. However, if this is a risk you prefer not to take, consider making the following recipe as a "carciofo" amaro by using cardoon or artichoke as your bittering agent, and omitting sage, which also contains thujone.

FALL "GÉNÉPI" AMARO

If you don't have access to wormwood or one of its relatives in the *Artemisia* family, you can easily source it dried; however, you'll only need to use a third the amount called for in the recipe below.

This recipe is based on the Amaro Master Recipe, page 80.

Makes approximately 1 qt/950 ml (prior to diluting with syrup and water)

---

2 medium apples, halved

120 g cranberries (approximately 1 cup)

50 g sumac berries (approximately 1 cup), or 1 Tbsp ground store-bought sumac powder

15 g rosemary (approximately three 6 in/15 cm sprigs)

12 g sage (approximately two 8 in/20 cm sprigs)

10 g fresh wormwood (approximately six 6 in/15 cm sprigs), or 60 g cardoon and/or artichoke leaves (approximately 2 large leaves) for a carciofo amaro

10 g fig leaves (approximately 3 medium leaves)

10 g dried hardy orange (*Citrus trifolata*) peels or dried common orange peels (approximately ¼ x)

2 Tbsp juniper berries (be sure to use the berries of an edible juniper species, like *Juniperus communis*; if unsure, use store-bought juniper berries)

2 Tbsp toasted pumpkin seeds (pepitas)

Laird's 100-proof "Jersey Lightning" unaged apple brandy, for topping (approximately 5 c/1.2 L)

Maple syrup, for sweetening

Water, for diluting

DIRECTIONS

Pack a 2 qt/2 L jar with the apples, cranberries, sumac, rosemary, sage, wormwood, fig leaves, orange peels, juniper berries, and pumpkin seeds and cover with the apple brandy. Allow the botanicals to macerate in the alcohol for 5 weeks.

After 5 weeks, strain out the solids and reserve the liquid. Add the strained liquid to a 3 qt/3 L oak barrel and age for an additional month (or longer), or skip this step if you don't have an oak barrel.

Next, add the water and maple syrup, starting with ¼ c/60 ml each, to dilute and sweeten to taste. Since the apple brandy is relatively low proof compared to the 151-proof vodka used in the other amaro recipes, minimal sweetening and dilution is needed. This will keep indefinitely at room temperature. Its flavors will meld and mellow over time.

BOULEVARDIER

Makes 1 cocktail

---

1 oz/30 ml bourbon

1 oz/30 ml Fall "Génépi" Amaro
(see page 252)

1 oz/30 ml sweet vermouth

Orange peel, for garnish

DIRECTIONS

To a mixing glass, add the bourbon, amaro, and vermouth. Add ice and stir for 15 seconds. Strain over a large cube in a rocks glass. Peel a long strip of orange zest and express over the drink (to release its oils) and drop the peel in the drink to garnish.

CHAPTER 6

WINTER

Winter Squash | Chicory | Beets | Barley | Citrus | Juniper
Sumac | Maple | Winter "Alpine" Amaro

Unlike many people, I'm thrilled each year when winter arrives. The time has finally come to put the garden to bed, loved ones arrive for the holidays, and the anticipation and excitement of the first snowfall are tangible. And while I can still go out and pick hardy herbs and chicories from the garden, storage crops like winter squash, beets, and grains have, like me, retired indoors for the year. These early days of winter are a time of hibernation, when I'm hunkered down and focused on rest and regeneration, fully embracing *hygge* and the slowness of this time of year.

After the calendar page turns to January and the deep freeze sets in, I find my mind beginning to drift back outside. I stay up late thumbing through seed catalogs, planning and scheming about the following year's garden and foraging trips. Though I try to keep myself occupied, I can't help but feel restless and antsy. These feelings are temporarily quelled with the arrival of citrus season, which breaks up the winter monotony with its bright colors and flavors. By February, I am able to return to the landscape in search of year-round staples like sumac berries, juniper, and other evergreens. Soon, when the time comes to begin tapping maple trees and sowing seeds, I know that spring is in arm's reach.

Many of the recipes in this chapter are my versions of familiar cocktails; creature comforts during the time of year when you need it most. These include crowd-pleasers like Sangria, a Hot Toddy, an Espresso Martini, a juniper-laden Gin and Tonic, and a tequila cocktail with spiced pumpkin. Other recipes, like winter amaro, homemade maple syrup, and sumac wine are longer-term projects that will help combat the winter doldrums. I've also included non-alcoholic recipes for each ingredient in this chapter (minus the amaro) in case you like to use the beginning of the year to reset after holiday indulgence. The resulting collection reflects my approach to drinking seasonally in the winter, even when there isn't much in season.

WINTER SQUASH | *Cucurbita*

In Guilá Naquitz, an archaeological site just outside of Oaxaca, Mexico, the oldest evidence of human consumption of wild pumpkin, *Cucurbita pepo*, was discovered in a cave, dating back approximately ten thousand years. Evidence from the site shows changes in the squash's shape, color, and the thickness of its skin and stem over the next two thousand years, indicating that the wild pumpkin was being altered by human selection. This process represents what is likely the oldest example of crop domestication in the Americas, and one that marked a monumental shift in how ancient humans ate and lived, as these thicker squashes could be kept for long-term storage after harvesting.

As it turns out, *C. pepo* was only the first of several species of *Cucurbita* to be independently domesticated in the ancient Americas. The same process took place with three other relatives of *C. pepo*: *C. maxima* in the southern cone of South America, *C. moschata* in northern South and Central America, and *C. argyrosperma* in southern Mexico. Each of the hundreds of winter squash species grown today, from miniature Jack-be-Littles to record-setting pumpkins weighing over 2,700 pounds/1,225 kg, belongs to one of these four species.

Winter squashes have since spread far and wide and tremendously impacted human history in the process. Calorically dense, nutritious, and long-lasting, they have offered food security for billions of people worldwide. Despite this fact, most people in the United States don't think of pumpkins as much more than Halloween decorations, pie filling, the Starbucks Pumpkin Spice Latte, or the equally divisive pumpkin ale, which many people don't realize is a style of beer that has been brewed in America since at least the 1770s. There is, however, another much older pumpkin drink that originated in pre-Columbian Mexico known as *xacualole* (pronounced cha-kwa-lo-le), which is part of a family of sweetened beverages known as *atole*, that are typically prepared with corn masa, piloncillo (Mexican raw cane sugar), and spices.

My first introduction to atole came from our wonderful team of Puebloan prep cooks at the restaurant: Evodia, her two daughters, and her daughter-in-law. In addition to the pivotal role they play in keeping the restaurant afloat, they also prepare the most incredible Mexican dishes for staff meals. On special occasions, these staff meals are accompanied by drinks, cold agua frescas in the summer and warm atoles in the winter.

CONTINUED

One day, when confronted with an abundance of pumpkins from our restaurant garden, I spoke to Evodia about making a pumpkin atole that could be used in a Mexican-inspired cocktail. That's how I first learned about xacualole. The recipe below is for a drink we called La Oaxacana (pronounced wuh-ha-ka-na) as an ode to the ancestral homeland of pumpkins. It's one of my favorite recipes in this book, and, more importantly, one that is Doña Evodia approved.

Curing tip: After you harvest or buy your pumpkins in the fall, let them sit in the sunlight for three days to cure (bring inside if it's going to be cloudy or rainy). After curing, most pumpkins can be stored at room temperature or in a basement or root cellar until well into the following year.

N/A Alternative: The spiced pumpkin atole recipe below is purposefully a thicker consistency to add body to the La Oaxacana cocktail. If you want to enjoy it as a non-alcoholic option, try thinning it out with water or milk and serving it warm.

SPICED PUMPKIN ATOLE

The recipe below is prepared with Mexican cinnamon (a.k.a. canela) and piloncillo, a raw Mexican cane sugar. Both can be found online or at a local Mexican grocer. If you can't find it, a single cinnamon stick and demerara sugar are good substitutes.

Makes approximately 3 c/720 ml

1½ lb/680 g unpeeled pumpkin flesh, (approximately one small pie pumpkin)

One 8 oz/225 g cone of piloncillo (or 1 c/200 g of demerara sugar)

2 c/475 ml water

1 dried pasilla chile (seeds, ribs, and stems removed)

1 dried ancho chile (seeds, ribs, and stems removed)

2 big pinches of kosher salt

One 1-in/2.5 cm piece whole canela, or substitute 1 cinnamon stick)

3 allspice berries

2 cloves

1 star anise

DIRECTIONS

Preheat the oven to 375°F/190°C. Cut the pumpkin and piloncillo into wedges and put in a roasting pan. Add the water, chiles, and salt. Wrap the canela, allspice, cloves, and star anise in cheesecloth and tie with twine, submerge in the water. Cover with tinfoil and roast for 2 hours. Take out of the oven and let cool. Discard the spices.

Once cooled, scrape the pumpkin flesh from the skin and discard the skin. Add all the ingredients to a blender and blend until smooth. This will keep in the refrigerator for up to 2 weeks.

LA OAXACANA

Makes 1 cocktail

1½ oz/45 ml añejo tequila

1¼ oz/37 ml Spiced Pumpkin Atole
(see page 263)

¾ oz/22 ml freshly squeezed lime juice

½ oz/15 ml mezcal

½ oz/15 ml spiced amaro, such as Averna
or Mexican-made Amargo-Vallet Cortezas
de Angostura)

½ oz/15 ml Agave Syrup (see page 25)

Pinch of kosher salt

1 dried chile de árbol, for garnish

DIRECTIONS

Fill a cocktail shaker with ice and add the tequila, pumpkin atole, lime juice, mezcal, amaro, agave, and salt. Shake and double strain into a coupe. Garnish with a chile de árbol.

CHICORY | *Cichorium* spp.

If you've ever visited the French Quarter in New Orleans, there's a good chance that you stopped by Cafe du Monde for their iconic coffee and beignets. Aside from the fact that they have been serving this winning combination for more than one hundred years, what makes their coffee special is that it's not just coffee, but a mix of ground coffee beans and chicory root. Though many think this is a Cafe du Monde invention, it is actually a practice that originated in France long before the café opened its doors, and still continues in many parts of the world today.

Chicory grows wild in northern Africa, western Asia, and Europe and has recently spread to North America where it has become an invasive species. Ancient Egyptians were the first to selectively breed varietals to be cultivated for food and medicine over five thousand years ago. As it spread up through the Italian peninsula and into mainland Europe, it was bred into bitter leafy vegetables like radicchio, endive, puntarelle, and closely related species like frisée and escarole. These bitter greens play an incredibly important role in Italian cuisine today.

Despite the fact that cultivated chicories are most commonly seen on winter menus, wild varieties can actually be found growing almost all year-long, and are easiest to identify when their bright blue flowers bloom atop leggy stems in late spring and early summer. While chicories are grown primarily for their greens, there is also immense flavor to be found in the taproot. This part of the plant is often tossed into the compost bin, but it can be cooked and eaten like a carrot, or roasted dry, and ground to make a drink that tastes remarkably like coffee.

In the early 1800s, chicory root coffee began to gain popularity in France as a homegrown way to stretch expensive imported coffee grounds. A few years later, Napoleon I imposed a blockade on British imports (including coffee beans), and chicory coffee consumption skyrocketed to a point where supply could no longer meet demand. This culinary custom followed immigrants to North America, including the first French immigrants to settle in Louisiana. When Union naval brigades blocked the port of New Orleans during the Civil War, these French descendants began to stretch their coffee rations with ground chicory just like their grandparents had done during the Napoleonic Wars. This practice, which was driven out of necessity, became embedded in the region's culinary customs.

CONTINUED

There are a few different ways to get your hands on chicory root, with the cheapest option being to forage for it. You can also grow it in your garden or find a local farmer who does. Chances are they just throw out the roots and would be happy to give them to you for a low price. Personally, I practice a combination of all three of these options, but if all of those seem too difficult, ground and roasted chicory root can easily be found online.

Now that you have your chicory, follow the recipe below for chicory root coffee and enjoy it by itself as a noncaffeinated beverage, or swap it into a cocktail where you would typically use coffee, such as an Irish Coffee, a bright and bitter coffee-spiked Gin and Tonic, or in an Espresso Martini as I've done below.

N/A Alternatives: Enjoy chicory coffee with or without cream and sugar as you would regular coffee. For a cold refreshing beverage, serve it over ice topped with sparkling water, or shaken with ice and simple syrup to make a chicory *shakerato*.

Regional Substitutes: Chicory and its relatives can be found throughout North America, as well as most other parts of the world. It is widely cultivated and prefers cooler temperatures. Dandelion root, a close relative, is also a perfectly fine substitute.

To prepare the chicory, pick the plants out of the ground and clean the roots thoroughly. Meanwhile, preheat the oven to 400°F/200°C. Coarsely chop the roots and spread on a baking sheet.

Roast the chicory in the oven until dark brown, which can take an hour or more depending on thickness. As they roast, the roots should give off a smell that is very similar to chocolate. Once cooled, grind in your coffee or spice grinder. Grounds can be kept in an airtight jar and stored at room temperature indefinitely.

CHICORY COFFEE

Chicory grounds are more soluble than regular coffee, so use half the amount you would with ground coffee if you intend to consume it on its own (approximately 1 Tbsp per c/240 ml). Here, I've increased the ratio of grinds to water to make a highly concentrated brew with a flavor that's more similar to espresso.

Makes approximately 1¾ c/415 ml

---

4 Tbsp/60 ml roasted ground chicory root (from approximately 1 ft/30 cm of ½ in/1.3 cm diameter root)

2 c/475 ml boiling water

DIRECTIONS

To brew, slowly pour the boiling water over the ground chicory root in a pour-over cone set on top of a large mug. You may also use a drip coffee machine. Drink it fresh or store it in an airtight container in the refrigerator and use within a week.

CAFÉ CHICORÉE

Makes 1 cocktail

1¾ oz/52 ml cognac

1 oz/30 ml Chicory Coffee (see page 269)

½ oz/15 ml coffee liqueur such as Caffé Borghetti, Kahlua, or Mr. Black

¼ oz/8 ml rich demerara syrup (see page 25)

Dash of Angostura bitters

DIRECTIONS

Fill a cocktail shaker with ice and add the cognac, chicory coffee, coffee liqueur, demerara syrup, and bitters. Shake vigorously and double strain into a chilled Martini coupe. Dry shake it again without ice if you want it extra foamy. No garnish.

Just a few centuries ago, there was a period in the agricultural calendar commonly known as the "six weeks want." This stretch referred to the time from the end of January until mid-March when both garden and nature were devoid of ingredients, and the only form of sustenance came from storage crops kept in root cellars or preserved ingredients that were put up for the winter. While storage crops are a vital source of calories during this lean time, many lend little in the way of nutritional value. One exception to this rule is the mighty beet—a highly nutritious vegetable that can be harvested from the garden just before the first frost, and, if stored right, will keep in the refrigerator (or root cellar) until well into spring.

Beets and their relatives come from a wild ancestor known as sea beets, which are native to the coasts of the Mediterranean where they have been utilized as forage crops for thousands of years. Sea beets were cultivated over time and gradually gave rise to the four subspecies of *B. vulgaris* that we know today. These varieties include chard (aka Swiss chard or spinach beet), which was selectively chosen for its leaves and thick stems, sugar beets, which were selected for their high sugar content and are responsible for approximately 20% of all sugar produced worldwide today, *mangelwurzel*, a fodder crop for livestock, and the root vegetable we know simply as beet or beetroot.

Beetroots come in a variety of shapes and sizes. They can be big or small, round or cylindrical, and exhibit a variety of colors from red, gold, white, and the candy cane-striped variety known as *chioggia*, named after a city of the same name in Northern Italy. Beets became ingrained in the culinary practices of many European, North African, and Asian cultures; however, no culture took to them quite as fondly as the Eastern Europeans, who prepared them in a variety of ways including raw, pickled, roasted, and fermented. Today, the most ubiquitous use for beets is *borscht*, a bright red soup whose slight sourness comes from the addition of fermented beet *kvass*.

Kvass is a generic term used in Eastern European countries to refer to any fermented, sparkling beverage with either zero ABV, or a very low alcohol content (less than 2%). Although there are many regional variations, the category can be broken into two main styles: white kvass made by fermenting a drink with stale rye bread, and red kvass made from beets. The stale rye bread style of kvass is the more widespread and ancient of the two. It's made by infusing cubes of stale, toasted rye bread

CONTINUED

in boiling water with dried herbs (especially mint), letting it sit overnight, straining out the solids, sweetening with honey, and culturing with yeast to begin fermentation. The earliest mention of this style of kvass comes from the celebration of Volodymyr the Great's baptism in Ukraine in 996 CE when it was served to the citizens of Kiev. The drink is still so popular today that you can purchase it from mobile kvass wagons in many Eastern European cities.

Beet kvass is different in that it's not so much a fermented soft drink as it is a sort of fermented pickle. It's typically made by placing beets in salted water, culturing with a starter, and allowing it to ferment for a few days, fueled by the beets' sugar and the lactic acid bacteria on their skins. It can be drunk as is for its health benefits (like sauerkraut brine), bottled and allowed to carbonate into a fizzy tonic, or used as a base for borscht.

The kvass I'm making here is a hybrid of the two styles. To make it, I first cube stale, toasted rye bread, add roasted beets, mint tea, caraway seeds, and a touch of salt, before topping with boiling water and allowing it to infuse overnight. The next day, I strain out all the solids, sweeten with honey, acidulate with lemon, and culture with my ginger bug. A few days later, I transfer it to glass bottles and allow it to carbonate. The scarlet red brew makes for a delicious savory soda or show-stopping highball when spiked with vodka.

If you live in a region that rarely dips below 30°F/-1°C, beets can be left in the ground to overwinter and then harvested all year. However, if you live in an area that experiences harsher winters (like I do), it's best to harvest your beets before the deep frost sets in. For long-term storage, harvest the beets when the soil is dry and immediately remove the greens. Store them, unwashed, in plastic bags with a few small holes poked in them for circulation. It's very important not to wash the beets before storing, as you will disrupt their protective coating. Wash the beets just before you are ready to use them. If purchasing beets that have been washed from the grocery store or farmer's market, you can remove the greens and store them the same way, but they will only keep for about a month or so.

BEET KVASS

This recipe is based on the Ginger Beer Master Recipe, page 43.

Makes approximately six 750 ml bottles

---

2 lbs/900 g medium beets, peeled

½ loaf toasted stale rye bread, cubed (approximately ¾ lb/340 g)

1 Tbsp dried mint (or 2 mint tea bags)

1 tsp caraway seeds

3½ qt/3.3 L boiling water

2½ c/590 ml freshly squeezed lemon juice

1 qt/950 ml honey syrup (see page 25)

½ cup/120 ml Ginger Bug, liquid only (see page 39)

DIRECTIONS

To roast the beets, preheat the oven to 400°F/200°C and place the beets in a baking dish with ¼ in/6 mm water in the bottom. Cover with aluminum foil and roast for 1½ hours, until the beets can be easily penetrated with a knife. While the beets are roasting, cube the rye bread and spread out on a baking sheet. Put in the oven with the beets for 10 minutes, flipping them at the 5-minute mark. Remove once the bread is well toasted.

Next, remove the beets from the water, cut into 1 in/2.5 cm cubes, and add them to a 2 gal/8 L food-safe container with the toasted bread. Add the dried mint leaves and caraway, then top everything with boiling water. Use a whisk to break up the beets and bread, then let sit at room temperature overnight.

The next day, strain out the solids (you should have about 2½ qt/2.4 L of liquid), add the lemon juice, honey syrup, and ginger bug, and cover with a towel or cheesecloth bound with a rubber band or other non-airtight lid. Let sit at room temperature out of direct sunlight for 2 days.

After 2 days have passed, strain out the solids and decant the kvass into swing-cap bottles. Allow to sit at room temperature for an additional 1 to 2 days, checking for carbonation after 24 hours to make sure it's not overly active (sometimes sweeter beets can cause a pretty active ferment). Once carbonated, place the bottle in the refrigerator and consume within 1 month.

KVASS HIGHBALL

Makes 1 cocktail

---

2 oz/60 ml vodka

Beet Kvass (see page 275), for topping

Mint sprig, for garnish

DIRECTIONS

Fill a Collins glass with ice and add the vodka. Top with the kvass and garnish with a mint sprig.

BARLEY | *Hordeum vulgare*

In the pantheon of botanical contributions to the history of alcohol, the undisputed champion is barley, for without it, we wouldn't have such staples as beer, whiskey, vodka, or gin. Barley may seem like an unlikely champion, as it doesn't possess easily fermentable sugars in the way that, say, apples or grapes do. Instead, barley requires a bit of coaxing to unlock its magic via a process known as malting.

Barley is a member of the genus *Hordeum* and one of the most important cereal or "staple" crops in the grass family, *Poaceae*. Other important members of this family include wheat, rye, corn, rice, and millet. Domesticated barley (*H. vulgaris*) is one of the most ancient domesticated grains, first cultivated in the Fertile Crescent ten thousand years ago when early humans realized that the seeds on some barley plants didn't drop, making them easier to harvest and store for later consumption. People saved these seeds and continued to plant them, altering the plant's genome in the process. Having large stores of shelf-stable,

nutritious, and calorically dense barley was one of the most important steps in the Middle East transitioning from hunter gatherers to larger agricultural settlements, and, later, civilizations.

Like all cereal grains, barley is a seed composed of a fibrous outer husk called the bran, which forms the protective envelope around the endosperm and germ. The germ is the part of the seed that will germinate into a plant, and the endosperm provides nourishment during this process. This nourishment comes primarily in the form of starch, a complex carbohydrate composed of sugars linked together in a chain. Starch molecules aren't sweet on their own, but their sweetness is revealed when enzymes activated during germination break them down into simpler sugar molecules to nourish the young seedling. This was discovered when barley seeds were soaked in water to soften the outer husk, and the next day the vessel was bubbling away as wild yeasts began to convert the sugars in the sweetened barley liquid to alcohol. This is malting on the most rudimentary level.

When we talk about malting today, it generally refers to a three-step, highly refined, and scientific procedure. The first step in the process is adding water to the dried grain and soaking it, often several times, in order to awaken the seed for germination. Once a certain level of hydration is reached, the barley is then laid out so that enzymes in the grain can begin to break down starch molecules for germination. If this process were allowed to continue, the germinating seed would go

CONTINUED

on to become its own barley plant; however, stopping the germination at this point means that these sugars are now captured and available for fermentation. This is achieved by heating the barley with hot air or smoke, the third and final step in commercial malting operations. Controlled variations in this final step are what produce differences in color and flavor that give rise to beers as varied as pilsners and porters and spirits as different as smoky Scotch whisky and neutral vodka.

The alcoholic lineage of barley drinks is only one part of its millennia-long history. Although many people don't realize they are familiar with nonalcoholic drinks made from barley, "barley's ghosts" as the food historian Ray Sokolov calls them, are all around us.

Take, for example, *orgeat*, a commonly used cocktail syrup made from almonds, and *horchata*, a sweetened drink consumed in Spain and Latin America that's typically made with rice, tigernuts, or sesame seeds. Both are derived from the Latin name for barley, *hordeum*, and are prepared by first brewing a tisane with the nut, seed, or grain from which they are made. Even the word "tisane," which is used today to refer to any herbal tea made without actual tea leaves, is derived from the Greek *ptisana*, which was the name given to barley tea.

Barley tea is commonly consumed in Eastern Asian countries where it is served warm like Korean *boricha*, or cold during the summer as with Japanese *mugicha*. Here, I have included a warm preparation of toasted barley tea along with two other barley byproducts—single-malt Irish whiskey and smokey Islay Scotch—to use in a hot cocktail, because sometimes you just need a nice Hot Toddy on a cold day.

Foraging Advice: If you live in North America and want to forage your own barley, try to find little barley (*Hordeum pusillum*), which grows wild in most parts of the continent and can be harvested in spring or fall. Little barley was cultivated by Native Americans and evidence suggests it was even briefly domesticated before it was overtaken by corn introduced from Mexico.

BARLEY TISANE

Makes approximately 3½ c/830 ml

¼ cup/46 g whole barley grains   4 c/950 ml gently boiling water

DIRECTIONS

To toast the barley, heat a dry skillet or frying pan over medium-high heat. Add the barley and occasionally stir until fragrant and caramelized, about 10 minutes. Transfer the barley to a mortar and pestle or spice grinder and grind into a powder. You should end up with ¼ c/60 ml ground barley. Add to a food-safe container and top with the boiling water. Let infuse for 5 minutes, then strain the solids through a fine-mesh strainer lined with a tea towel or cheesecloth. Consume while warm, or store in the refrigerator and drink within 1 week.

HOT TODDY

Makes 1 cocktail

---

2 oz/60 ml Irish whiskey

½ tsp peaty Islay single-malt Scotch, such as Laphroaig 10 (optional)

5 oz/148 ml hot Barley Tisane (see page 281)

1 oz honey syrup (see page 25)

Lemon wheel, for garnish

Cinnamon stick, for garnish

DIRECTIONS

Add Irish whiskey and Scotch to a pre-warmed mug. Top with hot Barley Tisane and honey syrup and stir. Garnish with a lemon wheel and a cinnamon stick inside the mug.

I debated including citrus in this book. Despite their ubiquity in cocktails, citruses are tropical plants and don't grow around me; yes, I would use citrus juice in recipes, but devoting an entire section to them would be like devoting a section to sugarcane. Although citrus trees are a huge part of the landscape in many southern and western states, most of the country is inhospitable to growing them. The one exception I considered was the trifoliate or hardy orange, *Citrus trifoliata*, which has naturalized here in North America since being introduced from its native China during colonial times.

The problem with hardy oranges, though, is that they aren't exactly crowd-pleasers. The fruit's flesh is riddled with seeds, the skin leaves a black tar-like substance on your hands when you handle them, they produce way less juice than other citrus fruits, plus they are bitter with an overwhelmingly perfumy aroma that many (if not most) find unpalatable. While I make a point of harvesting hardy oranges each year to use sparingly as a flavoring ingredient in amari and vermouth, I did not think that it was worth it to devote an entire section to them.

My outlook changed in early 2021, when I learned of Bhumi Growers, located less than a half hour from me in Florence, New Jersey. They sell exotic citrus varieties grown in onsite greenhouses to some of the top restaurants, bars, and breweries in the mid-Atlantic. Growing citrus indoors is not necessarily a new idea. During the seventeenth and eighteenth centuries in Europe, the most well-to-do families of the time constructed *orangeries*,

which were large greenhouses meant to grow oranges and other exotic fruits procured from tropical climates and faraway lands. Even today, many hobbyists keep a tree or two next to a window with the hopes of harvesting a few fruits each year. A few trees in your living room is one thing, a functional citrus farm operating in New Jersey is entirely different.

So how do they do it? A huge part of the success of Bhumi's operation comes from the aforementioned trifoliate orange, which is used as the hardy rootstock to which other, less hardy citrus varietals are grafted, such as calamansi, kumquats, and yuzu. The reason this works is that the citrus gene pool isn't very large, and each of the seemingly endless hybrids available today can be traced back to just a handful of ancestral species. These citrus progenitors include familiar varieties like mandarins (*C. reticulata*), pomelos (*C. maxima*), citrons (*C. medica*), and kumquats (*C. japonica*), plus others like yuzu, makrut lime, finger lime, and, you guessed it, the trifoliate orange. The result is that nearly every wild and cultivated citrus known today is genetically compatible for grafting and crossing with other members of the genus.

CONTINUED

This continued progress in citrus breeding gives me hope I'll one day be able to grow citrus right in my backyard. Until then, I'm happy to take the short drive to a citrus farm in New Jersey.

One of my favorite ways to use winter citrus is to make a Sangria. Long a Sangria naysayer, my mind was changed once I read about people treating the Spanish cocktail the way it was originally meant to—like a punch, rather than a liquid fruit salad.

For punches, the rind is macerated along with sugar and spices to make an oleo-saccharum, then the peeled fruit is juiced to convert the oleo- into a sherbet. I swapped brandy and red wine in the classic Sangria formula for lighter and brighter pisco and orange wine (wine made from white grapes with some skin contact). I finish it off with Italicus, a

bergamot orange liqueur from Italy (dry curaçao or another orange liqueur would be a fine substitute), and sparkling wine. If you've sworn off sangria because of the overly sweet versions served in chain restaurants, this version may change your mind.

N/A Alternative: The sherbet below is great when mixed with iced tea. To make it, shake 1½ oz/45 ml of the sherbet with 3 oz/89 ml of iced black tea and strain over fresh ice in a Collins glass.

TANGRIA SHERBET

Our bar team decided to name this cocktail "Tangria" due its similarities in appearance and orangey flavor to the powdered drink Tang, a staple of many of our childhoods. At the base of its flavor is this sherbet, which we will use to add sweetness, spice, acidity, and body to the Tangria cocktail (see page 287).

This recipe is based on the Oleo-Saccharum & Sherbet Master Recipe, page 89.

Makes approximately 3 c/720 ml, enough for about 20 servings

---

6 Meyer lemons (can substitute another tart citrus like kumquats, calamansi, or regular lemons; you may need more to make 1 c/240 ml juice)

6 Cara Cara oranges (can substitute another sweet citrus like blood orange, navel orange, or ruby grapefruit; you may need more to make 1 c/240 ml juice)

2 cardamom pods

5 coriander seeds

½ tsp fennel seeds

2 c/400 g sugar

¼ tsp ground ginger

DIRECTIONS

Using a Y-peeler, peel the 6 lemons and 6 oranges.

In a skillet over medium heat, toast the cardamom pods, coriander, and fennel seeds, stirring constantly until the spices become aromatic. Grind in a mortar and pestle or spice blender, then mix with the sugar in a food-safe container along with the ground ginger and citrus peels to make the oleo-saccharum. Cover and let sit overnight at room temperature.

In the meantime, juice the peeled citruses until you have 1 cup/240 ml from each (may need to supplement with additional fruit). Refrigerate in an airtight container. The next day, add the citrus juice and oleo-saccharum to a medium saucepan and gently heat until all the sugar dissolves. Pass through a fine-mesh strainer into a large bowl (this strained liquid is called a "sherbet"), being sure to squeeze as much liquid from the peels as possible. Discard the solids after straining and store the sherbet in the refrigerator for up to 1 month.

TANGRIA BASE

Makes 2 qt/1.9 L

---

3 c/720 ml Tangria Sherbet (see page 287)

1½ c/360 ml pisco (Chilean or Peruvian)

3 c/720 ml orange wine
(I love Oregon winemaker
Brianne Day's Vin de Days: L'Orange)

½ c/120 ml Italicus Rosolio di Bergamotto
(can substitute with Pierre Ferrand Dry
Curaçao or another orange liqueur)

DIRECTIONS

Add all the ingredients to a 2 qt/2 L mason jar and stir to dissolve. This will keep in the refrigerator indefinitely, though the flavors will mellow and change with time.

TANGRIA

Makes 1 cocktail

---

3 oz/89 ml Tangria Base (see above)

2 oz/60 ml sparkling wine,
like Spanish cava or Prosecco

Dried citrus wheel, for garnish

DIRECTIONS

Fill a wineglass with ice, add the Tangria base, and top with sparkling wine. Mix to incorporate the two, then garnish with an orange wheel.

This can easily be scaled up for a crowd: Pour half of the Tangria Base (see above) into an ice-filled pitcher with citrus wheels and top with a 750 ml bottle of sparkling wine.

JUNIPER | *Juniperus*

Come winter, I feel a deep sense of appreciation for conifers and evergreens. Although I tend to take them for granted during the rest of the year, once the landscape is brown and barren, their vibrant green color and bright flavor offer a welcome respite from the monotony of the cold months. And juniper, more than any other species of evergreen, has played an important role as a medicinal and culinary plant.

Junipers are members of the genus *Juniperus*, which includes around 60 species of coniferous trees and shrubs native to the entirety of the northern hemisphere. The most widespread species is common juniper (*J. communis*), which is found evenly distributed throughout Asia, Europe, and North America. In addition to being the most plentiful species, *J. communis* is also the most widely used in culinary applications due to the sweet berry produced by female plants. However, the term "berry" is a misnomer when talking about juniper, as these fruits are actually just cones with fleshy, microscopic scales that give them a berry-like appearance. In addition to being used in beverages, juniper berries and needles have a longstanding use as a food seasoning, most notably in the Nordic countries where it is frequently used to flavor game.

Juniper was an important part of traditional medicine across the northern hemisphere in many cultures spanning from ancient China to the Pueblo Nations of the American Southwest. The first written account of juniper in European medicinal traditions can be traced back to ancient Greece, although its use almost certainly predated that era. The practice of using juniper medicinally continued into the Middle Ages with European monks, the primary pharmacists of the time, who would extract the desired compounds by boiling, fermenting, and infusing the berries in wine. The healing powers of juniper were believed to be so great, that they were even stuffed in the elongated beaks of the masks sported by plague doctors during the bubonic plague that ravaged Europe in the fourteenth century.

Once the technology of distillation arrived in Europe, it unlocked an entirely different way of extracting the flavor, aroma, and beneficial properties of many plants, including juniper. The earliest evidence of this comes from Benedictine monks in Salerno, Italy, who distilled potent spirits from the berries of juniper trees that grew around their monastery. This tradition eventually spread throughout the continent and gave rise to the Dutch custom of distilling *jenever* (coming from the Dutch word for "juniper"), which originated as a pharmaceutical product, but eventually became an object of indulgence. After the Dutch and English fought alongside each other against the Spanish during the Dutch War of Independence, English soldiers grew fond of jenever, which they referred to as "Dutch courage." Not long after, they began distilling juniper spirits in England, which eventually gave rise to the style of London dry gin, which has become the most ubiquitous expression of juniper today.

CONTINUED

Beyond gin, juniper has been used to brew beer for centuries in the Nordic countries, especially in Finland where they have been brewing *sahti* from malted grains and juniper twigs since the time of the Vikings. In the Balkan region of southeastern Europe, they make a dry, tart, low- or no-alcohol juniper brew known as *smreka* (the local name for juniper berries).

Although smreka is traditionally brewed using only juniper berries, I wanted to experiment with brewing a soft drink by using juniper twigs and needles, as they are less laborious to collect. To do so, I used the branches of the eastern red cedar, which, despite the name, is actually a juniper species (*J. virginiana*) that is native to the eastern United States. Luckily, we have an abundance of this species that lines the entire parking lot outside the restaurant in a hedgerow that is about as long as a football field. Unlike smreka which utilizes a month-long cold extraction of the juniper berries and relies only on their inherent sugars, the sparkling juniper tonic I am able to make takes just four days because I brew a hot juniper tea to extract the flavor and ferment it using the ginger bug and supplemental sugar. Once it's spiked with gin (or vodka, if you prefer), the result is a juniper-laden beverage that tastes like Christmas morning.

Foraging Advice: Other edible juniper varieties are fine to swap in here, but keep in mind that not all species of juniper are safe for consumption (*J. sabina* and *J. oxycedrus* are two toxic varietals). Only use berries with a mild, sweet flavor, as an overly bitter flavor would indicate toxicity. As always with foraging, it is important to be certain you are harvesting the desired plant and not something that could harm you or anyone else. Consult a guidebook or an experienced forager in your area.

N/A Alternative: The juniper tonic that follows is exactly what I look for in an N/A cocktail—perfectly balanced, with texture from the bubbles, and complex flavors developed from the yeast during fermentation. It's got everything a Gin and Tonic does, minus the alcohol.

Safety: Don't consume juniper while pregnant or breastfeeding.

JUNIPER TEA

Makes approximately 3 qt/2.8 L

3½ qt/3.3 L water

3 qt/2.8 L roughly chopped
juniper needles, berries,
and nonwoody stems (about 350 g)

DIRECTIONS

Bring the water to a boil, then turn off the heat and allow it to cool for 3 minutes. Meanwhile, roughly chop your juniper with scissors or a knife and add it to a large bowl or food-safe container. Pour the water over the juniper and cover with a loose-fitting lid or tea towel. Let infuse for 30 minutes. Strain out the solids and move the tea into the refrigerator to chill before making the recipe below.

JUNIPER TONIC

This recipe is based on the Ginger Beer Master Recipe, page 43.

Makes approximately six 750 ml bottles

---

3 qt/2.8 L Juniper Tea (see above)

1 qt/950 ml simple syrup
(see page 25), plus 1 Tbsp per bottle
for priming (see page 43)

2½ c/590 ml freshly squeezed lemon juice

½ cup Ginger Bug, liquid only (see page 39)

DIRECTIONS

Add the tea, 1 qt of the simple syrup, the lemon juice, and ginger bug to a food-safe container and cover with cheesecloth or tea towel secured with a rubber band or other non-airtight lid. After 2 days have passed, strain out the solids and decant the soda into the 750 ml bottles primed with the remaining 1 Tbsp of simple syrup. Cap tightly and let sit out of direct sunlight for 48 hours. Check for carbonation and let sit longer if needed (juniper sometimes takes a bit longer to ferment, as juniper contains antimicrobial compounds). Once carbonated, place the bottle in the refrigerator and consume within 3 months.

JUNIPER GIN AND TONIC

Makes 1 cocktail

---

2 oz/60 ml London dry gin

Juniper Tonic (see page 293), for topping

Juniper sprig, for garnish

DIRECTIONS

Fill a Collins glass with ice and add the gin. Top with juniper tonic and garnish with a juniper sprig.

SUMAC | *Rhus*

The idea of foraging often conjures images of someone deep in the woods, hacking through the bush of some primeval forest to find exotic ingredients. Although this is occasionally true, the reality is that I spend much more time foraging along the edges of the woods rather than in them, as these liminal zones often contain more diversity than you'll find deep in the forest. This is due to a principle known in ecology as the edge effect, which states that the area between two adjacent biomes is often more diverse than the zones surrounding it. These edges can occur naturally, in the area between a forest and a meadow, for example, but these days you're much more likely to encounter them between a forest and human-made spaces like a farm, roadway, or parking lot. One of the few upsides to human-made disturbances in the landscape is the opportunity they create for wild edible plants to thrive. One species that I can almost always count on finding in these narrow edge zones is staghorn sumac, *Rhus typhina*, which is one of the first of the so-called pioneer species to establish itself in land recently disturbed by human development.

Staghorn sumac is just one of over two hundred sumac species in the genus *Rhus* that can be found growing in temperate and subtropical regions around the world, including in North America, Eurasia, Northern Africa, Australia, and the Pacific Islands. The name "sumac" is derived from the Syriac word *summāqā*, meaning "red," referring to the color of the dense berry clusters (or "bobs") that form at branch tips. Sumacs are members of the family, Anacardiaceae, along with cashews, pistachios, and mangoes, as well as the dreaded skin-irritating plants in the *Toxicodendron* genus—poison ivy, poison oak, and poison sumac. Although it may seem intimidating to forage for sumac knowing that you could potentially encounter poison sumac, the two are easily distinguishable as edible sumacs bear red berries that face up in tight clusters, whereas poison sumac's berries are downward-facing, white, and less densely grouped. Plus, poison sumac prefers very wet, swampy environments.

There are many varieties of sumac that are prized for their culinary usage, thanks to the acidic flavor and bright red color they impart to dishes. Sumac is a staple ingredient in Middle Eastern cuisine, where the berries of Sicilian sumac, *R. coriaria*, are dried and pulverized to be used as a spice most notably in Levantine fattoush salad and in za'atar seasoning. Sumac was also very important in various Western European culinary traditions as a source of acidity prior to wider availability of lemons in the fifteenth century.

Here in North America, home to the largest variety of edible sumac species in the world, Indigenous American groups have been using sumac as a food, medicine, dye, and tanning agent for millennia. Tart sumac beverages were an extremely popular delicacy consumed by tribal nations as wide-reaching as the Algonquin, Iroquois, Apache, Ojibwa, Hopi, and Navajo. They were most commonly prepared by soaking sumac berries in water and optionally sweetening the brew with

CONTINUED

honey or maple. This was consumed as a cooling refreshment similar to lemonade in the warmer months, or served warm during the winter. European colonizers adopted the practice of preparing this infusion and gave it many other names by which it is known today including sumac-ade, Indian lemonade, and rhus juice.

One of the great things about sumac is that even though it begins to ripen in early July, the berry clusters remain fresh on the branches through the winter, providing one of the only fruits in the landscape for animals and humans alike. You can find these tenacious plants growing in the most unlikely of places, like the entire interstate system of the Northeast, sports fields, parking lots, and the edge of farms.

I use sumac berries in a variety of ways each year: dehydrated and ground to use in homemade za'atar, infused into sumac-ade, or fermented into sparkling sumac kombucha and soda. However, sumac berries contain high levels of tannins and malic acid like some of the best varieties of cider apples and wine grapes, which I think makes it best suited to ferment into an alcoholic beverage. Enjoy it on its own or use it in a cocktail as I've done with the Stop and Smell the Rhuses (see page 301).

Foraging Advice: There are many different species of sumac growing around the world, with Sicilian sumac being the most important commercial variety. Here in the United States you can find smooth sumac (*R. glabra*) growing throughout all of southern Canada and each of the forty-eight states in the continental United States. In the entire area west of the plains you can find skunkbush sumac (*R. trilobata*), which still has sour, edible fruits despite its off-putting name. East of the plains you can find fragrant sumac (*R. aromatica*), winged sumac (*R. copallinum*), and staghorn sumac growing abundantly. There are also more isolated North American species including prairie sumac (*R. lanceolata*), Kearney sumac (*R. kearneyi*), lemonade sumac (*R. integrifolia*), and sugar sumac (*R. ovata*).

N/A Alternatives: The first step to making sumac mead is to make sumac-ade, so I'm always sure to make a little extra for a refreshing treat that the whole family can enjoy. It can also be fermented into a delicious sparkling nonalcoholic soda.

RHUS ROSÉ

This recipe is based on the Mead Master Recipe, page 55.

Makes approximately seven 750 ml bottles

---

4 qt/950 ml sumac berries, separated from the branches

6 qt/5.7 L warm water

4 ¾ c/1 L honey syrup (see page 25)

½ c/120 ml Ginger Bug, liquid only (see page 39)

DIRECTIONS

First make the sumac-ade by adding the berries to warm water in a large food-safe container, covering, and leaving to infuse at room temperature overnight. The next day, strain the sumac berries through a cheesecloth or tea towel to ensure all solids are removed (solids will prevent gasses from escaping and can cause your fermenting mead to explode). Add the honey syrup and ginger bug and transfer to a jug with an airlock and let ferment until bubbling subsides (between 4 and 6 weeks).

Once fermentation is complete, rack the wine off the lees (see page 51) and bottle. Like wine made from grapes, mead improves with age. This can be consumed while it is still young, but its flavor will be noticeably better after 3 to 6 months or more.

RHUS ROSÉ SYRUP

Wine syrups are a great way to add acidity, tannins,
and body to a cocktail with minimal effort.

Makes approximately 1½ c/360 ml

---

1 c/240 ml *Rhus* rosé   1 c/200 g sugar

DIRECTIONS

Add the *Rhus* rosé and sugar to a medium saucepan and gently heat until sugar dissolves
(don't let it boil). This will keep in a sealed container in the refrigerator for 1 month or more.

STOP AND SMELL THE RHUSES

Makes 1 cocktail

¾ oz/22 ml vodka

¾ oz/22 ml Rhus Rosé Syrup (see above)

¾ oz/22 ml Yellow Chartreuse (Strega also
works as a cheaper alternative)

¾ oz/22 ml freshly squeezed lemon juice

3 dashes of Peychaud's bitters

DIRECTIONS

Fill a cocktail shaker with ice and add all the ingredients. Shake vigorously until well-chilled
and double strain into a chilled Martini glass. No garnish.

MAPLE | *Acer*

One of the first home projects we undertook was to clear the property of nearly thirty trees in order to allow sunlight to reach the garden we dreamed of someday having. We decided that in addition to sparing the two sycamore trees on the side of the house that offered the perfect place to hang a hammock, we'd also leave the silver maple in the front yard and the Norwegian maple in the backyard because their shade helped keep the house cool in the summer. Never did we imagine that just a few years later we'd value these trees equally for what they provided us in the winter—maple syrup.

There are more than 130 species of maple in the genus *Acer*, which can be found growing across much of the northern hemisphere. Like all trees, maples produce sugars as a byproduct of photosynthesis, which they store in their sap to use during periods of growth. What makes maples unique is that the sugar concentration in their sap is quite high, ranging between 1 and 5%. This sap can be harvested each year when it begins to flow beginning at the end of January and extending into March. This is caused by a pressure gradient that forms when daytime temperatures are above freezing, and nighttime temperatures fall below.

This fact was well-known among Algonquian- and Iroquoian-speaking cultures of northeastern North America, who valued the sap as a means of energy and nutrition during an otherwise barren part of the year. To collect it, they would cut V-shaped incisions into the bark of the maple trees and insert a reed to direct the sap flow into a clay vessel. The raw sap was used both as a beverage and cooking liquid. The sap could then be further processed by boiling it down into maple syrup or until the liquid completely evaporates to make maple sugar. They taught this practice to European colonists, who eventually adopted the practice of making syrup as a means of subsistence and small-scale trade. Over time, maple syrup evolved into a major regional industry, and although the scale of the practice has changed, the general processes have mostly remained unchanged.

Each winter, people in the Northeast gather in their maple patches (known as "sugar bushes") to bore holes in the trees. Sap spouts are then inserted in the holes, and a collection mechanism is attached to the spout. In the old days that meant hanging a bucket from the tap, however in modern commercial operations, a vacuum-powered tubing system is often attached. The sap is then collected to be boiled down into syrup in small buildings known as "sugar shacks." The process of boiling sap down into syrup is incredibly intensive and time consuming, usually requiring between 40 and 60 gal of sap to yield 1 gal of syrup.

The species of maple most commonly used in syrup production is the sugar maple, *A. saccharum*, as they have the highest sugar concentration in the genus. One issue with sugar maples, though, is that they are most plentiful at higher elevations, which is why the majority of domestic maple syrup comes from the Appalachian Mountain regions of New England. Recently, however, there have been

CONTINUED

efforts to explore other maple species that are more plentiful at lower elevations to increase the range of maple syrup production. One such effort is underway at Stockton University, located in the Pine Barrens of southern New Jersey, where they are exploring the possibility of using the red maple, *A. rubrum*, which is the most plentiful tree both on the East Coast and the Stockton campus. After visiting their sugar bush last year, it got me thinking about whether I could harvest sap from the maple trees in our yard, so I decided to give it a go.

Later that week, I tapped our two trees and couldn't believe it when I woke up the following morning to find we had collected almost 1 gallon/3.8 L of sap! After we had accumulated 5 gallons/19 L, I spent a full day out in my backyard making syrup from the sap by reducing it over a fire to about 2% its original volume, which yielded about 1 pt/475 ml of amber syrup. I debated what to do with this precious maple syrup for some time, as it was surely too valuable to drizzle over a plate of pancakes. I decided to turn to New England for inspiration, and settled on making a maple beverage that has been consumed in the region for centuries: switchel.

Switchel was a popular drink in the eighteenth and ninteenth centuries among Christian Shaker communities in New England. It consists of apple cider vinegar, maple syrup (or another sweetener like honey or molasses), and ginger, which place it in the same family as other drinking vinegars like shrubs and oxymels. It was valued as a natural energy drink, and it was especially popular during the hay harvest, prompting its nickname

"haymaker's punch." It's great on its own as a healthy nonalcoholic tonic or spiked with rum as was the common practice with New England haymakers.

Regional Substitution: There are 132 maple species spread throughout Eurasia, North America, and northern Africa, with the highest concentration occurring in Asia. Here in North America, we have 13 native species and many introduced from abroad, each of which can hypothetically be tapped for maple syrup. The only stipulation is that nighttime temperatures must fall below freezing and daytime temperatures go above to create the pressure gradient necessary for the sap to run.

N/A Alternative: Top the switchel with club soda in a Collins glass for a bright and refreshing Shrub and Club.

MAPLE SYRUP

Making maple syrup is a true labor of love. If it seems too laborious or ambitious to try, no harm in purchasing it from the store or a local purveyor to make the switchel recipe below. If you feel inclined to try it, however, all you need to do is reduce any volume of maple sap by about 98%. I reduced 5 gal/19 L of sap to make 1 pt/475 ml of syrup.

SWITCHEL

This recipe is based on the Shrub Master Recipe from page 59.

Makes 2½ c/590 ml

---

6 Tbsp/36 g grated fresh ginger   ¼ c/60 ml maple syrup

1¼ c/300 ml Cider Vinegar (see page 221)

DIRECTIONS

Add the ginger to the apple cider vinegar and let infuse overnight at room temperature. The next day, strain out the ginger solids. Add the maple syrup to the ginger-infused vinegar and stir well to incorporate. This will keep indefinitely in the refrigerator.

SUGAR SHACK SWITCHEL

Makes 1 cocktail

2 oz/60 ml aged dark rum,
black rum if available

1¼ oz/37 ml Switchel (see page 305)

½ oz/15 ml freshly squeezed lemon juice

Candied ginger, for garnish

DIRECTIONS

Fill a cocktail shaker with ice and add the rum, switchel, and lemon juice. Shake vigorously and double strain into a rocks glass over a large ice cube. Garnish with a candied ginger skewer.

WINTER "ALPINE" AMARO

In the very hazily defined categories of amari, most are classified by their principle bittering agent. Rabarbaro, for example, is made with rhubarb, carciofo with artichoke or cardoon, tartufo contains truffle, and génépi must contain wormwood. Unlike the regulations given by the European Union to so many other liqueurs, wines, beers, and spirits, amari still remain loose in their definitions. Fernet is one such example. Former Chicago bartender Alex Bachman is quoted in Brad Thomas Parsons's book *Amaro* as saying that he could "walk out on the sidewalk outside the bar and do a maceration of the weeds in the cracks and call it fernet." The "alpine" category of amaro, which refers to an amaro made in the Swiss, Italian, French, or Austrian Alps, occupies similar territory. The only botanical specification for what it should contain is "alpine herbs." But I've always wondered, what exactly are alpine herbs? The answer came to me from a most unexpected place.

I was in the checkout line of my local pharmacy when I looked over and saw a bag of Ricola cough drops, which proudly stated on the front "Made with Swiss Alpine Herbs." I picked up the bag and saw illustrations of their proprietary blend of alpine botanicals, which included peppermint, elder, thyme, horehound, hyssop, mallow, lemon balm, linden flower, and sage. If these herbs were infused into an amaro, my guess would be that it would result in a final product that was herbaceous and floral. However, the most common descriptor you tend to see for the flavor of alpine amari is "piney." This flavor can be imparted by infusing pine in the amaro, which is the case with the Cappelletti family's Amaro Pasubio, or it can come from another evergreen species, such as juniper, a principle botanical ingredient used in the Braulio alpine amaro.

When I set out to make my version of a winter "alpine" amaro, I decided to make it decidedly piney, while infusing the hardiest of garden herbs to fit the "alpine herb" specification. Luckily, the herbs that survive in the Alps are usually the same ones that are still alive in the winter garden as they're built to withstand the cold. Depending on how harsh the winter is, I can usually wrangle mint, thyme, horehound, and possibly some sage into my alpine amaro. Next, I take a trip to the Pine Barrens to gather evergreens. I like to use juniper and pine, although any edible coniferous species would work. With each, I like to use the needles, as well as the fruits (berries for the juniper, cones for the pine) for the different flavors they impart. I'll also gather some birch bark and sumac berries while I'm there to add spice and citrus notes, respectively.

Once I'm home, I add the fresh ingredients to a 2-quart/2 L jar along with some dehydrated trifoliate orange peels, before covering with overproof vodka. I then let the botanicals macerate in the alcohol for 8 weeks, before letting it rest in a barrel for another 6 to 8 weeks. Once complete, I dilute and sweeten with homemade maple syrup (although store-bought works fine). I always make this at the end of the winter, knowing that by the time I get to enjoy it, summer will be right around the corner and taking a sip will transport me out of the heat to a cold late-winter's walk through the pine forest.

Below is a breakdown that's meant to be more of a rough guide than a rigid recipe. Of all the amari in this book, I'd say that I get the most mixed reactions to this one due to the strong flavor of the evergreens. However, that strong flavor is an integral part of two of the best-selling cocktails we've ever had on the menu at the Farm and Fisherman: The Pine Barrens Cocktail (see page 245) and one of my all-time favorite cocktails, the Rye Daisy (see page 313). This is a great lesson that sometimes, strong flavors need only be balanced correctly with complementary flavors to shine. I find this amaro is best enjoyed as a component in citrusy cocktails, however, it can also be consumed neat for a flavor that is as bracing and bitter as a cold winter's day.

Bittering agent: horehound

Acidic: staghorn sumac, dehydrated hardy orange peels (can substitute any citrus here)

Herbaceous: mint, thyme, sage

Spice: juniper berries, pine needles, juniper needles, birch bark

Depth of flavor: pine cones

WINTER "ALPINE" AMARO

This recipe is based on the Amaro Master Recipe, page 80.

Makes approximately 5 c/1.2 L

---

3 pine cones (approximately 100 g)

100 g pine needles (approximately five 6 in/15 cm branch tips)

100 g roughly chopped juniper needles, berries, and nonwoody stems (approximately three 1 ft/30 cm branches)

50 g sumac berries (approximately 1 c/240 ml)

20 g dehydrated trifoliate "hardy" orange (*Citrus trifolata*) peels or dried common orange peels (approximately ½ c)

10 g birch bark (approximately one 3- by 6-in/7.5 by 15 cm swath of bark)

5 g horehound (approximately three 6 in/15 cm sprigs)

5 g sage (approximately one 6 in/15 cm sprig)

3 g thyme (approximately five 6 in/15 cm sprigs)

5 g mint (approximately one 6 in/15 cm sprig)

2 Tbsp juniper berries

151-proof vodka, for topping (approximately 5 c/1.2 L)

3 c/720 ml water, plus more if needed

1½ c/360 ml maple syrup, plus more if needed

DIRECTIONS

To a 2 quart/2 L glass jar, add the pine cones, pine needles, juniper needles, sumac, orange peels, birch bark, horehound, sage, thyme, mint, and juniper berries and top with 151-proof vodka. Tightly secure the lid and let it macerate for 5 weeks.

After 5 weeks, strain out the solids and reserve the liquid (it should yield about 4½ cups/1 L). Add the strained liquid to a 3 quart/3 L oak barrel and let age for an additional month (or longer), or skip this step if you don't have an oak barrel.

Add the water and maple syrup. If the alcohol level feels too high or the flavor is too dry, add more water and maple syrup to adjust. This can be stored at room temperature indefinitely.

CHAMOMILE-INFUSED RYE

This recipe is directly out of the Death & Co. playbook. They describe it in their first book as one of their "most-used infusions," and after tasting it, it's not hard to see why.

This recipe is based on Infusions and Tinctures, page 72.

Makes 4¼ c/1 L

¼ c/60 ml dried chamomile flowers   4¼ c/1 L rye whiskey

DIRECTIONS

In a food-safe container, add the chamomile and rye and stir well. Allow to infuse at room temperature for 1¾ hours. Strain through a fine-mesh strainer lined with a tea towel or cheesecloth. This will store indefinitely at room temperature.

LEMON OLEO-SACCHARUM & SHERBET

This recipe is based on the Oleo-Saccharum & Sherbet Master Recipe, page 89.

Makes approximately 1½ c/360 ml

---

4 medium lemons (plus more if needed   ¾ c/150 g sugar
to yield 1 c/240 ml juice)   1 c/240 ml freshly squeezed lemon juice

DIRECTIONS

Peel 4 lemons and top with the sugar in a food-safe container. Muddle to release the oils, then cover and let the peels sit overnight at room temperature. Juice the peeled lemons until you have 1 cup/240 ml of juice. Refrigerate in an airtight container.

The next day, add the citrus juice and oleo-saccharum to a medium saucepan and gently heat until all the sugar dissolves. Pass through a fine-mesh strainer into a large bowl, being sure to squeeze as much liquid from the peels as possible. Discard the solids and store the sherbet in the refrigerator for up to 1 month.

RYE DAISY

Makes 1 cocktail

1¾ oz/52 ml Chamomile-Infused Rye (see page 312)

¾ oz/22 ml Lemon Sherbet (see page 312)

½ oz/15 ml Winter "Alpine" Amaro (see page 310)

½ oz/15 ml freshly squeezed lemon juice

½ oz/15 ml maple syrup

Sage leaf, for garnish

DIRECTIONS

Fill a cocktail shaker with ice and add the rye, sherbet, amaro, lemon juice, and maple syrup. Shake vigorously and double strain over a large cube in a rocks glass. Garnish with a sage leaf.

ACKNOWLEDGMENTS

To say it has taken a village to complete this book is an understatement. I'll start by thanking the person who has been by my side throughout: my wife and best friend, Katie. Katie, thank you for always encouraging me to follow my bliss even when I didn't know where it would lead, and for giving life to this project with your beautiful photos and endless advice. It's no exaggeration to say that without you, Slow Drinks wouldn't exist. Most of all, thank you for being the rock for the boys as I've written, edited, and rewritten this book. I can't wait to see our hard work come to fruition.

To our boys, Leo and Sonny, words can't describe how much we valued the distraction and much needed cuddles you provided during this process. Although writing and photographing this book while you were so young had its challenges, I would never trade the countless hours it forced us to spend in the garden, woods, and kitchen and the joys of watching you learn about the flavors and ingredients hidden all around us.

My deepest gratitude goes to my family and friends for a lifetime of cheering me on from the sidelines. I especially want to thank my mom, who has been the most selfless, amazing mother I could ever have asked for. My mom, along with my stepdad and sisters, continue to inspire me daily, leading by example with their "Press On" approach to all of life's challenges, not to mention the enormous assistance they provided with the boys during this process. To my dad, who left a bartending career to provide a brighter future for himself and his kids, thank you for supporting me when I later chose this path, and for always being there to lend a helping hand. Finally, I owe a great debt to my grandfather and Uncle Craig for helping shape my love of the outdoors and anthropology, to my grandmother for being our family recipe archivist, and to my cuzzos, Joe and Sam, for extravagant feasts and constant inspiration.

I'd like to also thank our restaurant "Farm Family" and especially our fearless leaders, Todd Fuller, Josh Lawler, and Ben Menk without whom this project would not have been possible. Thank you for taking a gamble on the kid living in the tent, for teaching me how to make things taste good, and for cultivating my interests over the better part of a decade; it allowed me to find something that I truly love. And a special thank you to all of our bar, server, and kitchen staff, past and present, with a special mention going to my friend and right-hand gal, Meredith Dabrowski.

There have been many important people whose influence helped shape this book long before I ever stepped behind a bar. First and foremost, thank you to my mentor, Dr. Peter Roe, whose teaching and academic advising started me on this botanical journey nearly fifteen years ago. I am further indebted to all of the village plant specialists and healers from Peru and Chile who shared their ethnobotanical knowledge with me. Special thanks go to my Shipibo guides, Manuel and Pablo, Mapuche elders, Miguel and Juanita, and my Likan-antai hosts, Cecilia and Luisa. Further appreciation goes to my South American friends who remain closer than family to this day, including Ximena, Luis, Felipe, Kenji, Michael, and Yerko. *Muchisimas gracias por compartir sus lindos paises, culturas, y casas conmigo.*

I'm also incredibly grateful to all those stateside who have helped me continue to learn about the bounty of my home region, none more so than Teddy and Faith Moynihan, who have shared their family farm in Bucks County, Pennsylvania with us. Thanks to Bob Toogood for sharing your knowledge of New Jersey's botanical riches, especially the magical pawpaw patch. Finally, to the entire Slow Food USA organization, especially Jeff Quattrone and the rest of our northeast Ark of Taste committee, I'm incredibly proud of the work we've done, and I hope this book makes a lasting contribution to this global movement.

The first person who ever saw potential in my writing was Jenn Hall, who after reading my first story on our fledgling bar program at the Farm and Fisherman said: "I think there's a book here." This led me to Teresa Politano who spent the next two years as my editor at *Edible Jersey*, helping me find my voice and aesthetic in my IACP-nominated "Slow Drinks" column and giving me the much-needed nudge to start writing a book proposal.

However, it wasn't until late 2020 when I met agent Jonah Straus (thanks to a tip from Kristin Donnelly), that Slow Drinks really began to take shape under his sage advice and countless hours of editing. After a full year of tirelessly reworking the proposal with Jonah and our graphic designer, Lou Forgione, we were finally able to ink a deal with the incredible team at Hardie Grant, thanks to the endorsement of our soon-to-be dream editor, Jenny Wapner. Jenny's expertise coupled with her ability to maintain the integrity and spirit of how we envisioned this book have resulted in a final product that is better than I could have ever imagined.

It is no understatement to say that this book would not be what it is if not for the incredible work of our illustrator, Molly Reeder, whose style perfectly encapsulates our ingredient-centered approach and attention to all life's tiniest details, as well as the incredible aesthetic expertise of our graphic designer, Ashley Lima.

Finally, I would like to acknowledge those people whose work has greatly influenced this book, including Pascal Baudar, Alex Day, Camper English, Emma Janzen, Sandor Katz, Deborah Madison, Dr. Patrick McGovern, Jim Meehan, Alexis Nikole Nelson, Brad Thomas Parsons, Michael Pollan, Sasha Petraske, Dr. Maricel Presilla, Sean Sherman, Dr. David Shields, Amy Stewart, Alice Waters, William Woys Weaver, and David Zilber.

Cheers, Danny

INDEX

Hardie Grant

NORTH AMERICA

Hardie Grant North America
2912 Telegraph Ave
Berkeley, CA 94705
hardiegrantbooks.com

Library of Congress Cataloging-in-Publication Data is available upon request.

ISBN: 9781958417300
ISBN: 9781958417027 (eBook)
Printed in China
Design by Ashley Lima
First Edition

"Danny Childs in *Slow Drinks* reminds us that the cocktail began its career as medicine, an amalgam of spirits, herbs, and syrups intended to mollify the soul and recharge the body. The traditional insights into the plants, distillates, and digestive decoctions have been gathered here, and the cocktail reframed within the Slow Food ethic of good, clean, and fair food. No dry academic survey this, but an engaging personal exploration of botany, material culture, and folk wisdom that contributed to shaping the iconic beverages. The splendidly illustrated profiles of key ingredients charm the eye while the text supplies plant lore mingled with scientific botany. Brillat-Savarin said that pleasure is enhanced by knowing what you ingest. *Slow Drinks* will enrich your every sip."

—**DAVID SHIELDS**, author of *The Culinarians*

"Danny Childs' training as an ethnobotanist and bartender uniquely situates him to shepherd readers from farms and foraging trips into the kitchen, where he combines those ingredients into spirited history lessons and handcrafted mixes. *Slow Drinks* is a deeply researched modern cookbook that sows the seeds for a seasonal mixology practice grounded in farm to table tenets like no bartending book has before."

—**JIM MEEHAN**, author of *The PDT Cocktail Book* and *Meehan's Bartender Manual*

"Danny Childs' fascinating journey is both universal and unique: He traveled extensively before coming home to New Jersey to see a familiar place with new insight and appreciation, informed by the experience gained in his ethnobotanical adventures. *Slow Drinks* is as much a love letter to the state and its botanical bounty as it is a thoughtful and creative guide to making very good drinks from scratch, from the plants that grow where you are. From juniper to sumac, crabapples to pawpaws, *Slow Drinks* offers techniques that can be applied broadly, as well as crafted recipes for drinks that will capture the time in which they were collected and the place where you live."

—**MARIE VILJOEN**, author of *Forage, Harvest, Feast*